THE REAL PUSHERS

The REAL PUSHERS

A CRITICAL ANALYSIS OF THE CANADIAN DRUG INDUSTRY

Joel Lexchin, M.D.

Foreword by Jim Harding

New Star Books
Vancouver, Canada

First printing September 1984
1   2   3   4   5   88   87   86   85   84

Canadian Cataloguing in Publication Data

Lexchin, Joel, 1948-
The real pushers

Includes index.
Bibliography: p.
ISBN 0-919573-26-6 (bound).--ISBN
0-919573-27-4 (pbk.)

1. Drug trade - Canada. I. Title.
HD9670.C22L49 1984   338.4'76151'0971
C84-091245-5

New Star Books is grateful for financial aid provided
by the Social Science Federation of Canada

The publisher also wishes to acknowledge the program
of annual support established by the Canada Council

Production co-ordinated by Jill Gibson

Printed and bound in Canada

New Star Books Ltd.
2504 York Avenue
Vancouver, B.C.
Canada V6K 1E3

To my mother and the memory of my father

Publisher's Note

This book has been published with the help of a grant from the Social Science Federation of Canada using funds provided by the Social Sciences and Humanities Research Council of Canada.

Contents

List of Tables

Foreword

The Real Pushers is the first comprehensive analysis of the pharmaceutical drug industry in Canada. Focusing on the power and the adverse effects of the industry, it tells the side of the story which has hitherto not been widely heard. It is a story of an industry dominated by foreign corporations which search out worldwide markets and profits while benefiting from the stress and disease of people who lack access to safer and more effective alternatives.

According to the mythology carried in the flood of drug advertising, and reinforced by the mainstream medical profession, the field of modern pharmaceuticals evolved rationally from medical research and scientific progress. Proponents of this view will likely say, perhaps without even reading this book, that the critical side of the story presented here portrays an exception to the rule. I think, however, that the scope and substance of *The Real Pushers* successfully challenges this one-dimensional view. It does so, first of all, by providing readers with the kind of information not easily available to the public. In case after case, the historical and structural context is carefully and clearly presented, enabling an understanding of a variety of drug problems, whether the devastating physical results on fetal development from thalidomide, or the widespread effect of drug dependency (especially among women) from the tranquillizer boom of the last two decades. The conventional view, that these are the unfortunate but unavoidable accidents of medical progress, is seriously considered in *The Real Pushers*. However, approaching the issues "systemically" (that is, investigating the drug industry, the medical profession, the government regulators, and the interrelations among them) clearly shows that such benign interpretations are inadequate and often

9

self-serving.

One of the strengths of this book derives from the fact that the author is both a doctor and critic of the drug industry, a rare combination. However, he does not write through the blind spots of a specialized profession or discipline. Rather, he has sought out evidence which links fields as seemingly diverse as pharmacology and medicine, medical sociology and health policy, political economy and women's studies.

The approach taken in *The Real Pushers* is sometimes discouraged by those with an interest in preserving established ideas. I experienced a blatant form of this when I was Director of Research for the Saskatchewan Alcoholism Commission in the late 1970s. We were conducting a research study on prescribing trends for central nervous system drugs. Our approach was systemic and critical, not unlike that taken in this book. A section in our first report reviewed pertinent literature on the pharmaceutical industry and medical profession, challenging practices in both areas. It was so controversial to some senior government officials, who did not want to imply any public criticism of the medical profession, that it was edited beyond recognition and finally had to be removed. When the second report, on prescribing trends to the elderly, was finally released, reference in the conclusion to the role of the drug industry, medical profession and government health care system regarding the problems of inappropriate and over-prescribing was replaced with a narrow mention of the elderly consumer and the need for more education. Although this research was about prescriptions issued under the Saskatchewan Drug Plan, and not about consumers or drug consumption, the term "prescribing" was systematically removed from the report and replaced by "utilization"—putting the emphasis on the largely powerless user, who is the potential victim of inappropriate and over-prescribing. As we learned, and as Lexchin amply documents, sensitivities run high in this field, where diplomatic distortions commonly substitute for truth.

Lexchin acknowledges that drugs can play an important role in medical treatment. He points out, however, that many of today's most serious medical problems (e.g., hypertension) are rooted in socio-economic and industrial stresses but are nonetheless treated with drugs. Many non-medical problems—including family crises, unemployment and problems related to the secondary status of women—have increasingly been labelled in medical terms and managed with drug products. In these cases, drug consumption, health costs and drug company profits all go up. Moreover, additional health problems result from the trend toward prescription drugs—e.g., adverse effects, drug dependency and decreased ability to address or prevent these problems at their social roots.

Perhaps the book's most challenging conclusion is that it is the expansion of the pharmaceutical market by the multinational corporations, and not the advancement of pharmacological research per se, which explains the escalating number of prescription (and over-the-counter) drugs to which the public is exposed. As in other commercial sectors, brand name marketing—not fundamental innovations—is the core strategy behind the drive toward power and profits in the pharmaceutical industry. The resulting proliferation of drugs—in one national market, as many as 14,000 products have been based on only 700 active ingredients—is the main reason why the World Health Organization has stated, "In recent years there has been a tremendous increase in the number of pharmaceutical products marketed; however, there has not been a proportionate improvement in health." The proliferation of drug products also explains why the World Health Organization has assembled and endorsed a list of safe, inexpensive and essential drugs; it views with urgency the need to limit and curtail irrational, uneconomic and hazardous prescribing throughout the world. Their list of over 200 essential drugs for use in developing countries contrasts sharply with the tens of thousands of pharmaceutical products currently under production worldwide.

Various constituencies engaged in human service work and social reform activities (including health professionals, women's health networks, consumer groups) will find the information on medicalization and product proliferation in this book challenging and enlightening. As more people face the disruption of unemployment, pollution, poverty and cutbacks, it will become even more vital to be critical of the medicalization of social problems and its role in social control. The information in this book will be very useful for promoting those social reforms which will shift health care priorities toward alternative treatments and primary prevention.

At a more specific level, *The Real Pushers* provides the reader with a context for understanding the current attempts of the multinational pharmaceutical firms operating in Canada to have patent protections reinstated for their products. These corporations, and likely the federal government too, would have the Canadian public believe that such protection for their profits is the only way to ensure investment, research and employment opportunities for this country. We are hearing the same corporate argument throughout the economy at present. In documenting the much more fundamental questions about the pharmaceutical industry's power and adverse effects, Joel Lexchin has provided a more thorough, critical background from which an informed and concerned public can view, and attempt to influence, this dispute.

Jim Harding
School of Human Justice
University of Regina
Regina, Saskatchewan
July 1984

Acknowledgements

Maryka Omatsu generously sent me a copy of her paper analysing the federal government's policy toward new drugs. Paul K. Gorecki obtained for me a number of publications that I was unable to get on my own. Discussions I had with Annalee Yassi helped formulate my ideas for the final chapter. John Crossley and Warren Bell also made valuable suggestions for the contents of this chapter. Kay Elgie, Alan Filewood, Manny Gordon, Bob James, Greg Kealey and Barb Lent all read a preliminary version of this manuscript and their critiques have made this a better book. In particular, I must thank John Crossley, Jim Harding and Warren Bell. John Crossley's suggestions led to a significant reorganization of the material in this book which has made it much more lucid. Jim Harding wrote nine pages of detailed comments on the penultimate draft and pointed out a number of weak points in the book which I have attempted to correct. Warren Bell's remarks forced me to rethink many of my positions, and while ultimately I might not have agreed with all of his points, they made me formulate my own in a clearer manner. He also provided me with information that I could not have obtained elsewhere. I was fortunate to find as good an editor as Lanny Beckman of New Star Books. His red pen contributed many improvements to what I had previously considered a flawless work. Finally, Catherine Oliver has to be thanked for tolerating me while I did endless revisions in the year before this book was ultimately published. Of course, I am the only one responsible for the final contents.

Introduction

Why write a book about the Canadian prescription drug industry?
The companies involved are not among the giants in the Canadian
economy. In the 1982 *Financial Post* rankings, only five companies
made the list of Canada's top 400 industrials and the highest of these
was 64th. Canadians spend only about 0.4 percent of their
disposable income on prescription drugs.[1] So why investigate the
drug companies?

In this case, size is not the important consideration. Because the
industry is so intimately bound up with people's health, its
significance is far greater than the magnitude of its net earnings and
gross profit margins. People trust the integrity of drug companies
when they are ill. Whether the companies have honored or betrayed
this trust is the issue this book is concerned with.

There are three groups that are central to the drug industry—the
companies, the government and the medical profession. And, of
course, there is a fourth group that is on the receiving end—the
public. This book will examine each of the first three groups. We will
see how, in general, both the government and organized medicine
have become subservient to the interests of the industry, and we will
explore the effects of this development on the public.

The industry is dominated by subsidiaries of American, British
and Swiss multinationals, with Canadian-owned companies having
less than 10 percent of the market. This structure, with such a high
degree of foreign control and restricted competition, allows the
companies to set and maintain prices at artificially high levels. The
drug industry thus provides a disturbing example of how human
misery and profit-making can become intertwined. But the
companies go further than just profiting at the expense of illness.

15

They have knowingly deceived doctors about the drugs that they make, as the examples of chloramphenicol and MER/29 will show. The research efforts of the drug industry are also distorted. The development of drugs is biased toward producing the ones with the greatest sales potential, and not necessarily the greatest social benefits.

In order to sell their products, the companies generate a constant bombardment of advertising directed at doctors. Physicians rely on this advertising for much of their knowledge about drugs. When this reliance is superimposed on an initially deficient base of knowledge, the result is overuse and misuse of drugs, often leading to injurious consequences.

In another effort to expand the use of drugs, the industry has even tried to create new diseases that require drug treatment. This process is easily observed in the cases of Valium and Ritalin and is one that is called "medicalization." What this term means is that problems that were formerly social or family ones now become diseases for doctors to deal with; however, most of these problems cannot be solved on an individual basis. When people are depressed because they are unemployed, the answer is not to give them an antidepressant, but that is the choice many physicians make. Drug advertising encourages doctors to view loneliness or marriage breakdown as medical problems. Medical education is grossly deficient in equipping doctors to help people with these problems. The easiest solution for doctors, especially when they are trying to see a patient every ten minutes, is to take the advice in the ads and prescribe a pill.

The way to overcome the power of the drug industry does not lie in reformist solutions. Governments at both the federal and provincial levels have attempted to increase competition in the industry as a means of driving prices down. Everybody urges more continuing education for doctors to decrease the misuse of drugs. But neither of these measures has proved to be effective, and in the final chapter we will look at some new approaches to these problems.

Non-prescription, or over-the-counter, drugs are beyond the scope of this book. They are advertised directly to the public; they can be bought without a doctor as an intermediary; and government regulations covering their manufacture and marketing are different from those for prescription medications. To explore the problems associated with these drugs would require a separate book.

Pharmacists and drugstores have also been largely ignored in this book. This is not to deny that they are a factor in determining drug prices and in other aspects of the industry. According to a couple of surveys, prices for the same drug can vary up to 300 percent depending on the store.[2] In Toronto, the highest prices were charged by druggists in the lower income areas of the city.[3] But pharmacists remain peripheral to the central themes of this book—the power of the drug industry and its adverse effects on our health.

It will quickly become obvious that I have very little good to say about the drug companies. As a doctor I have seen how the industry appeals to physicians through blandishments and how it distorts the facts about its products. The companies have plenty of defenders as it is and it is not my intention to present "both sides of the story."

It will sometimes be necessary to use words which may be unfamiliar to people outside the health-related professions. Most of these are explained in the text when they occur. Some terms, however, are used so often that it is probably best to introduce them now. Among these are the terms "brand (or trade or proprietary) name," "generic name" and "chemical name." Generic name is not actually an official Canadian term, the correct one being "proper name," but generic name seems to be the term that has the most general usage, and it is the one I will use. A generic name is an abbreviated scientific name for a drug and is generally used in prescribing, naming and identifying drugs. The true scientific name is called the "chemical name." The brand or trade or proprietary name is that assigned to a drug by the manufacturing company and is usually a registered trademark which identifies the drug as a product of a single manufacturer. As an example, Miltown is Horner's trade name for a tranquillizer. The generic name is "meprobamate" and the chemical name is "2-methyl-2-propyl-1,3-propanedioldicarbamate."

The information in this book is as current as possible, but until recently, the early 1970s was the last time that there was any sustained interest in the Canadian pharmaceutical industry from any quarter. Consequently some of the information available has not been updated for fifteen or twenty years. In those instances where it has been necessary to use older material it might be thought that the conclusions based on that information would be open to challenge as being outmoded. However, whenever it has been possible to compare data from the 1960s with data from the 1970s or 1980s, the conclusions have always remained consistent. Updating the information does not substantially alter the arguments for and against the drug industry. The major trends of twenty years ago continue unabated. As newer information becomes available, I am confident that it will reinforce, in broad outline, the central contentions that follow.

Finally, although this is a book about Canada and the Canadian industry, occasionally it will be necessary to use American or, rarely, British findings. Given that the Canadian industry is almost totally foreign dominated, this should make little difference to the arguments that I will be making. The companies are the same; the drugs are the same; and the motives of the companies are the same.

Chapter 1
Valium for the Adults
and Ritalin for the Kids

Valium

Librium appeared on the market in 1960 to compete with the original "minor tranquillizer," meprobamate (Miltown, Equanil). Librium is Hoffman-LaRoche's brand of chlordiazepoxide. Soon after it became available, Librium had taken away the sales lead from meprobamate. Valium (diazepam) was synthesized soon after Librium and although some Roche executives did not expect much of it, it was put on the market in 1963 and the rest is history. By 1972, it was the most widely prescribed drug in the United States. In 1974-75, according to figures from the Pharmaceutical Manufacturers Association of Canada, it was second only to 292s on the Canadian market.[1] That same year, Horner's brand of diazepam, Vivol, was the eighth most frequently prescribed drug. Overall, diazepam was probably the top selling drug in the country. Between March 1977 and March 1978, Canadian physicians wrote almost 2.25 million prescriptions for diazepam, 1.17 million for Valium alone, and another 390,000 for Librium.[2]

Roche's annual profits from worldwide sales of Valium and Librium are roughly $100 million.[3] (Profit estimates are approximate since Roche, a Swiss-based company, provides very little public financial information.) In 1970, Roche Canada sold $3.74 million worth of Librium and $9.72 million worth of Valium.[4] The selling price of Valium in Canada is twenty times the total production cost.[5]

In Britain, the government challenged the price of Librium and Valium it was being charged by Roche and demanded that Roche justify its price on the basis of its costs. Roche refused to allow the government to audit its books but finally agreed to refund $30 million to the British Treasury.[6] In addition, price reductions of 75 percent for Valium and 60 percent for Librium were ordered by the government.

In 1980, Roche was convicted by the Supreme Court of Ontario and fined $50,000 for violation of a section of the Combines Investigation Act which makes it an offence to sell a product at an unreasonably low price if the effect is to lessen or eliminate competition. Never before had there been a federal prosecution under that particular section of the Act. In his judgment, Mr. Justice Allan Linden found that during the period of time under question, sales of Valium were an "extraordinarily profitable operation for the defendant company."[7] Between 1970 and 1974, Roche had given away 174 million units of Valium worth an estimated $5 million at market price. One reason for Roche's act of uncommon generosity was to head off competition from Horner's Vivol. But Roche was also very anxious to get its products into hospital pharmacies. Roche secretary-treasurer Charles Nowotny testified as to the reasons: There, the drugs "would be used by top doctors. They will tend to influence the prescribing habits of their residents and interns [who] will tend to use this particular brand in their private practice."[8]

The longer Valium is on the market and the more it is used, the more apparent it is that Valium is not the safe drug it had always been thought to be. Information to this effect was coming to light in the early 1970s. But between 1970 and 1975, advertisements for Valium in the *New England Journal of Medicine* referred to side effects as rarely serious and usually controlled by adjusting the dosage.[9] As late as 1976, an ad for Valium in the *Canadian Family Physician* trumpeted in large extrabold type: "characterized by safety." But previously held myths about benzodiazepines, the class of drugs including Valium and Librium, are being challenged by a growing body of medical literature.

It was commonly believed that benzodiazepines were not associated with tolerance or withdrawal symptoms, although it was usually conceded that a few people who would abuse other drugs might also abuse Valium. Reports now indicate that dependency may well be a problem for a broad range of patients.[10] One study cited by Cooperstock and Hill[11] looked at withdrawal symptoms in patients who had been on low doses of benzodiazepines for a mean of 3.6 years. Between 27 and 45 percent showed clear withdrawal symptoms. The authors concluded: "The high incidence of withdrawal symptoms suggests that a substantial minority of

patients taking benzodiazepines are pharmacologically dependent."[12] Sudden withdrawal of large doses of Librium has been shown
to produce severe reactions including seizures,[13] and stopping even
moderate to low doses can lead to symptoms.[14] Of a group of 50
patients referred from a variety of outpatient clinics, 60 percent
admitted to viewing themselves as being at least slightly dependent
on Valium.[15] Cooperstock and Hill also reviewed studies showing
psychomotor, learning and memory impairment following the use of
benzodiazepines.[16]

Users of tranquillizers are also more likely to use both legal and
illegal drugs. A survey of Toronto adults reported that those who
used tranquillizers were over four times as likely to also be users of
stimulants or barbiturates as were non-tranquillizer users.[17] The
Ontario Addiction Research Foundation found that 44 percent of the
patients on methadone maintenance therapy (for heroin addiction)
used benzodiazepines regularly or most of the time.[18] The use of
illegal drugs extends to the children of tranquillizer users. Dr. R.
Smart testified before the U.S. Senate on the results of his study in
Toronto: "The conclusion is inescapable that the parents who are
users of tranquilizers . . . are likely to have children who are users of
drugs, such as marijuana, LSD, speed as well as prescription drugs
and alcohol and tobacco."[19]

Benzodiazepines are frequently prescribed to lessen anxiety, fear
or irritability, but in some minimally anxious subjects they have
been shown to actually increase anxiety.[20] It was found that violent,
aggressive incidents occurred significantly more frequently when
prisoners were on Valium than when they were not.[21]

Few people who use only Valium succeed in committing suicide,
but that does not make it safe in that regard. Combined with other
central nervous system depressants such as barbiturates or alcohol,
benzodiazepines can be lethal. A number of reports have emphasized
the risk of suicidal thought induced by Valium or Librium.[22]
According to one review on the subject: "Benzodiazepines are given
freely to a large group of patients, some of whom may already be at
high risk for suicide and others who become at high risk after taking
the benzodiazepines."[23] Between 1970 and 1976 there was a 46
percent increase in the reporting of Valium poisonings in Canada.[24]
Studies done in Canadian emergency rooms between 1973 and 1980
found that from one third to one half of patients with drug overdoses
used a benzodiazepine.[25]

Based on short-term studies, Valium has been generally found to be more effective than a placebo in reducing anxiety. But in two studies which have extended beyond four to six weeks, the difference between Valium and a placebo diminished and eventually became statistically nonsignificant.[26] Reports of this kind suggest that a substantial fraction of persons suffering from anxiety or other psychiatric symptoms can improve spontaneously in a few months without any treatment.[27]

In many cases, a prescription for Valium has become a substitute for careful consideration of patients' problems. In some of their ads, Roche ranks the use of Valium second to counselling and says that Valium is just "for the few. . . who can't or won't help themselves." (Notice how the wording explicitly places the source of the problem in the individual.) But reality is a doctor with a maximum of fifteen minutes to solve any problem a patient may present. Issuing a prescription at the end of a visit tells the patient that the visit was necessary, because medication is needed. A prescription also gives the physician a feeling of having done something useful. More and more, general practitioners are seeing people who are lonely, having marital problems, having trouble sleeping or are unhappy at work. In other words, people with social problems. Little stress is laid on dealing with these kinds of problems during medical school or internship. Advertising encourages doctors to look upon them as being solvable with a prescription. Valium has been promoted for a wide range of dissimilar problems: "psychic support for the tense insomniac," for the "always weary," and for the housewife "with too little time to pursue a vocation for which she has spent many years in training."[28] Librium has been advertised for the relief of anxiety in the new college student whose new friends and experiences "may force her to reevaluate herself and her goals" and whose "newly stimulated intellectual curiosity may make her more sensitive to and apprehensive about unstable national and world conditions."[29]

The use of tranquillizers for these types of "problems" is explicitly rejected in a monograph prepared under the sponsorship of the Health Protection Branch of the Department of Health and Welfare:

> There is no justification for the regular use of anxiolytic drugs in overt or covert manifestations of anxiety if they are considered to be within the normal range of human living. Anxiolytic drugs should not routinely be used for anxiety associated with normal

tensions of unhappy personal or family situations, loneliness, interpersonal difficulties, normal grief or bereavement, expected reactions to everyday stresses, normal frustrations, trials and tribulations of human existence or transient complaints of a nonorganic nature.[30]

As the analysis of advertising in Chapter 8 will show, it is women who are most likely to be targeted as needing these drugs. And in some cases the ads merely reinforce the feeling doctors already have about women. Dr. Mary Sims, formerly with the Addiction Research Foundation in Ontario, studied the day-to-day activities of 68 general practitioners. Here is a not atypical example of their attitudes: "Women are frailer vessels: More time to brood and not enough good honest work"; "You can't give men that kind of drug, their work demands concentration."[31] Ruth Cooperstock has found a 2:1 ratio of women to men in the receipt of prescriptions for psychotropic drugs; the finding cannot be explained by the greater use of physicians' services by women.[32] Indeed, women 25 to 44 years of age with the same psychosocial diagnoses as men received prescriptions for anxiety reducing agents significantly more often than men.[33]

Doctors are inclined to prescribe mood modifying drugs because of time constraints, advertising, general societal pressures and a lack of alternatives. But they also believe in the use of psychotropic drugs. In one survey, 80 percent of doctors agreed that "certain medications are often very helpful in handling the special demands and stresses of everyday living."[34] One third of doctors accepted daily use of Librium for a middle-aged housewife having marital troubles as "very legitimate." Occasional use by physicians themselves was judged by 17 percent of doctors to be "very legitimate" when stress and demands of their practice become too great. An additional 40 to 50 percent accepted each of these uses as "somewhat legitimate."[35] As would be expected, such attitudes influence actual prescribing behavior; those doctors who accepted the use of psychotropic drugs for social problems and everyday stress prescribed more psychotropic drugs.[36]

Using drugs to treat problems of everyday living can be dangerous to patients in a number of ways, not the least of which is the risk of side effects of the medication. But this type of treatment also cheats both the patient and the doctor. The real reasons behind problems remain buried, leaving patients with a diminished chance of discovering the basis of their difficulties and working toward a solution. In 1979, the staff at Bryony House, a transition house in Halifax which serves "battered wives" and run-away women, concluded from its survey that women on tranquillizers took longer to leave violent, abusive marriages than those who were drug free.[37] Doctors who freely prescribe psychotropic drugs are left with an essentially false sense of achievement, and are deprived of the true intellectual and emotional insights that they can realize by helping the patient.

The use of Valium to treat problems which are social in origin, and whose solutions are therefore social, has been explored in a study by Ingrid Waldron. She shows that the period of rapid growth in the use of minor tranquillizers in the U.S. coincided with a dramatic rise in social stress as measured by suicides, homicides and alcohol consumption. The next part of her argument is particularly important:

> Thus, use of Valium and Librium increased rapidly during a period of increasing social problems...This particular method of responding to increasing social problems would appear to have significant social consequences. Perhaps most significantly, it focuses attention on individual malfunction and the alleviation of symptoms of distress, rather than on seeking to understand and deal with the problems and their causes. As a consequence, social and economic problems are dealt with in the framework of a medical model of relief of individual distress rather than in a social and political context of cooperative efforts for societal change. It is tempting to speculate that the "medicalization" of these problems reduces pressures for societal change and that this outcome is advantageous from the point of view of those who profit from the existing economic and political order.[38]

Ritalin

> *I got my Rit-lin; you got your Dex.*
> *Slip us a pill. We won't be wrecks.*
> —Schoolyard song of the seventies[39]

Is Johnny causing trouble at school? Sally won't sit still to do her homework? Maybe they are hyperactive and require Ritalin to control them. Actually, hyperactivity as a diagnosis has been subsumed by the more general term "minimal brain dysfunction" or MBD. What is MBD and how does it get diagnosed? One writer drew up a list of 99 of the most prevalent symptoms. They include: "achievement low in some areas, high in others," "general awkwardness," "slowness in finishing work," "sleep abnormally light or deep," "possibly negative and aggressive to authority" and "sweet and even-tempered, cooperative and friendly."[40] Sound like any child you know, or possibly every child you know? MBD is not easily defined, and that is why the label is so easy to pin on a child, because there are no strict diagnostic guidelines. According to two authors who did a comprehensive review of the medical literature on the subject, the reasoning behind the acceptance of MBD was "circular—that is authors have assumed that behaviors such as hyperactivity were signs of brain damage independent of neurologic indexes, and, therefore, that many behavior problem children had brain damage."[41] They also point out that "to date, no neurological sign or test or combination of tests has been established through cross-validation to differentiate hyperactive children or those with minimal brain dysfunction from normal control subjects."

Simple acceptance of the diagnosis of MBD just on the basis of behavior can be very dangerous. One five-year-old girl who seemed to be hyperactive turned out to have heart problems. Another child had behavioral problems from sleeplessness—caused by pinworms.[42] This is not to imply that a condition called hyperactivity, or to be more medically correct, hyperkinesis, does not exist. It does, but only in a very small number of children who usually have objectively demonstrable brain damage.

If the diagnosis is in doubt, the treatment is not. It is Ritalin (methylphenidate) made by CIBA, one of the giant multinational drug companies. Ritalin is an amphetamine congener, that is, it is not an amphetamine but its structure is similar to that family of drugs. Initially, it was believed that Ritalin had a paradoxical effect on hyperactive children. Whereas normally it would be expected to speed them up further (as is true with adults), it "paradoxically" slows them down. Now the predominant theory is that Ritalin works not by changing the level of activity, but by allowing the child to focus his or her activity on a single subject. Clearly, beliefs about Ritalin and its effects are not very scientific.

A positive response to Ritalin is one of the ways cited for confirming the diagnosis of MBD. Therefore, in order to promote Ritalin, it is necessary to promote the whole concept of MBD. Many of the authorities in the field of MBD conduct research supported by CIBA or other companies which make similar products. As one doctor said of his MBD research budget, "Whenever we need money they'll [the drug companies] give me some."[43]

One of the keys, of course, to successfully promoting the drug and the disease is a good advertising campaign. In one journal ad, two side-by-side pictures showed an angry looking child staring at a book on his desk with his fist raised, while in the second panel the same child was peacefully working.[44] The implication was obvious—Ritalin caused this change. In large type doctors were asked: "What medical practitioner has not, at one time or another, been called upon to examine an impulsive, excitable hyperkinetic child? A child with difficulty in concentrating. Easily frustrated. Overly aggressive. A classroom rebel." Just a little further down the page, doctors were informed that MBD was "now readily diagnosed," and there was a "special role for Ritalin." (Whether as a nod to the truth or as a means of self-protection, the ad did point out that Ritalin was not effective for all childhood behavior disorders.) As with Valium, Ritalin provides an easy way to avoid probing into causes of behavioral problems. And advertising reinforces the busy physician's tendency to treat problems quickly and cleanly.

Ritalin ads were reinforced with other material. In 1973, CIBA published a 96 page *Physician's Handbook: Screening for MBD*, available free to any doctor who wished it. A second booklet, *Minimal Brain Dysfunction: Guidelines to Diagnosis/Guidelines to Treatment* was also produced. The text of the second urged that "the MBD child should be treated now" and warned that "drug therapy can make the difference between keeping the MBD child in his normal class and having him placed elsewhere."[45] Nowhere in either of these publications was it said that many of the assumptions and definitions were disputed by serious scientific research.

To date, four studies have evaluated the effects of long-term treatment with Ritalin.[46] One of these was conducted at the Montreal Children's Hospital in the early 1970s.[47] Three groups of hyperactive children were studied over a five-year period. One group received no treatment, one group was treated with Ritalin for three to five years, and the third group was treated with chlorpromazine (a major tranquillizer) for eighteen months to five years. At the end of the five years, there were no statistically significant differences between the three groups as measured by emotional adjustment, delinquency, IQ, visual-motor ability or academic performance. All groups also showed the same degree of improvement in hyperactivity and family stability. Ritalin made the children more obedient at school and at home but this group differed in no other way from the group receiving no drug treatment at all. The study also suggested that Ritalin might slow down a child's rate of physical growth. Interestingly, growth retardation is not mentioned as a possible side effect in the promotional literature for Ritalin. The other three studies all confirmed the lack of long-term effectiveness of Ritalin. According to Dr. Sydney Walker, a neuropsychiatrist, "It may well be that stimulant drugs produce greater harm in the long run than the hyperactive symptoms they are meant to control."[48]

Despite these reports and other literature critical of Ritalin, some 200,000 to 300,000 children in the U.S. were taking the drug *daily* in the early 1970s.[49] The number using Ritalin in Canada is not known, but in 1971 Sidney Katz wrote in the Toronto *Star* that "daily doses...of amphetamine like drugs...are being used to control the behaviour of a large number of unruly school children."[50]

Schrag and Divoky, in their book *The Myth of the Hyperactive Child*, point out that the most common defence for using drugs such as Ritalin is that the use of medication to alter children's behavior is better than failure and punishment. A common rationalization offered by the proponents of drugs is that no one has the right to deprive a child of a chance for treatment and thereby to increase the child's risk of subsequent failure and more serious problems. But according to Schrag and Divoky, such statements are generally made by the same people who define failure and determine punishment. These statements, and the people making them, assume that there exists a connection between present diagnosis and future behavior, and that the remedies provided will be at least as effective as no intervention at all. Neither of these two assertions has so far been proven. Moreover, the use of drugs teaches children that they cannot control their own behavior; that they need a medication, an external influence, to make them "good." And if they are not good, it is because they forgot their pills or their pills are not working.

Schrag and Divoky reach essentially the same conclusion as did Waldron. They state that the ideology that encourages drug therapy is one that seeks to eliminate nonconformity by defining it as a medical problem. Individuals lose both the ability to assert themselves and the personal rewards that such assertiveness brings. The political possibilities that could be realized by confronting the system are also lost:

> By converting social problems into medical cases or into subjects for "behavior modification," the ideology obviates legal and institutional due process and encourages the individual to surrender his right to confront, question and challenge, however rudimentary that right may be.[51]

The histories of Valium and Ritalin combine to illustrate the practices of the drug industry that were alluded to in the introduction. Prices are kept high by limiting competition and these high prices in turn lead to high profits. Massive advertising campaigns directed at doctors play on biases that some doctors already hold and encourage physicians to view an ever-widening range of problems as coming within the purview of medicine, and therefore being subject to drug therapy. These same ads ignore real health hazards associated with the drugs they promote. People's health actually suffers from the over-consumption of drugs. Society's health suffers as the underlying social and political problems are turned into problems of the individual. Governments usually sit on the sidelines as passive observers of the drug industry, acting only when the situation becomes so intolerable that not acting is no longer an option.

Chapter 2
The Industry:
Ethics and Organization

The calling of a pharmaceutical manufacturer is
one dedicated to a most important public
service, and such public service shall be the first
and ruling consideration in all dealings.
—Principles and Code of
Marketing Practice, Pharmaceutical
Manufacturers Association of
Canada[1]

The pharmaceutical industry has never claimed
to be motivated by altruism, but rather by
profit for survival.
—W.M. Garton, President
Pharmaceutical Manufacturers
Association of Canada[2]

Ethics
The key to understanding the industry lies in the second quote. The
motivation for the pharmaceutical industry is profit; considerations
such as public service take second place. The incompatability
between public service and private profit becomes evident when the
stated ethics of the industry clash with the realities of turning a
profit.

In 1982, the *Globe and Mail* reported that the Canadian Pediatric
Society was very concerned that most drugs have never been tested
in children and that doctors were left largely on their own to

determine safe and effective dosages.[3] The society was seeking research funds to investigate proper pediatric doses of important drugs. In its quest for money the society approached the drug industry but was turned down. The PMAC also refused the Canadian Institute of Child Health when it asked for money. The 1981-82 annual report of the pediatric society, quoted in the same *Globe* article, drew the following conclusion: "Since the PMAC board is composed of marketing-oriented executives and no medical representatives, one must assume that their rejection is based on a failure to perceive the commercial importance of the pediatric drug market." Bluntly put, the drug industry did not foresee adequate profitability in the pediatric market and therefore was unwilling to spend the money necessary to determine the safety of drugs in children.

In 1975, medical reports began appearing which warned that sudden withdrawal of a drug called propranolol, marketed by Ayerst Laboratories as Inderal and used for treating high blood pressure and angina (heart pain), could lead to heart attacks in some cases. Warnings to that effect were appearing in advertisements in American medical journals, but not in Canadian ones. (Since then such warnings have also been included in advertisements in Canadian medical journals.) When asked about this discrepancy, a representative for Ayerst said, "This is of no concern to the consuming public...We're getting into more complex drugs. We can't inform the public on them all."[4] At that time Inderal was the twelfth most frequently prescribed drug in Canada.

According to the PMAC:

> Preparations must be labelled and merchandised only in a manner free from misrepresentation, misleading practices of all kinds and in entire harmony with the highest standards of commercial morality and professional ethics.[5]

In 1965, Merck Sharp and Dohme was preparing a mass campaign in Canada and the United States to introduce indomethacin, an anti-arthritic drug marketed under the name Indocid. By early 1966, medical journals in both countries were running eight-page color ads stating that indomethacin was "the most promising antirheumatic agent that has been made available for clinical investigation since the introduction of cortisone."[6] This statement could have been, and probably was, misinterpreted by doctors to mean that the drug could be used in all forms of rheumatic disease, but in fact it had been tested in only four types. Indocid was described as "safer" and "more effective," but the ads never did say safer or more effective than what.

Nothing was known about the drug's effects on children and it was recommended by government monitoring bodies that the prescribing directions should warn against use in children. Merck altered this warning in the actual directions to read "not recommended for use in children" and the fine print in the ads further changed this to: "Safety in pediatric age groups...has not been established," thereby implying that the drug might be safe in children, but more experience was needed. By November 1966, the Food and Drug Directorate in Ottawa had become concerned enough about deaths in children using Indocid that it sent letters directly to every physician in Canada stating: "We recommend that indomethacin should not be used in children until the results of further studies become available."[7]

The Merck ads also contained testimonials from physicians, one of whom claimed to have used Indocid and found it "extremely helpful in over 500 patients." Unfortunately, as later revelations showed, he had never treated anywhere near 500 people with the drug.[8] The ads further claimed that the drug did not increase susceptibility to infection, but they did not mention that this claim was based on experiments with rats involving a procedure which could not assure the same results in humans. In fact, the drug does increase human susceptibility to infection.[9]

Not quite an example of merchandising "free from misrepresentation, misleading practices and in harmony with the highest standards of commercial morality and professional ethics." But then there is a potential $6 billion a year market for an arthritis "cure,"[10] which is essentially what Indocid was being marketed as.

Organization

The early Canadian drug industry was divided into domestically owned companies, the first one established in Toronto in 1879 by E.B. Shuttleworth, and foreign-owned subsidiaries, the original being started in Windsor in 1887 by Parke, Davis and Company. The branch plant operations were set up to take advantage of provisions in the Canadian tariff laws designed to protect domestic manufacturers from competition from foreign imports. Companies that made their finished products in Canadian facilities with 20 to 25 percent of the value of the products being added in Canada qualified to have their drugs designated as "made in Canada." This designation meant that the fine chemicals used in the production process could enter the country with only a 15 percent duty or could come in duty free. Any foreign company importing a competing product which had no value added in Canada found its drug subject to a tariff of 20 percent. Therefore, in order to undercut a competitor's price a company would establish a manufacturing facility in Canada. The size of the Canadian operation would then grow with sales and as new products were introduced. However, the branch plants usually confined their activities to secondary manufacturing and sales as there was no incentive for backward integration into the manufacture of fine chemicals, or for undertaking research or any other activities that could be done at the corporate headquarters.[11]

In the 1940s, the Canadian industry underwent a dramatic transformation. As potent new drugs, especially antibiotics, were rapidly developed and marketed the location of pharmaceutical preparations shifted from the drugstore to the factory, where sophisticated technological processes were employed in the synthesis of the active ingredients in the new drugs. Economies of scale became possible in the manufacture of these drugs and production was centralized in a few centres. This centralization coupled with a reduction in the transportation costs and an increasing openness of world trade spelt the end for many small domestic Canadian companies. Unable to compete on the scale demanded by the new technology most of them fell under foreign control. Prior to World War II a significant portion of the industry had been Canadian controlled, but the postwar wave of acquisitions left only one domestically owned company of any consequence, Connaught Laboratories.

Ayerst, McKenna and Harrison provides a good example of the fate of most of the Canadian firms.[12] In the prewar years, Ayerst had a large and vigorous research and development organization that was, in the Canadian context, quite successful in discovering new products. However, the Canadian market was too small to generate the gross profits necessary to continue this R&D activity. The testing, marketing and other requirements that would have been necessary for Ayerst to expand into foreign markets would have meant further investment that was large and risky in relation to the firm's size. At the same time, the U.S. firm American Home Products had the resources and expertise necessary for entry into the American and other markets, and was interested in entering the pharmaceutical field. Consequently, Ayerst was purchased by American Home Products in 1943. Over the next twenty years, other large Canadian companies were also bought out: E.B. Shuttleworth Chemical Company, by Pitman-Moore in 1957; Frank W. Horner, by Carter Products in 1963; and Charles E. Frosst, by Merck Sharp and Dohme in 1965.

In 1981, there were 138 companies competing in the Canadian pharmaceutical market. These firms can be divided into three distinct types: 1. subsidiaries of multinational companies; 2. generic companies that manufacture drugs that are ineligible for patents, drugs for which patents have expired and patented drugs for which they have obtained compulsory licences; and 3. biological companies, such as Connaught, that produce such products as vaccines, insulins and blood by-products. A number of the generic companies are Canadian-controlled and there are two associations of domestically owned companies: the Canadian Drug Manufacturers Association with twelve members in Ontario, Quebec and British Columbia, and the Association des Fabricants du Quebec de Produits Pharmaceutiques representing about ten Quebec-based manufacturers. The subsidiaries of the multinationals dominate the Canadian market, controlling over 90 percent of it. All of the large multinationals belong to the PMAC, including Ayerst and Merck Sharp and Dohme, now Merck Frosst Canada Inc., two of the four largest companies in Canada (see Table 2-1). The PMAC membership is overwhelmingly made up of foreign-owned corporations. In 1961, when the PMAC had 57 members, seven were Canadian owned, but by 1981 that number was down to four of 66 (see Table 2-2). These 66 firms control about 90 percent of the dollar volume of prescription drugs sold in Canada.[13]

The PMAC acts as the voice of the multinationals. Despite its lofty "Principles of Ethics," some of which were quoted above, the PMAC's main purpose is to ensure that no action is taken, especially by government, that might endanger the profitability of the industry. It began life in 1914 under the name of the Canadian Association of Manufacturers of Medicinals and Toilet Products, but

Table 2-1: The 21 Largest Pharmaceutical Firms in Canada—1981

Rank	Company Name	Canadian Sales $(000,000)	Country of Ownership	PMAC Member
1	Merck Frosst Canada Ltd.	84.2	United States	Yes
2	Smith Kline & French Canada Ltd.	62.3	United States	Yes
3	CIBA-Geigy Ltd.	52.0	Switzerland	Yes
4	Ayerst Laboratories Inc.	47.5	United States	Yes
5	Wyeth Ltd.	45.3	United States	Yes
6	Parke, Davis Canada Inc.	40.6	United States	Yes
7	Abbott Laboratories Ltd.	38.7	United States	Yes
8	Travenol Canada Inc.	33.9	United States	Yes
9	Syntex Inc.	33.2	United States	Yes
10	Upjohn Company of Canada	32.3	United States	Yes
11	Glaxo Holdings Ltd.	31.8	United Kingdom	Yes
12	Schering Canada Inc.	27.2	United States	Yes
13	Ortho Pharmaceuticals (Canada) Inc.	27.2	United States	Yes
14	Sandoz Ltd.	25.1	Switzerland	Yes
15	Eli Lilly Canada Inc.	24.8	United States	Yes
16	Sterling Drug Ltd.	24.0	United States	Yes
17	Burroughs Wellcome Inc.	23.8	United Kingdom	Yes
18	Hoffman-LaRoche Ltd.	23.4	Switzerland	Yes
19	Pfizer Canada Inc.	22.7	United States	Yes
20	Searle Pharmaceuticals	21.1	United States	Yes
21	Squibb Canada Inc.	20.0	United States	Yes

Note: All divisions of a single parent company are combined under one listing for purposes of this table if the divisions all operate out of the same physical facilities. Companies that are owned by the same parent, but which maintain separate Canadian corporate headquarters are listed separately. An example of the first case is Merck Sharp and Dohme and Frosst which are grouped under Merck Frosst Canada Ltd. An example of the second case is Ayerst and Wyeth, both owned by American Home Products but which are listed separately in this table.

Table adapted from: R.C. Kennett, *Profile of the Pharmaceutical Industry in Canada,* Supply and Services Canada, Ottawa, April 1982, p. 8.
Compulsory Licensing of Pharmaceuticals: A Review of Section 41 of the Patent Act, Consumer and Corporate Affairs Canada, Ottawa, 1983, p. 8.

Table 2-2: PMAC Membership—Nationality of Firm

	American	British	Swiss	Canadian	Other
No. of Companies	42	6	4	4	10

Sources: *Who Owns Whom—North America 1977/78*, Dun & Bradstreet, London, 1978.
Inter-Corporate Ownership 1978-79, Statistics Canada, Ottawa, 1979.
A Profile, PMAC, Ottawa, 1980.
Drug Merchandising, 64:26-42, April 1983.

a year later that name was shed for the more distinguished sounding Canadian Pharmaceutical Manufacturers Association (CPMA). The present name was adopted in 1965. Initially the CPMA had offices in Toronto, but in the early 1960s the headquarters was moved to Ottawa. According to the then-general manager S.N. Condor, this relocation was made so that the headquarters would be readily accessible to the full membership of the CPMA, which was about equally divided between Ontario and Quebec.[14] A more honest reason for the move was given by Condor's successor, Guy Beauchemin, who said, "The CPMA was being designed to pressure."[15]

Ronald Lang, in his book *The Politics of Drugs*, makes the point that at the time of the move, the federal government had begun to take a more active interest in the drug industry. The Director of Investigation and Research in the Combines Division in Ottawa had started an investigation in 1958 and this report prompted an inquiry by the Restrictive Trade Practices Commission between 1961 and 1963. Both of these reports called Canadian drug prices the "highest in the world" and suggested the patent system was the major cause of this situation. Some form of government action seemed to be on the horizon.

With the office move, the PMAC was also restructured into six major divisions, each with its own vice-president. According to Lang the titles of these divisions alone show that the industry was mobilizing itself in order to be able to call on influential groups and organizations to help it stand up to the government: government relations division, pharmacy relations division, professional (or medical) relations division, public relations division, special projects division and sections operations division. CPMA general manager S.N. Condor said that "through these six operating divisions, supplemented by experienced staff personnel, CPMA had the administrative machinery with which to meet any major problem affecting Canada's pharmaceutical manufacturing industry."[16] In 1968, the PMAC occupied a suite of offices a few blocks from the parliament buildings and was preparing for its first major battle with the federal government, a battle over the issue of patents that we shall examine later.

Chapter 3
Prices and Profits

*I can't honestly say that drug prices are cheap. I
think they're reasonable only for those who can
afford to pay the price.*
—V.D. Mattia, M.D.
President of Hoffman-LaRoche
(U.S.)[1]

Prices

The price of drugs is not an easy topic. All kinds of figures measuring
different parameters clutter up the issue. A look at Table 3-1 should
make that obvious. The average cost of a prescription more than
tripled between 1956 and 1980, but what does that mean? The price
could have gone up because more expensive drugs were being
prescribed; because there was more medicine per prescription; or
because prescriptions were being written to cover longer periods of
time. The rise in per capita expenditure could be similarly explained.
According to Peter Ruderman,[2] if the outpatient prescription
expenditure is revised to take into account changes in both
population and prescription prices, then the number of prescriptions
per capita exactly doubled between 1960 and 1971, thereby
accounting for much of the rise in per capita expenditure.

The drug industry loves to refer to the Consumer Price Index
(CPI), since that seems to indicate a remarkably slow rise in the price
of drugs.[3] But the CPI should be used with caution. It measures the
changes in prices of only a small "basket" of drugs. To be sure that it
is an accurate reflection of drug prices we would have to know the
answers to a number of questions. Are the products whose prices are

37

Table 3-1: Changes in the Price of Drugs: 1956-1981

	Overall Consumer Price Index (1961=100)	CPI for Prescribed Drugs (1961=100)	Outpatient Prescription Expenditure (1960=100)	Personal Income (1960=100)	Per Capita Expenditure on Prescribed Drugs ($)	Average Cost Per Prescription ($)
1956	–	–	–	–	5.69	2.49
1961	100.0	100.0	102	102	7.87	3.14
1966	111.4	97.9	175	156	–	3.34
1971	133.4	93.8	319	248	18.64	3.73
1976	198.6	113.6	–	–	31.66	5.02
1981	316.0	170.3	–	–	57.00 (est.)	8.19 (1980)

Sources: *Restrictive Trade Practices Commission Report Concerning the Manufacture, Distribution and Sale of Drugs*, Queen's Printer, Ottawa, 1963, p. 388.
Report on the Provision, Distribution and Cost of Drugs in Canada, A Study Prepared for the Royal Commission on Health Services, Queen's Printer, Ottawa, 1964, p. 68.
A.P. Ruderman, "The Drug Business in the Context of Canadian Health Care Programs," *International Journal of Health Services*, 4:641-650, 1974.
A Survey on Prescriptions 1977, Conducted for Drug Merchandising and Le Pharmacien, Maclean-Hunter Research Bureau, Toronto, July 1977, p. 29.
Background Information on the Canadian Pharmaceutical Manufacturing Industry, PMAC, Ottawa, 1979, Appendices 1, 4.
Consumer Prices and Price Indexes—October-December 1981, Statistics Canada, Ottawa, 1982.
Halifax Chronicle Herald, July 26, 1982, p. 18.

being measured truly representative of what people are buying? Are the drugs patented, which ensures a higher price, or not? Are brand name or generic name drugs being used? How often are the drugs changed which are used in the index? This last point would seem to be particularly important, because between revisions, the CPI would not reflect the introduction of any new drugs. In fact, the CPI covers only five drugs on a weighted basis, and as a result the index reflects price changes of only a small fraction of the thousands of drugs used today in Canada. The Royal Commission on Health Services concluded that "any examination of drug prices requires more intensive inquiry than reliance on the general purpose price index on drugs currently used."[4]

Although it may be difficult to come to any conclusions about the movement of drug prices, it is much easier to discover who bears the heaviest burden of the cost of drugs. One group is people 55 to 64 years of age. In most provinces, they do not qualify for government assistance in the purchase of drugs, but they are reaching the point where their health is starting to deteriorate and their incomes are declining. In Saskatchewan in 1978, people in this age group received benefits from that province's drug plan of $52.75 a year, compared to an average per capita cost of $31.91.[5] In most other provinces, where this group of people would not have drug insurance, they would have to shoulder this extra cost individually.

The poor spend a far greater proportion of their income on prescription drugs than do the wealthy, as can be seen in Table 3-2. Not only that, but, surprisingly, a much lower percentage of the poor than of the rich report spending any money at all on prescription drugs. This difference is surprising because it is well known that income is inversely related to illness.[6] It may be that the cost of prescription drugs is deterring the poor from purchasing them. At least one study partially confirms this conclusion. A follow-up study was done on patients who were taking "essential medication" upon discharge from a hospital in London, Ontario. It was found that almost one third of the time the cost of the drugs was a significant factor in explaining why medications were not taken properly.[7]

On an international scale, three different studies between 1961 and 1972 concluded that Canadian drug prices were among the highest, if not the highest, in the world.[8] (Even representatives of the drug industry, such as William Robson, president and chief executive of

**Table 3-2: Income and Expenditure on Prescription Drugs, 1978,
All Families and Unattached Individuals**

| | Income (per year) | | | |
	Less than $6000	$6000-7999	$30000-34999	Greater than $35000
Expenditure on prescription drugs ($)	18.4	27.1	44.4	59.8
Percent of group reporting expenditure	30.0	38.3	69.7	67.3
Expenditure on prescription drugs as a percent of total expediture	0.35	0.35	0.15	0.15

Source: *Family Expenditure in Canada,* Volume 2, Statistics Canada, Ottawa, 1981.

Smith Kline and French Canada, conceded that "drug prices probably were higher than they should have been in the 1960s."[9]) How did the pharmaceutical industry respond to these studies? Sometimes, the industry resorted to what I refer to as the "drugs are inexpensive (relatively)" argument. Drug costs in various countries were compared with the number of hours of work required to pay for prescription drugs. "Labor indices" were prepared which showed that Canadians were able to buy their drugs with fewer hours of work than people in most other countries. This argument, however, is not acceptable because it avoids the question of whether the prices were reasonable with respect to manufacting costs and profit levels.[10]

Equally fallacious were claims about the comparative cost of drugs in relation to the benefits derived. Again we were told nothing about the reasonableness of the prices. By that standard we should be willing to pay a hundred dollars for a pint of brake fluid if our car breaks down on a remote highway in the middle of the night. After all, that brake fluid would provide relief from misery, permanent disablement or even death.[11]

The industry's third line of defence was to claim that costs for research and quality control were so high as to justify the prices charged. The expenses involved in research and quality control will be explored in later chapters, but for now it should suffice to say that neither of these was considered significant by the Royal Commission on Health Services.

Since the early 1970s, the multinationals have continued to maintain drug prices at artifically high levels. The explanation for the high cost of drugs in Canada seems to revolve around two themes—competition, or the lack thereof, and foreign domination of the Canadian industry.

I. Competition

The selling price of a drug does not reflect the cost of its production. Even the drug companies admit this,[12] although occasionally the industry has trouble keeping its arguments consistent. For instance, testifying before the Restrictive Trade Practices Commission, the counsel for several of the drug companies said: "They [the drug companies] have been supplying the market at prices which people in the industry know what it costs to make these things, prices which are related to these costs."[13] Drugs are priced at the level of the products already on the market with which they must compete, regardless of the production costs. Tolbutamide is an oral antidiabetic drug produced by a relatively inexpensive process compared to the production costs for insulin. However, when it was introduced, its price was identical to that of insulin, because insulin was the competition.[14]

New semisynthetic penicillins were introduced into the Canadian market in the mid-1950s. Despite manufacturing costs which varied from $54 per kilogram to $196 per kilogram, they were all sold at almost the same price. A similar situation prevailed with the drugs of the tetracycline family.[15] The industry claimed that essentially identical prices were not the result of patent control, but represented exactly the result to be expected from active competition. "The [Restrictive Trade Practices] Commission, however, does not find this argument convincing... The Commission's view is strengthened by the fact that the prescribing physician does not pay for the drug and, according to the evidence before us... very frequently does not know either the price of the drug he prescribes or those of alternatives."[16]

In 1977, the PMAC published a table of the most frequently prescribed drugs in Canada.[17] The purpose of this table was to show that drug prices had remained stable or decreased, since their introduction. Analysing this table differently, according to whether or not these products were subject to significant price competition, yields far different results. (Price competition, in this instance, was defined as a 25 percent difference between the highest and lowest priced brands of the same drug.) Of the eleven products where price competition existed, the price decreased on nine. Of the eleven where there was no price competition, the price increased on eight. This difference in price changes is a clear indication of the effect of competition on the movement of drug prices. Leslie Dan, president of Novopharm Limited, the largest Canadian-owned pharmaceutical manufacturing company, gives two further examples illustrating the effect of competition on drug prices. In the first example, he notes that for the first twelve years of Inderal's existence, Ayerst continually increased the price. In 1980 when a competitor was marketed, the price of Inderal suddenly dropped by 25 to 35 percent. Similarly, when a competitor to Smith Kline and French's Dyazide (triamterene-hydrochlorthiazide) appeared in 1982, the price for Dyazide also dropped by 25 to 35 percent.[18]

Mr. Dan's observations are backed up by Patrick Tidball, the manager of British Columbia's Pharmacare program. According to Mr. Tidball: "The average per hundred price of multisource products has remained low and has actually declined from 1974 to 1979. Where products are available from only one manufacturer, however, the average per hundred price has remained high and has increased during the same period."[19] The reality is that for most products there is only a single supplier. The July 1, 1982, edition of Ontario's *Drug Benefit Formulary* lists a total of 1,335 different preparations. (This figure includes different dosage forms of the same drug and different formulations of the same drug; for instance a drug may be marketed as pills, capsules, solutions, creams or ointments.) Almost 75 percent of these preparations were available from only one manufacturer. In only 138 cases, or 10 percent of the total, was there significant price competition. (The definition of significant price competition is the same that applied above.)

Finally, we can look at the effects of price competition on the prices of drugs in Canada as compared to prices internationally. A 1978 PMAC study[20] compared the price of the nineteen top selling drugs in Canada with the price of the same drugs in seven other industrialized countries. Of the nineteen drugs, seven were subject to competition. For those seven the Canadian price was, on average, 55 per cent of the price in the other seven countries. For the twelve drugs immune to price competition, the Canadian price was, on average, almost 75 percent of the international price. Clearly, if Canadian drug prices are dropping below those in other parts of the world, competition in Canada must be a major force in the drop.

Even when new methods of production for the same product are developed the price often remains unchanged. The price of corticosteroids, for example, was established when oxbile was used and it was necessary to slaughter hundreds of animals to yield a few grams of steroid. This laborious, costly process was described by the Upjohn company: "...oxbile is not a readily available commodity on the market in large quantities. It was scarce. It was expensive. The process...had some 40 steps or more. It was an extremely complicated chemical synthesis...The costs of the material were very high." In place of this older process Upjohn devised a new method referred to as "the most ecnomical and versatile steroid processes presently available anywhere in the world today."[21] Despite this change in production techniques, the price of steroids did not change at all.

In fact, according to a 1976 study on competition in the Canadian drug industry, price cuts in drugs are usually applied only during the last stages of the product's life cycle, when the decision to withdraw the product is being made.[22] This stability in prices exists because "the control exercised over the manufacture, distribution and sale of certain drugs through patents has virtually eliminated price competition in respect of such drugs."[23] Some industry representatives maintain that price competition is not necessarily desirable from the social point of view. They argue that in a research-oriented industry the profits resulting from having a temporary monopoly on the drug through the mechanism of patent protection are needed to sustain a reasonable flow of innovations. However, this same study analyses the magnitude of the discrepancy between the prices charged by the large companies for their brand name products and the smaller companies for their generic equivalents. It concludes that the significantly higher prices charged by the research-oriented companies could not be accounted for by their research and development expenditures.[24]

In place of price competition, the industry has given us product competition. In product competition drugs are promoted not on the basis of being less expensive than other equivalent products, but on the grounds that they are superior in their action, whether or not that is in fact the case. Companies identify successful drugs sold by their competitors and then expend large quantities of money in an attempt to invent new drugs that circumvent existing patents and thereby secure their own product for which they can obtain a patent.[25] "Above all, regular new marketable discoveries are absolutely vital in the fight for...sales," was what one industry-oriented magazine had to say.[26]

Product competition is a formidable entry barrier into therapeutic markets, especially for small companies. (A "therapeutic market" consists of drugs used in the treatment of a particular problem or disease, such as arthritis or ulcers. All drugs can be placed into one, or more, therapeutic markets, depending on how many uses the drug has.) In order to develop a new patentable product a company must be able to expend substantial capital, first on research and later on marketing. Smaller companies lack the necessary funding and therefore are denied entry into the market. The strength of the entry barrier into the pharmaceutical manufacturing industry is illustrated in a 1974 study of 71 Canadian manufacturing industries. The entry barrier was measured against the following five characteristics: empirically observed ability to meet capital requirements, advertising intensity, research and development intensity, risk and level of concentration within the industry. Of the 71 industries, the pharmaceutical industry had the twelfth highest entry barrier.[27]

The net result, has been a high level of concentration within therapeutic markets. Among the large firms, a pattern of specialization has emerged that tends to break the companies into smaller, rather exclusive groups. Each group shares a market such as antibiotics or steroids. In the late 1960s, an economist who had closely studied the industry concluded that "while the exact order of firms in a market may change, the positions of leadership are effectively preserved for the large firms specializing in that area. Concentration thus tends to be both high in degree and stability."[28]

The PMAC tries to hide this type of market concentration by talking about overall industry concentration statistics instead. In

1976, the latest year for which figures are available, the top four drug manufacturers, all foreign controlled, accounted for less than 25 percent of total pharmaceutical industry shipments. The PMAC weighs these figures against the comparable figure of 50 percent for all Canadian manufacturing industries and proclaims that "drug manufacturing is relatively unconcentrated."[29] However, these figures ignore the relatively high degree of concentration in therapeutic markets just referred to. In 1982, in 28 out of 38 major therapeutic markets, two companies accounted for more than 50 percent of sales. For example: two companies had 100 percent of the respiratory stimulant market; two had 66 percent of the diuretic ("water pill") market; and two had 60 percent of the anticonvulsant market.[30]

A look at Table 3-3 shows that by 1976, the top four companies controlled over 50 percent of sales in ten of the fourteen markets listed. Moreover, in at least seven of these markets concentration had increased between 1964 and 1976. Finally, there was a high degree of stability in terms of company leadership in these fourteen markets between 1964 and 1976. Of the top four companies in each of these markets in 1964, three were still in the top four in 1976 in five markets; two were still in the top four in another five markets; and in four markets one company was left in the top four.

Since patents inhibit competition, it is also reasonable to assume that they allow companies to maintain prices at unduly high levels. The price of antibiotics during the 1950s provides an example of this practice. By 1953, there were three patented broad spectrum antibiotics on the market: Aureomycin (chlortetracycline), manufactured by Lederle, Chloromycetin, (chloramphenicol), manufactured by Parke, Davis, and Terramycin (oxytetracycline), manufactured by Pfizer. All three sold at exactly the same price, $5.10 for sixteen capsules of 250 milligrams. Between 1953 and 1960, two more patented broad spectrum drugs were introduced and both sold at $5.10 for sixteen capsules. During the seven year period to 1960, the price of all five drugs remained unchanged. When it eventually did drop in 1960, the reason was the importation of lower cost European drugs, which introduced a measure of price competition. According to the Restrictive Trade Practices Commission, "it was as if the price established in 1953 had come to be regarded as the right price."[31] During this same period, the price of "old" penicillin, which was unpatented, went down 80

Table 3-3: Concentration in Fourteen Therapeutic Markets

Therapeutic Market	Percent of Market Controlled by Top Four Companies 1964	1976	Percent Change in Market Concentration 1964-1976	Number of Companies in Top Four in 1976 That Were in Top Four in 1964
Bronchial Dilators	51.8	72.9	40.7	1
Ethical Cough and Cold Preparations	42.9	54.3	26.6	3
Hormones, Plain Corticoids	60.2	72.3	20.1	2
Penicillin	78.8	89.7	13.8	3
Hematinics	34.0	38.1	12.1	1
Ethical Laxatives	43.8	46.8	6.8	3
Sex Hormones	81.0	82.2	1.5	2
Hormones, Corticoid Combinations	64.9	63.5	-2.2	3
Ethical Analgesics	69.4	67.0	-3.5	3
Other Hypotensives	104.8*	98.1	-6.4	2
Nutrients	74.7	68.1	-8.8	1
Tranquillizers	77.6	64.7	-16.6	2
Antibiotics, Broad and Medium Spectrum	55.7	46.0	-17.4	1
Vitamins	44.5	33.2	-25.4	2

* There appears to be an error in these figures and therefore concentration movement in this market cannot accurately be assessed.

Source: J.J. Friedman & Associates, *Pharmaceutical Prices in Canada: Guiding Principles for Government Policy,* PMAC, Ottawa, 1981, pp. 177-204.

percent. Considering that the costs of producing broad spectrum antibiotics fell by about as much as the costs of producing penicillin did, it seems that the difference in their price reductions can only be due to the presence or absence of patent protection. Commenting on the difference in price changes between the broad spectrum antibiotics and penicillin, the report issued under the Combines Investigation Act said, "it would appear that the larger drug manufacturers have in recent years attempted to avoid a repetition of the experiences with penicillin...and any manufacturer discovering a new drug has sought to control its sale and distribution."[32]

Another example of the inflationary effects of patents on prices derives from a United States Senate Antitrust Subcommittee which found that the average price of twelve major drugs was 60 percent lower in countries that did not issue product patents than in countries that did. Further investigation showed that the higher prices could not be accounted for by any greater rate of inventiveness in the countries granting the patents.[33]

Eventually other companies are able to market competing drugs either as a result of acquiring a compulsory licence, a licence to manufacture or import a drug in return for payment of a royalty fee to the patent holder, or because the originating company's patent has expired or by developing a therapeutically similar product. But even under these circumstances the first firm to offer and promote a new type of product has a substantial and enduring sales advantage. According to a study done for the U.S. Federal Trade Commission:

> In each market the success of the first brand did stimulate other firms to enter with therapeutically substitutable products. Yet such follow-on brands failed to dislodge the early entrant from a dominant position.[34]

The market power gained by being first permits the companies that introduced the drugs to continue to charge higher prices than their competitors and still maintain a dominant share of the market.[35] Due to the higher prices of brand name drugs, the multinational companies end up with about 80 percent of the market share, based on dollar sales.[36] A 1980 survey of pharmacies across Canada dealt with the question of which drug was used in filling a prescription when selection was allowed. (Product selection means that a pharmacist is allowed to substitute one therapeutically identical drug for another.) For eight of thirteen drugs surveyed, the first brand on the market, and still the one with the highest price, was either the most frequently or second most frequently used product.[37]

II. Foreign Control

Foreign control is a fact of life for the Canadian industry. In 1981, of the 21 largest companies by sales, none was Canadian-owned (see Table 2-1). Foreign companies controlled about 92 percent of the industry in 1972. That figure is probably several percentage points higher by now; according to a 1980 report from the Department of Industry, Trade and Commerce, the percentage of assets under Canadian control has been declining since 1975.[38] Domestically owned companies supplied only 15 percent of the Canadian pharmaceutical market in 1975, ranking us below countries such as Mexico, Iran, India and the Philippines. Any concerns that may be voiced about such a high degree of foreign ownership are dismissed by the PMAC as the result of "a brooding insular sense of nationalism [which] pervades political thought."[39]

Even when Canadian firms make the same product as U.S. multinationals, it is usually the American product that sells in Canada. Canadian doctors attend the same meetings as their American counterparts, see the same drug company displays and read the same advertisements in U.S. scientific journals. Hence, Canadian doctors are subjected to a constant barrage of information and promotion about drug products developed in the U.S., which are available in Canada through branches or subsidiaries of their U.S. parents. On the other hand, smaller Canadian companies which make generic products have limited promotional budgets. Under these circumstances, it is natural for Canadian physicians to rely on the American brand name product, which is also usually higher in price.

The degree of foreign control over the Canadian market leads to what the Royal Commission on Health Services, in 1964, called "the quite unparalleled payments for research or know-how made by the Canadian subsidiaries to foreign parent companies."[40] These payments, of course, will be included in the price of the drugs.

In 1981, Canada had a trade deficit of over $301 million in pharmaceuticals, versus a $29 million deficit in 1968.[41] Between 1968 and 1979 the fraction of the Canadian market served by imports originating from parent countries or other subsidiaries abroad increased from 13.9 percent of sales to 26.3 percent, while the fraction of the market served by Canadian subsidiaries fell.[42] The PMAC would like us to believe that the 1969 changes in the patent laws have lead to a decline in the growth of pharmaceutical manufacturing in Canada and therefore a more rapid increase in imports than in exports. (See Chapter 11 for a discussion of the changes in Canadian patent laws.) According to James Doherty, PMAC chairman, the bill "has created the impression that Canada is not a good host country and has meant a reduction in plant investment here...The industry has geared down to the Canadian market only."[43]

The PMAC is right about the increase in the trade deficit but at least part of the blame for that growth can be laid at the door of the multinationals. Foreign parent companies, for example, often charge their Canadian subsidiaries exaggerated prices for raw materials, thereby falsely elevating the value of the imports. According to Gorecki, the effect of compulsory licensing on the balance of trade for prescription drugs was of minimal importance.[44]

The PMAC is also right about drug manufacturing in Canada; it is declining relative to total world production of drugs. Between 1967 and 1981, Canada's contribution to the world output of pharmaceuticals fell from 2.6 to 1.6 percent of the total.[45] But the slowdown in manufacturing has little to do with any patent law changes, since these have affected less than 17 percent of total 1981 drug sales.[46]

To begin with, even in the late 1960s drug manufacturing in Canada was minimal. Of all manufacturing, 85 percent was confined to the conversion of imported material into final-dosage form. As well, the Canadian industry imported a number of finished products which were just packaged and marketed here. (Packaging of a drug product in Canada, including merely labelling it for reshipment to pharmacists, apparently qualifies a product for the designation "made in Canada.")[47] The real reason why growth in the manufacturing of drugs in Canada is decreasing from its already low level is that the multinationals are finding that they can generate greater profits by consolidating production in other countries.[48] An analysis of import and export figures confirms that the multinationals are centralizing their production. Between 1968 and 1977, the country which had the largest relative gain in exports to Canada was

Puerto Rico. The rise in imports from Puerto Rico is the result of U.S. companies moving their manufacturing operations there to take advantage of tax concessions.[49] Gordon and Fowler conclude:

> For Canada, importing fine chemicals had been the rule, but what took place during the seventies was the massive transfer abroad of the secondary stages of drug manufacture, including the production of the end product.[50]

Accompanying this shift in production was a predictable decline in production and nonproduction employment in Canadian establishments as a percentage of total employment.[51] The employment shift may also account for the failure of wages in Canada to rise as rapidly in the drug industry as in other Canadian industries.[52]

The companies claim that in addition to the patent laws, another reason for discontinuing manufacturing activity in Canada is because the small size of the Canadian market makes production uneconomical. However, studies have shown that manufacturing costs do not decrease as plants get larger, and that only a relatively small plant is required for economical production.[53]

Because of the high level of imports, the effect of dumping duties becomes an important consideration in the price of drugs in Canada. Dumping duties are applied to drugs imported into Canada if the import price is less than the "fair market value" of the equivalent drug sold in the exporting country. In order to avoid this duty the parent company may jack up the price to its Canadian subsidiary. The Special House of Commons Committee on the price of drugs concluded that "for this reason, imported finished dosage forms of drugs might well be priced higher than would normally be the case, especially in those instances where the importer was a subsidiary of the parent exporting company."[54]

The ability of Canadian branch plants to export drugs is also limited by foreign control. With most patents on drugs foreign-owned, subsidiary companies of the parent patentees control the market within their own jurisdictions. Export activity has to be confined to world areas where patents are not taken out; areas that are commercially insignificant. As a representative of a Canadian subsidiary of one U.S. company said, "We have so many plants all over the world I just do not know where we would export to."[55] Finally, having a successful Canadian operation takes second place to achieving an optimal overall international performance. This situation leads to the finding by the Department of Industry, Trade and Commerce that Canadian subsidiaries are usually "not encouraged or permitted by the head office to assume responsibility for exports of their products."[56]

Foreign domination and a lack of price competition are the factors that allow the pharmaceutical industry to maintain prices in Canada at artificially high levels. However, even if these conditions were changed, there is no guarantee that prices would drop. In the U.S., where the industry is domestically controlled, prices are higher than those in Canada. Furthermore, as we will see in Chapters 11 and 12, government attempts to introduce price competition have been largely unsuccessful, owing to the domination of the industry by a relatively small number of powerful multinationals. Although an industry run by Canadian capitalists, with numerous companies competing in each therapeutic market, would probably lower prices, that is not the ultimate solution to the problem of the cost of drugs. As long as the industry is governed by the profit motive, drugs will always be more expensive than they need be.

Profits

If prices run high, can profits be far behind? Listening to the description of the head of the PMAC offered by a writer for the trade publication *Drug Merchandising* one might believe that the pharmaceutical industry was at death's door: "It's easy to imagine him [PMAC chairman James Doherty] gritting his teeth in private frustration when he considers how tough it is to make a buck in pharmaceuticals in a deteriorating economic climate."[57] The director of marketing for CIBA, Paul Baehr, was more honest about conditions in the industry: "I think in the context of the Canadian environment and looking at other businesses in the Canadian environment, the pharmaceutical business is very healthy."[58] According to a 1980 report from the Department of Industry, Trade and Commerce, "pharmaceutical manufacturing remains among the more profitable manufacturing activities in Canada."[59] A 1983 report by the investment firm of Walwyn Stodgell Cochrane Murray Ltd. of Toronto called the pharmaceutical industry "a particularly attractive area for long-term investment. The field is characterized by high profitability and consistent growth. Favorable demographics assures that this growth will continue well into the foreseeable future."[60]

In all their publications, the PMAC tries to obscure the true rate of profit in the industry, and thereby deflect criticism aimed against it, by referring to profits *after* taxes, when comparing the pharmaceutical industry to other businesses. But in order to compare the profits in the drug industry with all other manufacturing industries, the *before* tax figures should be used. The after-tax rate of profitability of two companies may differ solely because of variations in the rate of income tax depending on the scale of corporate income. The U.S. Task Force on Prescription Drugs suggests that the most useful measure of profitability is probably the rate of return based on invested capital, since the most important consideration for stockholders is generally the relative success of their investment in a company. The Consumers Association of Canada agrees that this is the best index to use and, at one time, so did the PMAC.[61]

Table 3-4, which uses this criterion, contains some revealing findings. It shows that the average rate of return on investment over the eleven year period 1953 to 1963 was 19.71 percent for the pharmaceutical industry as compared to 10.40 percent for all manufacturing, the pharmaceuticals being approximately 90 percent higher. During this period, the return on investment to the drug industry tended to increase, from 16.62 percent in 1953 to 21.92 percent in 1963. At the same time, the return on investment for all manufacturing showed a substantial decline, from 15.03 percent in 1953 to 9.49 percent in 1963.

A similar pattern exists when comparing only companies that made a profit. Over the eleven-year period in question, the average rate of return for all profitable pharmaceutical companies was about 75 percent higher than for all profitable manufacturing companies: 23.2 percent as compared to 13.3 percent. While the rate of return of all profitable manufacturing firms declined by 36.9 percent from 1953 to 1963, that of the profitable pharmaceutical manufacturing firms increased by 31.9 percent.

The PMAC's explanation for this level of profits during the 1950s and early 1960s was that "the period under analysis was a period of growth and upswing for the industry, under the impetus of the development of new drugs, and other wider application in medical treatment, as contrasted with a general stickiness of a considerable part of the period as far as the manufacturing sector of the economy

Table 3-4: Rate of Return on Capital Invested, Before Taxes, 1953-1963, Profit and Loss Companies

	All Manufacturing (%)	Pharmaceuticals (%)
1953	15.03	16.62
1954	11.42	17.63
1955	13.69	18.73
1956	11.68	21.93
1957	9.54	20.47
1958	8.26	19.59
1959	9.25	23.05
1960	8.74	20.55
1961	8.11	18.57
1962	9.20	17.79
1963	9.49	21.92
Average	10.40	19.71

Adapted from: *Second (Final) Report of the Special Committee of the House of Commons on Drug Costs and Prices,* Queen's Printer, Ottawa, 1967, p. 73.

as a whole was concerned." Furthermore, "the rate of profit . . . would seem to be higher than one might expect in the future, both because of indications of more difficult competitive pressures and higher costs."[62]

To be fair to the drug industry, I examined the rate of return on capital employed from 1968 to 1980. (Statistics Canada does not report profit as a percentage of capital invested. The closest category is capital employed.) The results can be seen in Table 3-5. Once again the pharmaceutical industry is much more profitable than manufacturing in general. The average over the thirteen-year period for the drug makers is more than 80 percent higher than for all manufacturing. During the entire period under consideration, the pharmaceutical industry has always been among the top fifteen manufacturing industries. Furthermore, far from declining, the rate of return actually increased over what it had been in the 1953 to 1963 period.

One major factor contributing to the rise in profits was the advent

Table 3-5: Rate of Return on Capital Employed, Before Taxes, 1968-1980, Profit and Loss Companies

Year	All Manufacturing (%)	Pharmaceuticals (%)	Ranking of Pharmaceutical Industry of 87 Manufacturing Industries
1968	10.6	24.9	4
1969	10.7	22.1	6
1970	8.2	20.9	3
1971	9.5	23.8	2
1972	10.8	23.8	3
1973	15.2	22.3	11
1974	17.3	25.0	8
1975	13.4	22.6	10
1976	11.7	19.4	13
1977	10.8	18.7	13
1978	12.8	20.4	12
1979 (prelim)	16.1	24.7	11
1980 (prelim)	14.7	27.0	4
Average	12.4	22.7	7.7

Source: *Corporation Financial Statistics—Detailed Income and Retained Earning Statistics for 182 Industries*, Statistics Canada, Ottawa, Various Years.

of medicare. While the multinational companies cry loud and long about the patent law changes of 1969, they fail to mention that medicare, which started around the same time, gave a substantial boost to their fortunes. More patients visiting doctors meant more prescriptions being written and that, of course, translated into greater sales. A look at the annual increases in the number and dollar value of retail pharmacy prescriptions bears this out. Between 1966 and 1969, the annual growth in the number and value of prescriptions was 4.4 and 7.8 percent respectively. Between 1970 and 1973, the increases were 9.7 and 12.8 percent respectively. In 1970, the changes were most dramatic. The number of prescriptions filled grew by 14.9 percent and their value grew by an incredible 22.6

percent.[63]

As robust as these profits seem, it is quite likely that they are an underestimate of the industry's true profit picture. To start with, the profit figures take into account non-prescription drug making activities,[64] which usually yield lower rates of profit. In 1964, the rate of profit (before taxes, royalties and management fees) on total resources employed was 18.2 percent for the total operations of drug companies in Canada, but their profit on just the manufacturing of pharmaceuticals destined for human use was 24.5 percent.

The 1964 Report of the Royal Commission on Health Services said that "the earnings of the Canadian drug industry are not a satisfactory test of the overall pricing policies of the industry because they are understated."[65] This statement recognizes that multinational firms tend to charge the most advantageous "cost" of raw materials supplied by their plants in other countries, so as to have lower profits in high-tax countries than in low-tax countries. For example, support for this view is found in the Restrictive Trade Practices Commission Report. In the early 1960s, the average rate of profit on sales, before taxes, was 15.7 percent for nine Canadian pharmaceutical branches or subsidiaries, compared to 25.0 percent for their American parents.[66] This trend would appear to be continuing. From 1970 to 1975, the profits of the American pharmaceutical industry on stockholders' equity, after taxes, averaged 16.2 percent, while in Canada, it was only 13.3 percent.[67] Figures for 1979 yield the same result: after tax profit on equity in the U.S. was 18.0 percent compared to 16.1 percent in Canada.[68]

Still more evidence on the same topic is provided by Gordon and Fowler. They conclude that the terms under which resale products (finished products that are imported into Canada for sale), raw materials and business services were transferred from foreign parents to Canadian subsidiaries were designed to transfer profits out of the Canadian subsidiaries. In 1976, the cost to Canadian subsidiaries for resale products was 73.4 percent of sales. This figure, which is more than twice the production cost in the United States on these products, provides the parent companies with substantial profits. Furthermore, the 26.4 percent gross margin did not begin to cover the selling and other overhead expenses incurred by the Canadian subsidiaries, with the result that no profit was reported in Canada. (In 1976, resale products accounted for almost 20 percent of sales in Canada.)[69]

In 1980, the Department of National Revenue launched an industry-wide audit of the international transactions of the pharmaceutical industry. A sampling of fourteen major drugs in Canada, covering the period 1977 to 1979, revealed that prices charged by one subsidiary to another subsidiary of the same company were more than three times higher than the prices paid for the same drugs when the transaction was between two independent companies.[70] Findings of this sort led a representative of the department to comment that "profits were not being reported in Canada but somewhere else."[71] It is believed that because of the government audit, $20 to $25 million in additional tax reassessments were filed and promptly paid by several companies in order to avoid court action.[72] The opinions of the Department of National Revenue were also echoed by Statistics Canada, which felt that many non-arms length import transactions between multinationals and local subsidiaries did not follow the free trade pattern which should normally apply; in other words, these transactions were not based on factors such as production costs and foreign exchange movements that normally favor trade with one country over another. The Statistics Canada report concluded: "Widespread tied trade [trade between subsidiaries of the same company] means that there is a considerable scope for transfer pricing, which may work to undermine tax revenues in Canada."[73]

Looking at the figures in Table 3-5 and all the evidence just presented suggesting that these figures are an understatement of the industry's true profits, it would seem difficult to deny that there are huge profits to be derived from manufacturing pharmaceuticals. But deny it the PMAC does. The claim is repeatedly made that the high profits are an accounting illusion created by the standard accounting practice of treating research and development expenditures as expenses against current income rather than capitalizing these outlays as an investment item.[74] However, as Gary Gereffi, professor of sociology at Duke University, makes clear, the accounting explanation of high profitability is inadequate for several reasons.[75] First, the accounting bias is not just confined to the pharmaceutical industry but is present in all "discovery-intensive" industries such as oil and gas and in industries with high levels of research and development expenditures. Under certain circumstances the accounting rate of return could actually *understate* rather than overstate the "real" or economic rate of return.[76] Second, as we have just seen, under any method of calculating profitability, the declared profits of the industry in Canada are likely to be artificially depressed. Finally, by allowing pharmaceutical companies to treat research and development costs as a current accounting expense, the government, in effect, is granting them an indirect fiscal subsidy to encourage their risk-taking efforts. This accounting method thus serves to raise the drug firm's profitability in fact as well as on paper. In two U.S. studies, even after "correcting" profits by treating research and development expenditures as an investment, the drug industry was still one of the most profitable industries around.[77]

Sometimes the PMAC takes another approach and maintains that high profits are necessary because they finance the various philanthropic efforts of the industry. As was argued before the Restrictive Trade Practices Commission: "Many pharmaceutical manufacturers carry 'public service' products on which they actually lose money or break even on cost. Some of these drugs are actually given away free . . . In many cases these 'public service' products are the result of extensive research."[78] However, the industry's record with respect to philanthropic ventures is at best spotty. By 1978, Dr. J.M. Walshe of Cambridge, England, had been purifying and encapsulating triethylene tetramine (trien) for patients in his own laboratory for over nine years. Trien is an effective substitute for penicillamine in those patients who cannot use penicillamine because of its side effects. Both drugs are used to treat Wilson's disease, a rare neurological condition, and these drugs have transformed the disease from a fatal one to one that is curable in 90 percent of patients. Dr. Walshe continued to make trien on his own because no pharmaceutical company was interested in producing it commercially. By 1983, not a single pharmaceutical company was manufacturing the drug. In the 1960s, the manufacturer of penicillamine discontinued production because the anticipated financial return was too meagre. (Public pressure later forced a reversal of the decision.) L-5-hydroxytryptophan (L-5HTP), useful in another type of neurological disease known as myoclonus, is another example of a drug without a manufacturer. L-5HTP is a plant extract and drugs made directly from plant or animal sources are not patentable in the U.S. or in Canada. Not having a patent on a drug markedly decreases its profitability. The low profit potential plus the small North American market for L-5HTP, about 2,000 people, renders it a drug of little commercial value and as such it is not produced by any pharmaceutical firm.

The pharmaceutical companies' main justification for needing high profits is that theirs is an inherently high risk industry.

> The industry is characterized by a fairly high degree of risk, in the sense that there is a continual introduction of new products, which generally operate to displace existing products...This leads to an indicated rate of product obsolescence of a fairly high order...A fairly high rate of profit is to be expected under such conditions in order to induce the firms to continue to invest in what is an uncertain environment...High risk is expected to bring higher rewards, to compensate for the taking of risk.[79]
> And it's risky. Almost 200,000 substances are investigated each year, but only one in every 7,000 compounds yields a usable drug—after seven years' research and an investment average of $700,000![80]

Let us examine these claims. The contention that "profits" are needed to supply the funds to finance research and development seems fallacious. Profits, by definition, are the residual left after all costs, including those for research and development, have been met. To add to costs an additional element for future research, which, of course, will also be paid for by future sales, is to charge consumers twice for the research component.[81] Charging the consumer twice means that the consumer pays the stockholder twice, once in dividends and again in plant and equipment. These payments are added to the stockholders' holdings, although the investment comes out of the patient's pocket.[82] Who ends up paying twice for the research costs? The elderly and the ill, the ones who use proportionately more medicine, and the ones who can least afford the cost.

Dr. Dale Console, a former medical director of Squibb, has testified about the risk involved:

> They [the drug firms] stress that there are many failures for each successful drug. This is true since it is the very essence of research. The problem arises out of the fact that they market so many of their failures.
> I doubt that there are many other industries in which research is so free of risks...with a little luck, proper timing, and a good

promotion program, a bag of asafetida with a unique chemical side chain can be made to look like a wonder drug.[83]

According to evidence presented by Cyanamid to the Restrictive Trade Practices Commission, there is a strong degree of brand loyalty among doctors, and superior products do not easily replace older ones. "Achromycin...has been widely used by many physicians," testified the Cyanamid representative. "When Declomycin, which we think is an improvement, became available we set out thinking that physicians were entitled to know about this new drug...We encountered the most conservative form of loyalty to Achromycin that you can imagine."[84]

A drug's lifespan is another concept thrown into the debate on industry profit. The initial marketing costs of new drugs are usually recovered about 8.8 years after the drug first appears.[85] According to one estimate from the president of the PMAC, the average lifespan of a drug from its introduction to its withdrawal is about ten years;[86] another estimate, in a study commissioned by the PMAC, places the average product life at fifteen years and states that most drugs remain in the market for considerably longer periods.[87] The average drug, therefore, enjoys a range of one to six years of pure profit.

In one study, 71 Canadian manufacturing industries were ranked on the basis of risk. The drug industry was 67th, showing itself to be almost the lowest risk industry in Canada.[88] The Special House of Commons Committee on the price of drugs concluded:

[A] review of the evidence before this Committee seems to indicate that, in comparison to manufacturing in general, the effects of losses on the pharmaceutical firms as a group does not indicate the presence of greater risk. In fact the rates of return on investment demonstrate that, over the period 1953-1964, the pharmaceutical industry in Canada has been increasingly less risky as compared with manufacturing in general.[89]

Analysis of the profits of the drug industry for the 1970s suggests nothing to indicate that it is any riskier now that it was in 1964.

Excessive, and unjustifiable, prices ultimately yielding excessive, and unjustifiable, profits would be a concise description of the economics of the industry. Underlying this state of affairs is a drug market dominated by a small number of large multinationals. These companies have effectively divided up the various therapeutic submarkets among themselves and then have used their market power to inhibit price competition by limiting access of the generic manufacturers to these markets. The high prices have consistently maintained profits at levels exceeding those of nearly all other manufacturing industries and, in fact, profits are probably under-reported through dodges such as transfer pricing. Finally, as we have just seen, none of the justifications that the drug companies give for needing large profits can stand up to close scrutiny.

Chapter 4
Generics:
What's in a Name?

Two of the PMAC's "Principles for the Provision of Drugs to Canadians" deal directly with the question of how brand name drugs ought to be regarded:

3. It is the right of the physician to prescribe the drug preparation of his choice.
4. Nothing must be allowed to interfere with the duty of the pharmacists to respect the integrity of the physician's prescription.[1]

Translated, these mean that the PMAC believes that doctors should prescribe by brand name, and pharmacists should not be allowed to substitute equivalent, but less costly, drugs.

The industry does not have to worry about the government moving to eliminate brand names. The last time a government body conducted a comprehensive examination of the pharmaceutical industry, it concluded that "it seems clear that any regulations that could now be imposed that would prevent the use of brand names in marketing and sale of drugs would be out of character with present day commercial practice."[2]

Still, the multinational industry is worried about competition from the so-called generic companies. These are the smaller, often Canadian-controlled, companies that sell their products either under generic names or their own brand names. Although sales of drugs from these companies accounted for only $45 to $65 million of the total human pharmaceutical market of $1.01 billion in 1981,[3] the Canadian Drug Manufacturers Association has estimated that the presence of competition forced the multinationals to reduce the prices on their products by $85 to $165 million in 1982.[4]

When products are available under their generic names there is usually a considerable savings to the consumer. By substituting just one of the generics for a brand name drug, the British Columbia drug plan has saved about $700,000. The Ontario drug plan's annual cost of $285 million would rise by $40 million if generics were eliminated.[5] An analysis of the July 1982 Ontario *Drug Benefit Formulary* showed that drugs sold under generic names were, on the average, only 67.5 percent of the price of the most expensive brand name. Unfortunately, there were generic equivalents for only 91 of 1,335 products listed.

Despite the considerable potential savings to be realized from generics, to date doctors seem reluctant to prescribe by generic names and pharmacists seem equally reluctant to dispense generic products. (The term "generic products" here includes both drugs sold under generic names and the brand name drugs of the smaller companies.) In 1980, prescriptions were written using generic names only 21.4 percent of the time. In 1976, pharmacists were filling these generically written prescriptions with non-brand name products in only slightly more than 50 percent of the cases.[6] Admittedly, these figures are a distinct improvement upon the previous decade when only 9.1 percent of prescriptions were written generically and only a third of those were filled with a generic manufacturer's product. However, statistics for 1981 show that there is still a long way to go. Of the 175 million prescriptions written in Canada in that year, only 8.7 million were filled with generic products.

What is the secret of the drug companies' success in keeping down the use of generic products? The full answer includes the use of catchy trade names and a blizzard of advertising, persistent attacks on the quality of the drugs of generic manufacturers, support from organized medicine for the multinational companies' brand name drugs and, in the past, support from officials in the federal government.

One reason why doctors use brand names is that they are simple and easy to remember. Why try to pronounce or write "acetazolamide" when "Diamox" means the same thing? Ever wonder why some generic names are so long and cumbersome? Until 1964, any drug developed by an American company had both its trade and generic names assigned solely by that company. Since the companies wanted to encourage prescribing by brand names it was in their best interest to make the generic name almost impossible to remember or spell.

Although brand names are convenient, they can prove dangerous to the health of the public. Trade names often give no indication of what type of drug is involved, whereas generic names usually do. Dr. Mark Nickerson, then-head of the Department of Pharmacology at the University of Manitoba, testified before the Restrictive Trade Practices Commission about the drug phenylbutazone, first marketed by CIBA-Geigy as Butazolidin. This is a very effective medication for inflammation, but one that can have very serious, and sometimes fatal, side effects. "The new derivative is hydrophenylbutazone," said Dr. Nickerson, "but the trade name is teandril [sic, Tandearil]. I couldn't prove this point, but I suspect this is an attempt to get around many physicians' concerns about the toxicity of the older drug. The generic name tells you immediately that this is almost the same thing. The trade name leads you to think it is not related in any way, nor does the promotional literature."[7]

When drugs are identified by their trade names, the public is generally unaware of the nature of the medications they are taking. Pharmacists in Manitoba cited cases of people taking both Lanoxin and digoxin, Mobenol and tolbutamide, and Vivol and diazepam, without realizing that they were double dosing themselves.[8] In at least some of these cases, there could have been serious health problems from this double dosing.

Trade names are a matter of concern to Canadian pharmacists because of the possibility of confusing similar sounding names and mistakenly dispensing the wrong product. Leroy Fevang, the executive director of the Canadian Pharmaceutical Association, says that "the deliberately granting of similar trade names is sheer irresponsibility." Mr. Fevang contends that drug companies want the names of their new products to sound like those of already successful drugs. "A good name is money in the bank," he says. Despite pharmacists' reservations about the naming of drugs, Canadian authorities seem unwilling to block a company's selection of a trade name. Health and Welfare Canada refuses to act because it is unsure whether its authority covers such matters, and the registrar of trademarks in Ottawa cannot refuse to approve a name based on the possibility of confusion with other names.[9]

It is not very comforting to read an article in the *Canadian Medical Association Journal* about physicians' knowledge of the components in brand name drugs. Sixty doctors in the Montreal area were asked to name the contents of 23 fixed-dose combination brand name drugs they had been using. (Fixed-dose or fixed-ratio combination means that the medication contains more than one active ingredient, and that these ingredients are combined in specific and fixed amounts.) The authors concluded that if their sample is representative, then "in the majority of instances when a physician signs his name below a drug-combination prescription he does not know exactly what he is signing for."[10]

Until 1959, a number of commonly prescribed penicillin-strepto-mycin brand combinations contained dihydrostreptomycin. By 1951, it was known that dihydrostreptomycin would cause permanent hearing loss, and on this basis doctors were understandably reluctant to use it. In 1961, it was discovered that because physicians did not know what was contained in the combination drugs they were prescribing, a number of cases of permanent deafness had resulted from the presence of dihydrostrep-tomycin.

During the time that thalidomide was still on the world market, a child with phocomelia (malformations of the limbs) was born in Brazil. A journalist with the Brazilian magazine *Ocruziero* investigated, and was told that thalidomide was not on sale in Brazil. It was later determined that thalidomide was being sold under five different names in that country. None of these names provided any clue that the drugs contained thalidomide.

The large drug companies are fond of impressing doctors with the great sums of money they spend to ensure the quality of their products. The unstated corollary, of course, is that small generic manufacturers could never afford to spend so much, and therefore the quality of their goods must be suspect.

> To give you an idea of the costs involved, a recording spectro-photometer for use in the ultraviolet and visible regions of the spectrum costs around $15,000. Infra-red equipment can cost more than $20,000 for a single instrument not much larger than a suitcase. These are but two of many such instruments required to test this medicine. It does not include the salaries paid to the scientists who operate the instruments.[11]

However, in 1963, when the above statement was made, these types of expenses amounted to only about 3.6 percent of the cost of goods sold.[12] In 1960, the technology of adequate quality control was not deemed to be particularly complex, and according to Dr. Walter Modell of Cornell University, did not require a large scale of operation for its effective utilization.[13]

Occasionally the drug companies still try to disparage the quality of generic products, as did Bill Robson, the president of Smith Kline and French Canada, in a 1982 newspaper feature.[14] Generally, however, that line of attack has faded out as accumulated evidence has demonstrated that the quality of generic products is comparable to that of brand name drugs.

In the mid-1960s, the U.S. Food and Drug Administration released a study disclosing that about 7 percent of a sample of generic products on the market failed to meet United States Pharmacopeia or National Formulary requirements for potency. However, an almost equal percentage of brand name products similarly failed to meet these standards.[15] On this side of the border, we have evidence, released in 1967, from the Food and Drug Directorate (now the Health Protection Branch) on the generally high quality of both brand name and generic name drugs: "The instances of a significant hazard to health involving the quality of pharmaceutical products is relatively rare in Canada, a total of five over a period of seven years."[16]

When the federal government was still publishing *Rx Bulletin*, a drug information journal for health care workers, the names of the companies whose products had to be recalled were listed in it. I did a survey covering the period November 1973, when the recalls were first published, until June 1975, when the government stopped publishing *Rx Bulletin* for budgetary reasons. During that time 49 companies had drugs recalled, 34 of them PMAC members. Dr. Warren Bell, a long-time observer of the Canadian drug industry, was told in the late 1970s by officials in the HPB that generic and brand name drugs were equally likely to fail the federal government's quality assessment tests.[17]

Another tactic employed by the drug companies to discourage the use of generic products involved having their sales representatives (commonly referred to as "detail men") secure from practising physicians and pharmacists all possible clues to the clinical failure of generic products.[18] Similarly, detail men made the rounds of hospitals trying to convince the people in charge not to order drugs from generic manufacturers.[19] (Although a number of sales representatives are now women, "detail men" is still the commonly used term.) In the early 1960s, representatives of the PMAC circulated stories about the generic brand of tolbutamide (an oral drug useful in mild to moderate cases of diabetes). It was claimed that the drug failed to dissolve in one particular patient's stomach. But in 1965, a study was undertaken to compare two different brand name tolbutamide preparations and three generic ones. It concluded that all five were equally effective.[20]

The attack was directed not only against domestic generic manufacturers, but also against imported generic drugs. "There is a movement on foot," testified E. Clyde Gregory of the Ayerst corporation, "to undermine the North American pharmaceutical industry by the importation of foreign-made chemicals and compounds of obscure origin."[21]

The drug companies' campaign was helped along in the 1960s by the then-head of the Food and Drug Directorate in Ottawa, Dr. C.A. Morrell. He stated that he "personally would always buy a brand-name drug, to ensure that he obtains the quality and efficacy guaranteed by the reputation of a well-known manufacturer."[22] In 1965, Dr. Morrell left the FDD for a position on the CIBA board of directors.

Dr. Morrell's successor as head of the FDD, however, testified that "there does not appear to be any significant difference between drugs sold under a generic name and those sold under a brand name. Similarly, imported drugs appeared to be of the same general quality as domestic production."[23] The Canadian Hospital Association has admitted that generic drugs are not inferior, and finally, since the 1950s, the Canadian federal government has bought drugs by generic name.

The PMAC often gets a boost from organized medicine in the fight against generic products. On February 27, 1971, a letter appeared in the *Globe and Mail* from the assistant secretary of the Ontario Medical Assocation warning the public about generic drugs. The *Canadian Medical Association Journal* has run an editorial reminding physicians that "the best guarantee in drug products is still the manufacturer's reputation as represented by his name or his trademark."[24] The same sentiments were echoed in the *CMAJ*'s pages in 1982 by the director of publications for the Canadian Medical Association.[25]

On the question of the quality of imported drugs, the Director of Investigation and Research for the Combines Investigation Act said:

> The importer's product may be disparaged as foreign, cheap and not brand names; but the crux of the matter appears to be that the importer is a small firm which allegedly does not exercise proper quality control. Nobody in the industry would criticize Poulenc which imports chlorpromazine from France and sells it under the trade name Largactil at a high price, rather Largactil is simply regarded as another product of a reliable drug firm and on a par with a domestic product. But when a small dealer imports meprobamate from Italy and sells it under its generic name at a low price, the product is immediately questioned. Regardless of the merits of the criticism, it should be recognized, as the illustration shows, that the criticism is of the small firm's product. The fact that a particular drug is imported is not the issue. Neither is the fact that it is sold under a generic name except on the [incorrect] line of reasoning that all drugs sold under generic names are necessarily of inferior quality.[26]

Lately, the drug companies have shifted to the issue of "bioavailability" in defence of brand names. Although two drugs may have the same active ingredients in the same dosage form, they are not necessarily therapeutically equivalent, and therefore they may not be equally effective in treating the patient's disease. If they are therapeutically equivalent, then they are said to be equally bioavailable. Factors that can affect bioavailability include particle size and shape and the nature of the so-called inert ingredients contained in the drug product. A booklet published by the PMAC marshals quotes from thirteen different authorities, all designed to convince the reader that generic drugs cannot be trusted to be therapeutically equivalent. The section ends with the sermon: *"Conscientious physicians and pharmacists consider it part of their obligation to the patient to select manufacturers who will supply the drug required in a proven, therapeutically effective form."*[27] (Emphasis in original.) Upjohn has published a book entitled *Basics of Bioavailability*. The documentation upon which the book was based was submitted to Dr. Allan E. Dyer, Director of Drugs and Therapeutics of the Ontario Ministry of Health. He wrote: "We are aware of much of the literature quoted in Upjohn's paper and, as you probably know, most of it is not relevant to the subject of interchangability of comparable dosage forms. It is unfortunate that data like this is presented as representing comparative bioavailability of like formulations since indeed most of the references relate to 'unlike' formulations."[28]

In August 1968, the Pharmaceutical Manufacturers Association in the U.S. published a bibliography of 501 articles in the medical literature which, according to PMA president C. Joseph Stetler, would refute "the astonishing myth that there are not significant differences among dosage forms of the same drug."[29] This bibliography was analysed by the U.S. Task Force on Prescription Drugs. It concluded that at most two or three articles demonstrated a statistically significant lack of biological equivalency. In one of these cases, the differences were without any practical clinical importance.[30]

A paper which appeared in the *Journal of the American Medical Association* made the claim that the generic form of tolbutamide was much less effective than Upjohn's brand, called Orinase. There are a few additional details which are pertinent to this scientific discovery. First, the article was written by a member of the Upjohn staff. Second, the "inferior" product had never been marketed, had never even been proposed for clinical use, and finally, it had been developed for the article by the Upjohn laboratory.[31]

In the U.S., a report on bioavailability was commissioned by the Office of Technology Assessment. The panel was chaired by Dr. Robert Berliner, Dean of Yale University School of Medicine. His conclusion was that the great proportion of chemically equivalent products, 85 to 90 percent, presented no problems of therapeutic equivalency and could be used interchangeably.[32] Eldon Boyd, professor of pharmacology at Queen's University in Kingston, wrote that in Canada the lack of therapeutic equivalence in brands of drugs meeting all other statutory requirements was not extensive and was not a hazard to public health.[33]

But the multinational drug companies are still implicitly claiming superior bioavailability of their products in their advertising. An ad for Anturan from Geigy claims that it is "the only sulfinpyrazone available to Canadian physicians that has been subjected to extensive world-wide clinical investigation." A prescription for Anturan is shown with the words "no substitution" written across the bottom of the prescription.[34] A similar message accompanies an ad for Tegretol.[35]

Pierre Biron of the Department of Pharmacology at the Universite de Montreal, put the issue of bioavailability in the proper perspective:

> Compared with insufficient dosage and insufficient compliance, insufficient bioavailability is a marginal factor leading to insufficient blood concentrations of prescribed drugs. Much more energy and financial support should be directed towards educating physicians in prescribing correct dosage and obtaining proper compliance, rather than towards increasing the number of sophisticated and costly bioavailability trials.[36]

Professor Biron's statement reinforces the belief that the drug companies' campaign against generic names and products has less to do with the health of people and more to do with the health of company profits. In fact, as we have seen, the use of brand names potentially has negative effects on health by confusing doctors as to the true contents of the medicines they are prescribing.

Chapter 5
Chloramphenicol and MER/29

*Quality conscious manufacturers stake
their reputation on, and are answerable
for, the integrity of medicines bearing
their name.*
—PMAC[1]

When all the other defences that the drug industry uses to justify brand names and patents fail, there is one final line to fall back on. *"The greatest guarantee remains the integrity of the maker,"* trumpets the PMAC.[2] (Emphasis in original.) One of the PMAC's past presidents proudly boasts, "I don't know anybody who has successfully fooled physicians over any extended period of time with a drug."[3] The underlying message is always that reputable manufacturers would lose the trust of doctors and go broke if they knowingly marketed drugs of questionable quality. But according to the Royal Commission on Health Services, "there are a number of historic—and, indeed, recent—instances where large-scale manufacturers have failed to fulfil the promises implicit in their national stature."[4] The history of two drugs, chloramphenicol and MER/29, shows that the Royal Commission's concern is somewhat of an understatement. The events that surround these two drugs took place largely in the United States, but exactly the same drugs, with the same names, were marketed in Canada by the same companies.

Chloramphenicol
Chloramphenicol was discovered in 1947, and in the following year it became the first antibiotic to be prepared synthetically. In

1949, it was put on the U.S. and Canadian markets by Parke, Davis, under the name Chloromycetin. It was promoted as a broad spectrum antibiotic, useful for a wide variety of infections including respiratory tract infections, urinary tract infections, as well as for rarer diseases such as typhoid, typhus, other rickettsial infections and brucellosis. Commercially, the drug was a great success. North American sales in the first year exceeded $9 million, and by 1951, sales of Chloromycetin had reached $52 million. Parke, Davis had become the world's largest selling pharmaceutical manufacturer.

But there was a cloud on the horizon. As early as 1949, there were reports that chloramphenicol could cause blood disorders. In June 1952, an editorial appeared in the *Journal of the American Medical Association* about the link between chloramphenicol and aplastic anaemia. Doctors were advised to be very cautious about administering this drug, since deaths had been associated with its use. Aplastic anaemia is a condition in which the bone marrow stops making all types of blood cells. People are left vulnerable to infection because of the lack of white blood cells and they are also anaemic because they are deficient in red blood cells. Frequently, aplastic anaemia can be fatal. Fatal aplastic anaemia occurs in only one in 25,000 to one in 40,000 cholramphenicol users, depending on the dose. This is not a very high percentage, but the risk of acquiring aplastic anaemia in the absence of the drug is only one in 500,000. To make matters worse, it seems that children are especially susceptible to developing the condition from exposure to chloramphenicol.

When the early reports about chloramphenicol toxicity started coming out, Parke, Davis hinted at a devious plot marked by "the unethical tactics being employed by representatives of certain competitors."[5] Journalists were attacked for "careless or illogical deductions, lack of scientific understanding, use of material out of context, and lack of proper perspective."[6] In 1952, the U.S. Food and Drug Administration reviewed the data on chloramphenicol in light of the fatal reactions. Some physicians wanted to remove the drug from the market completely; but it is the drug of choice for typhoid fever, Rocky Mountain spotted fever and a few other diseases where other antibiotics have proven ineffective. Therefore, the decision was made to let it remain on the market in the U.S. However, the FDA did require labelling changes to indicate that serious blood disorders were associated with using the drug and that "*Chloromycetin should not be used indiscriminately or for minor infections.'*[7] (Emphasis in original.)

As a result of this investigation, the sales of Chloromycetin dropped $5 million in 1952, and in 1953 and 1954 sales were below the $26 million mark. Parke, Davis did not take this situation lying down. On August 12, 1952, the president of Parke, Davis, Henry Loynd, advised detail men that Chloromycetin had been "officially cleared by the FDA and the National Research Council with *no restrictions* on the number or range of diseases for which Chloromycetin may be administered."[8] A month later, the firm wrote their detail men saying, "The recent decision reached by the Food and Drug Administration with the assistance of the National Research Council and a board of nationally known medical experts was undoubtedly the highest compliment ever tendered the medical staff of our Company."[9] In November, detail men were "instructed to memorize and repeat verbatim to the physician: '. . . intensive investigation by the Food and Drug Administration, carried on with the assistance of a special committee of eminent specialists appointed by the National Research Council, resulted in the unqualified sanction of continued use of Chloromycetin for all conditions in which it has been previously used.'"[10] Detail men were warned not to mention toxicity "unless the physician brings up the subject."[11]

These tactics succeeded admirably, and by 1959 Chloromycetin was being administered to four million people annually in the U.S. Had it been used properly, fewer than 200,000 people a year would have been treated with it. In 1960, sales were $86 million. According to the American Medical Association's Council on Drugs, people were receiving chloramphenicol for "the common cold, bronchial infections, asthma, sore throat, and tonsilitis, miscellaneous urinary tract and ear infections, undiagnosed low-grade fever, and even disseminated lupus erythematosis, gout, eczema, malaise, and iron deficiency anemia."[12]

The U.S. Senate, led by Estes Kefauver, conducted hearings on the drug industry during 1960, and one of the focuses for its investigations was chloramphenicol. Testimony during the hearings showed that Parke, Davis had watered down warnings in direct mail ads to physicians. Detail men were alleging that Chloromycetin was no more dangerous than any other antibiotic and insisting that their information was "based on figures supplied them by their home office."[13]

In Canada, a second company started manufacturing and selling chloramphenicol in 1960 by virtue of a compulsory licence from Parke, Davis. (A compulsory licence, issued by the Commissioner of Patents, permits a company to import or manufacture a product already being sold in Canada in return for payment of a royalty fee to the patent holder.) Parke, Davis' response was to send a letter to all Canadian physicians denouncing this second brand now on the market, and boosting its own product. It is interesting to read this letter to see what Parke, Davis said, and did not say, about their brand of chloramphenicol. In part the letter read: "How has CHLOROMYCETIN'S effectiveness been proved?...The efficacy of CHLOROMYCETIN has been proved by clinical use in millions of patients all over the world."[14] No mention was made in this letter of any toxic effects, and by talking about the use of Chloromycetin in millions of people, the impression was left that it was safe to go on using it in millions of people.

In 1960, the first edition of the *Compendium of Pharmaceuticals and Specialties(CPS)* was published in Canada. It contained the names and descriptions of most of the brand name prescription drugs available in Canada. (See Chapter 9 for more on the *CPS*.) Chloramphenicol was listed as being useful for, among other things, urinary and respiratory tract infections and viral pneumonia. Most cases of respiratory tract infections and all cases of viral pneumonia are caused by viruses. Antibiotics are completely useless for treating any viral illness. There was also no mention in the *CPS* of any side effects at all. Most of the information used in compiling the *CPS* comes from the manufacturers.

In 1961, as a result of the U.S. Senate hearings, the sales of Chloromycetin once again dropped, this time by 20 percent. The president of Parke, Davis blamed the Kefauver hearings, which, he said, "caused some very unfavorable publicity, I might say unjustified and some of it ridiculous, which cost us a volume loss on *Chloromycetin* of about $15 million."[15] However, again a strong promotional campaign pushed Chloromycetin back to near record sales levels. In 1967, 3.7 million Americans received the drug.

The final decline for Chloromycetin sales started with another set of U.S. Senate hearings, led by Gaylord Nelson, in 1967. The drop in prescribing, in the U.S., started in mid-1968, and has continued. In Canada, Chloromycetin still sold strongly for a few more years. One reason for the lag in falling sales in Canada relative to the U.S. was the continued flow of misinformation supplied to doctors. The fourth edition of the *CPS*, in 1967, had listings for both chloramphenicol and Chloromycetin. When the drug was listed under its generic name, the indications for using it did not mention urinary or respiratory tract infections. Under the Chloromycetin heading, both kinds of infections were given as reasons to use the drug. In 1969, sales of Chloromycetin in Canada were $697,000, enough to rank it twelfth in volume among all antibiotic products, and 62nd among 650 pharmaceuticals with sales volumes over $75,000 in that year. It was not until 1972 that the Health Protection Branch felt obliged to send a letter about chloramphenicol to Canadian physicians.

Parke, Davis' profitability did decline in the 1970s, and eventually the company was taken over by another giant American multinational, Warner Lambert. But it was not Parke, Davis' conduct with regard to Chloromycetin that caused this situation. Rather, while Parke, Davis held its seventeen-year monopoly on chloramphenicol, it introduced few, if any, significant new drugs on the market. This lack of innovation was Parke, Davis' downfall. During the 1960s while Chloromycetin's sales were temporarily down because of publicity over its side effects, Parke, Davis' profit rate was substantially *above* the all-industry average.[16] Parke, Davis obviously had not lost the trust of doctors in the rest of its products. In fact, doctors continued to trust Parke, Davis about chloramphenicol from 1952 to 1968 in the U.S., and even longer in Canada.

There is a footnote to the chloramphenicol story. Sales of the drug have not declined throughout the world. In the late 1970s in Mexico, Equador and Columbia, Parke, Davis was still promoting Chloromycetin as effective for "tonsillitis, pharyngitis, bronchitis, urinary tract infections, ulcerative colitis, pneumonia, staphylococcus infections, streptococcus infections, eye infections, yaws, and gonorrhea."[17] In Central American states as late as 1977 no warning was given to physicians about the possibility of aplastic anaemia.

MER/29

This story is somewhat different from the chloramphenicol one. It involves not only deceptive advertising, but also, at best, gross negligence in research, and at worst, deliberate fraud.[18]

It has been known for some time that people with high cholesterol levels have a greater chance of developing heart disease, or of having a stroke. Consequently, many scientists and doctors believe that lowering cholesterol levels would be beneficial. Cholesterol levels can be reduced either by decreasing the amount in the diet or by decreasing its synthesis in the liver by chemical means (that is, by drugs.) But, and this is a very big but, until 1984 there was no evidence that lowering cholesterol by either means will reduce a person's risk of heart disease or stroke. Recent information also indicates that there are two different kinds of cholesterol, and one of these may be protective against heart disease.

Nevertheless, in the 1950s, there was much research being conducted to develop a drug that would decrease cholesterol levels. By the late 1950s, Richardson Merrell, whose Canadian subsidiary brought thalidomide to this country, had synthesized triparanol, which looked promising. The drug was given the brand name MER/29, and in June 1960, was launched onto the Canadian and American markets with lavish two page ads in medical journals across the continent. Merrell had high hopes for this drug, calling it "the most successful drug in Merrell's 133-year history."[19] Some people at Merrell hoped that MER/29 would eventually be taken by every person over 35—one-a-day, just like vitamins. In April 1962, MER/29 was removed from the market forever. By that time, hundreds of people had developed cataracts (clouding of the lens of the eye) because of MER/29. Before the story reached its conclusion, three Merrell executives would be tried and placed on probation for six months; Merrell would be fined $80,000 in criminal court; and law suits would cost the company $45 to $55 million in lawyers' fees and settlements.

The events that finally caused MER/29 to be withdrawn began when an official in the U.S. Food and Drug Administration learned that a former employee of Merrell's had been ordered to falsify information. During the drug's experimental phase, a monkey to whom MER/29 had been administered had lost weight; this could have indicated toxic effects of the drug. Mrs. Beulah Jordan, a research employee, was told to eliminate the sharp decline in the graph showing the weight loss. "Dr. King [head of Merrell's toxicology and pathology laboratories] ordered her to never mention the substitution. She was told that this order had come from higher up and there was nothing she could do about it but obey the order and do as the 'higher-ups' wanted."[20]

Subsequent investigations by the FDA and by lawyers for the

complainants suing Merrell turned up numerous other instances of research data being either changed or ignored.

During some of the initial experiments on MER/29, two dogs developed cataracts, but Merrell neglected to inform the FDA about this. When Merrell's advertising agency wanted to know "about the corneal changes recently noted in dogs," Merrell replied, "There are none."[21] (The cornea is a transparent membrane covering the pupil and the iris.) Merrell did not mention the cataracts.

Rats developed corneal changes in studies conducted by Merrell. Dr. Lauretta E. Fox, associate professor of pharmacology at the University of Florida, wrote to Merrell, saying she had administered MER/29 to rats and noted an "opaque cornea" and cataracts in three of six rats. Merrell told the FDA that in its experiments control rats (those not getting the drug but otherwise treated exactly the same as rats receiving the drug) also developed corneal changes, thereby implying that rats naturally develop corneal problems. What Merrell did not tell the FDA, was that 25 out of 36 rats on MER/29 developed corneal changes, but only two of 28 control rats were so affected. As for Dr. Fox's observations, Merrell wrote to the FDA that it had observed no eye changes in dogs, and that Merrell's scientists found Dr. Fox's study confusing.

Merrell sanctioned use of MER/29 in a military hospital although they "were not thinking here so much of honest clinical work" as they were of "pre-marketing softening prior to the introduction of the product."[22] (Pre-marketing softening is industry slang for the practice of making large numbers of doctors aware of a product before it has been approved for marketing.) As part of the softening phase, Merrell awarded a grant of $500 to Dr. Hyman Engelberg in order to delay the publication of what they feared would be a negative report. Dr. Robert McMaster, associate director of Merrell's medical research department, explained that "although it begins to appear that any report from this study may be a negative one, we may find that we are money ahead to keep Dr. Engelberg busy at it for a while longer than to take a chance on his reporting negatively."[23] Under the right circumstances, it appears that the medical laboratory, where scientific truths are to be revealed, can as easily be a site for suppressing such truths.

As part of its introductory campaign for MER/29, Merrell sponsored a conference on the drug. One of the participants, Dr. Robert W. Wilkins, was asked to summarize the results. As part of his concluding remarks, he noted that there had not been "sufficient experience" with the drug and that he found "drug companies reluctant to accept" the fact that "you cannot tell what a drug will do after four or five years of treatment without waiting four or five years."[24] When Merrell abstracted the conference proceedings and distributed the precis to the medical community, it deleted Dr. Wilkin's caveat and oblique condemnation.

Even before the drug was on the market, Merrell had started to receive negative reports from doctors conducting human trials with MER/29. Some patients had noted watering of the eyes, and a few were even experiencing blurred vision. Merrell already knew that "corneal opacities" had been observed in rats and that two dogs had developed cataracts, but did not pass any of these observations along to doctors. Instead, detail men were instructed to tell physicians that if any toxic effects showed up, Merrell would "be the *first* to know it and *report it to you!*"[25] (Emphasis in original.)

Two months after MER/29 was released for general use, Merrell was still promoting it as "virtually nontoxic." If doctors reported side effects to Merrell's salesmen, they were told their immediate reply should be: "Doctor, what other drug is the patient taking?" The rationale behind asking this question was explained to the salesmen: "Even if you know your drug can cause the side effect mentioned, chances are equally good the same effect is being caused by a second drug."[26]

In August 1961, after Merrell had received earlier complaints of blurred vision, its medical staff still wrote to a physician that "we have received absolutely no reports of this type of reaction."[27] In April 1961, a physician wrote to Merrell about serious liver changes in one of his patients taking MER/29. In June, a doctor on Merrell's payroll replied to another doctor concerned about liver problems with MER/29: "Let me assure you that we have received absolutely no reports of liver toxicity."[28] On October 31, 1961, Merrell had knowledge of four cataract cases. However, Dr. McMaster replied to a physician who had reported that two of his patients on MER/29 were complaining of "black spots before their eyes" (this can be one of the first indications of cataract formation): "This is so unusual a report that I would like to ask you to provide us with additional details...In fact, we have never before heard of anything remotely resembling this."[29]

Merrell's final regular mailing of information on MER/29 to

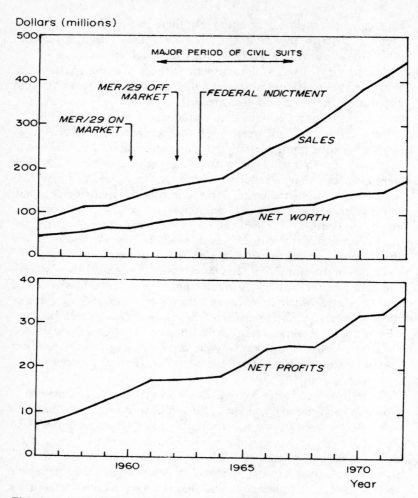

Dollars (millions)

MAJOR PERIOD OF CIVIL SUITS

MER/29 OFF MARKET

FEDERAL INDICTMENT

MER/29 ON MARKET

SALES

NET WORTH

NET PROFITS

1960   1965   1970

Year

Figure 5-1. The Impact of MER/29 Litigation: Richardson-Merrell Sales, Net Worth, and Net Profits, 1956-1972.

Source: M. Silverman and P.R. Lee, *Pills, Profits and Politics,* University of California Press, Berkeley, 1974, p. 93.

physicians was in late October 1961. Despite reports of liver damage, cataracts, hair loss and potentially severe skin changes, Merrell was saying that there was "no serious toxicity (and few significant side effects) reported in three years' clinical use." This denial of problems with MER/29 coincided with the theme of Merrell's October-November sales campaign: "Taking patients off MER/29 is bad medicine!"[30]

In August of 1972, four months after MER/29 was withdrawn from the market, the Deputy Food and Drug Commissioner in the U.S., John L. Harvey, admitted: "It is apparent that the drug should not have gone on the market in the first place."[31]

What effect did all the adverse publicity, convictions and law suits have on Richardson-Merrell? At first, the company's stock went down on the New York Stock Exchange, and it remained depressed for several years. But as Figure 5-1 shows, the company's sales, net worth and net profits all continued to rise.

Cyanamid of Canada has said: "It is far better to disclose than to conceal side-effects, for otherwise the drug product and the drug manufacturer would soon become regarded with distrust."[32] The stories of Chloromycetin and MER/29 show otherwise. A brand name or a "company's reputation" does not guarantee anything to doctors or to the public. All a brand name seems to guarantee is a big profit to the company.

Chapter 6
Research

. . . an industry which has probably done more for mankind through the saving of lives and relief of suffering in the past 30 years than any other industry in history.
—W.W. Wigle, M.D.
President, PMAC[1]

The Contribution of Drugs to Health

The opening quote is very impressive, but is it really true? In almost all the literature published by the PMAC, there are charts and tables showing decreases in the death rate from various diseases, increases in life expectancy and drops in the number of people in psychiatric institutions, all of these changes being attributed mostly to the wonders of modern pharmaceuticals. As a patient, I have been on the receiving end of drugs a number of times. As a doctor, I write prescriptions every day, so it would be foolish of me to deny that drugs can be useful or even, at times, life-saving. Still it would be interesting to examine the claims of the drug industry.

By 1971, Canadian life expectancy at birth, for men, had increased by over nine years since 1931, and for women by over fourteen years, as the PMAC claims. But between 1931 and 1971, the lifespan for men who reached forty years of age went up less than 1.5 years, and for women just slightly under six years.[2] The nine and fourteen year increases in overall life expectancy were largely due to a sharp decline in infant mortality rates. Infant mortality decreased partly because of pharmaceuticals, but mostly because of improved overall living and nutritional standards.

The PMAC cites statistics to show that the mortality rate from diptheria dropped from 9.7 per 100,000 population in 1926, to 0.1 in 1956. The implication is that this fall was due to the availability of antibiotics and vaccinations. Immunization against diptheria was introduced in Ontario in the early 1930s, but again, we have to put this fall in perspective. In the 1880s, mortality from diptheria was 90 per 100,000. So before we had medical therapy for diptheria, there had already been a decline of almost 90 percent in the death rate from the disease. Furthermore, once you caught the disease, your chances of dying were the same in 1955 as they were in 1900, despite antibiotics and any other medicines available to doctors.[3] Similarly, the decline in death from rheumatic fever, lobar pneumonia, tuberculosis and scarlet fever had started long before the era of vaccinations and modern drugs. Again, the reasons lie in better nutritional and hygiene standards and better living conditions in general. One study analysed U.S. mortality statistics and concluded that, at most, 3.5 percent of the total decline in mortality in that country since 1900 could be ascribed to the introduction of vaccines and antibiotics.[4]

Citing more statistics, the PMAC trumpets a 35 percent drop in the number of patients in Canadian psychiatric hospitals from 1963 to 1974 due to the introduction of psychoactive drugs such as the phenothiazines. It further proclaims that "the availability of an armamentarium of psychotherapeutic drugs...has made revolutionary progress into the overall treatement of the disease of [mental illness.]"[5] But once again the PMAC is guilty of using selective statistics. The inpatient psychiatric population may be dropping but according to an Ontario Public Service Employees Union (OPSEU)-financed study of Ontario's mental health care system, readmission rates in that province climbed from 25 percent in 1941 to 70 percent in 1971, and currently two thirds of all admissions to psychiatric hospital units are readmissions. The OPSEU study notes that in 1961 there were 56,000 cases of admissions to mental health care—27,000 to provincial psychiatric hospitals, 19,000 to general hospitals and 10,000 to community outpatient services. By 1979-80 there were 237,000 admissions—17,000 to provincial psychiatric hospitals, 70,000 to general and community hospitals and 150,000 to community outpatient services.[6]

It is far from clear that the introduction of the phenothiazine group of "major tranquillizers" has had very much to do with the exodus of psychiatric inpatients. Andrew Scull closely scrutinized the role of these drugs in the decarceration of the mentally ill.[7] He points out that in the late 1940s and early 1950s, well before the introduction of the phenothiazines, some hospitals had already embarked on programs of early discharge or of reducing admissions. Scull cites a series of studies of changes in mental hospital populations "which failed to show that any relationship whatsoever existed between the introduction of drugs and the fall in resident population."[8]

Scull goes on to explore an even more damaging objection to the pharmacological claim for the decline in the inpatient population: the growing volume of evidence suggests that the claims about the therapeutic effectiveness of the phenothiazines have been greatly exaggerated. Most of the early studies documenting the effects of these drugs were riddled with biases and failed to meet even minimal criteria of scientifically acceptable research design. According to Scull, "the extreme optimism which greeted the advent of psychoactive drugs, and which persisted for a number of years reflected the weakness and poor design of many of the evaluations made at the time far more than the actual efficacy of the drugs themselves."[9]

Currently, the *sine qua non* of clinical drug research is the double blind study. In this technique two groups of subjects are used. One receives a specific drug (or other form of therapy). The second group is treated similarly in all respects, except that its members get an inactive substance, a placebo, instead of the drug being studied. Neither the person receiving the therapy, nor the person administering the therapy, knows whether the substance is the drug or the placebo. Such a study tends to eliminate bias, either on the part of the patient or the investigator. Without these double blind studies, doctors may believe that drug "A" is useful from observing its effects on patients, but there is no scientific proof that it is actually better than drug "B" or "C" or no drug at all. Double blind studies have usually shown that the phenothiazines, when given in sufficiently high doses, are more effective than a placebo in controlling a patient's behavior. But even proponents of the drugs do not contend that the phenothiazines cure their patients, merely that they provide a measure of symptomatic relief.[10] At lower, more routine doses the evidence of their value is at best ambiguous. One double blind study involved 28 men, 26 of whom had a diagnosis of chronic schizophrenia. Treatment with what is considered an average dose of chlorpromazine, the first and still one of the most widely used phenothiazines, produced a positive response in only one of the 28.[11] A review of another twelve double blind studies using chlorpromazine to treat chronic schizophrenics showed a mean rate of improvement of only 17.5 percent. "Improved" patients in these studies included those whom drugs simply rendered less troublesome in a hospital context, but who, it was conceded, were not fit for release.[12]

Scull's inescapable conclusion:

> If phenothiazines are ineffective for substantial portions of the target population, and if in any event the types of maintenance doses generally prescribed are largely ineffective, how can anyone seriously contend that the advent of drug therapy is the main reason for the decline in mental hospital populations (the more so since the drugs are apparently *least* effective with the groups whose release has been *most* crucial to the running down of mental hospital populations—the old chronic cases)?[13] (Emphasis in original.)

In the United States, modern medical care, including modern drugs, was introduced and delivered to a group of about 2,000 Navaho Indians, who had primitive living conditions and little medical care, but adequate nutrition. Some conditions such as tuberculosis and ear infections were reduced, and drug therapy certainly had a role to play. But other medical problems such as trachoma (an eye infection caused by organisms known as chlamydiae), pneumonia and diarrhoea, were all unaffected.[14]

A 1977 report by the World Health Organization found that only about 230 of the many thousands of drugs currently marketed are really indispensible for health care.[15]

The polio vaccine has been of great benefit; antibiotics have drastically reduced the length of illnesses and have saved many lives; and drugs to lower blood pressure help to prevent heart attacks and strokes. But the usefulness of drugs must always be examined in perspective. We have to take into account other changes in society, and we have to carefully examine the evidence that is cited in favor of drugs.

While the usefulness of some drugs is in question, the uselessness of others is not. In the mid-1960s, the U.S. Food and Drug Administration set up expert scientific panels from the National Academy of Sciences and the National Research Council (NAS/NRC panels) to evaluate the claims made for all drugs introduced into the U.S. prior to 1962.[16] (Significantly, the Canadian government has never undertaken a similar review, largely due to budgetary restrictions. See Chapter 12 for more details.) Of the 4,000 products considered, 2,000 were cleared as "effective," but 760 were categorized as "ineffective" or "ineffective as a fixed-ratio combination." The remainder were classified as "probably effective" or "possibly effective." Six hundred were banned from the market, and hundreds of others required substantial changes in their labelling.[17] The large companies' products did not escape being labelled ineffective: 29 came from Squibb, 27 from Upjohn, 21 from Pfizer, 20 from Lederle, nineteen from Lilly, fifteen from Wyeth and fourteen from Merck. Of 16,000 therapeutic claims made for the products under investigation, 66 percent could not be scientifically substantiated.[18] The NAS/NRC panels concluded:

> Many of the presentations submitted by manufacturers in support of the claims made for their drugs were far from convincing. The lack of evidence based on controlled studies by seasoned investigators was conspicuous. In its place, we were asked to evaluate bulky files of uncontrolled observations and testimonial-type endorsements. Moreover, independent searches of the medical literature indicated that there exists little or no scientifically convincing evidence to support many of the claims made for many drugs that have acquired a significant place in medical practice.[19]

One group of drugs that came in for particular criticism was the fixed-dose combinations. They were ruled against for the following reasons:

> 1. The fixed dosage form made rational therapeutics difficult or impossible since necessary titration of one ingredient was made impossible by the presence of others.
> 2. Some of the formulations had no rational basis.
> 3. Some ingredients were present in too small a dose to be effective.

4. Though several ingredients were active and contributed to the therapeutic effect, a similar effect could be obtained by the use of one of the ingredients if used in a normal dose.

5. The therapeutic effect of one ingredient ran counter to the therapeutic effects of another.

6. An ingredient was present for which there was no evidence of effectiveness.[20]

7. The combination is often given a trade name distinct from the names of the component drugs, and often bearing no relation to them, and thus does not readily identify the components to the physician.

8. Although savings are achieved in some cases, in others the fixed combination is significantly more expensive than the total cost of the ingredients dispensed separately.[21]

Forty antibiotic combinations were found to be ineffective by reason of being no more effective than their components used singly. Fifty antibiotic combinations were judged dangerous, not just to the individual user, but also to the public at large, because they could permit resistant strains of bacteria to proliferate.

Significantly, of a total of 2,131 new products introduced into the American market between 1958 and 1967, 1,440 were combination products, more than two thirds of the total.[22] Since the Canadian market is such a carbon-copy of the American one, it is safe to assume the same situation prevailed here.

Fixed-dose combination drugs are still a problem as far as the Quebec Order of Pharmacists is concerned. In 1982, its president, Jean-Claude Marquis, stated: "Because it is better and safer to prescribe individual drugs, we are not in favor of any fixed combination drug products."[23]

What Research Gets Done and Why

Why were so many combination products developed and marketed? Or, to put the question more broadly, what motivates the drug companies to undertake the research that they do? Jim Russo, a representative in the U.S. for the Pharmaceutical Manufacturers Association, has admitted that drug companies do not undertake research on relatively uncommon diseases, because drugs for them would generate insufficient profits.[24] These same sentiments were echoed in 1980 by Joseph Williams, president of Warner Lambert, who said: "Our focus is to develop major drugs for major markets."[25]

The key word is obviously "profit," and volume of sales is one of the prime contributors to profits. Over the past twenty years a great deal of research has gone into developing drugs to lower cholesterol and triglyceride ("fat") levels, although until 1984 no conclusive data existed that showed that reducing the levels of either, or both, of these substances is going to lower the risk of having a heart attack or stroke. But since millions of people suffer from these diseases, the sales potential is great, and so the research went on. On the other hand, we have already seen how profit interfered with the production of penicillamine, trien and 5-HPT, drugs needed for serious and potentially fatal diseases.

Another key influence on the direction, or misdirection, of pharmaceutical research, is whether or not the product can be patented. New uses of already existing chemicals cannot be patented and therefore industry research tends to ignore these substances. This point was supported in testimony by George Wright, a professor of chemistry at the University of Toronto, before the Special House of Commons Committee:

> Some significance must be attached to the observation that new drugs emanating from commercial drug research laboratories are almost always new-and-therefore-patentable compounds, despite a reservoir of about two million known chemicals, the majority of which have not been examined pharmacologically.[26]

Again, the reason for the companies' deep disinterest is related to the effect that patents have on profits. Two examples of how existing chemicals are not developed by the drug industry involve lithium and L-dopa, medications that may be very beneficial in manic-depressive disorders and in Parkinson's disease respectively. Reports of lithium's effectiveness began appearing as long ago as 1949. But lithium, which is a naturally occurring element, cannot be patented. Only when it was found that lithium could be compounded into a patentable slow release form did the drug companies start researching and manufacturing it.[27] The existence of L-dopa has been known since the early 1930s, but for two reasons its development was delayed until the late 1960s. First, the pharmaceutical industry considered the potential U.S. market—1.5

million Parkinson's sufferers—to be too small. Second, L-dopa is derived from fava beans, and as a natural substance it could not be patented. When the drug companies devised a way to make L-dopa synthetically, they could then get a patent on it, and as with lithium, it was then manufactured commercially.[28]

The Royal Commission on Health believed that much of the research done by companies was directed toward duplicating already existing drugs; in effect, inventing around other companies' patents in order to capture a share of the particular market. Frequently the new products are no better than the old ones (see Chapter 12 for an example of this phenomenon involving the benzodiazepines), and may have new and more dangerous side effects. In its brief to the Special House of Commons Committee, the province of Alberta severely criticized the effect of patents on applied research:

> Hence patents have not only induced a distortion between basic and applied research, but in making the latter budgets relatively too large have induced wasteful duplication of effort and the misdirection of effort toward rivalry-oriented molecular manipulation, the development of often irrational combinations of existing drugs, which lack flexibility and compound the problems of dosage and toxicity, and the devising of additives which represent often questionable and perhaps unnecessary flourishes in the direction of increasing the absorption rate of a drug, guarding against side effects and the like.[29]

Naturally, the drug industry opposes that line of thought. Its claim is that patents provide the incentive for significant research discoveries. In its investigation into the effects of patents, a U.S. Senate Antitrust Subcommittee classified 176 important drug discoveries according to the place of discovery, and then broke that list down into countries that grant product patents and those that do not. Among the latter, discoveries within the U.S. were further subdivided into those made in commercial or non-commercial laboratories. The results are very revealing. Not including the U.S., the performance of those countries not granting product patents was far superior to those which did, 82 discoveries to fifteen. When the contribution of the U.S. was added, the advantage shifts slightly in favor of the countries that do grant patent protection, 94 to 82. However, if the discoveries made in non-commercial U.S.

laboratories are deleted, then the countries without product patents have the advantage, 82 to 75. Therefore, it would appear that pharmaceutical innovation is not dependent upon patent protection.[30]

In Canada, it is hard to see how the existence of patents has done anything to encourage research and development. This was the conclusion of the Restrictive Trade Practices Commission in the early 1960s.[31] A few years later, the Royal Commission on Health found that of 395 patents on fourteen "important pharmaceutical products," only nine, or less than 3 percent, were held by genuine Canadian firms.[32] While this finding does not offer conclusive proof, it suggests that little is to be lost by abandoning the patent system and that much might be gained.

Directing research toward patentable chemical therapy means discouraging research in other fields such as nutrition, public health, biochemistry and preventive medicine, since the funding is not available. If the drug industry is ignoring these areas as priorities, then what happens to the priorities of people interested in research in therapeutics? How much does the knowledge of where funding can come from influence the kinds of questions that researchers are even willing to consider?

The stress placed on the discovery of new processes and patents means that properties and therapeutic possibilities of existing medicines are not studied as intensively as they should be. In an industry where product—not price—competition is the chief form of rivalry, it is essential to keep churning out new products. Pierre Garai, who was an advertising executive and a staunch supporter of the pharmaceutical industry, and the free enterprise system in general, wrote that "to continue to thrive in the highly competitive sphere in which they exist, the drug companies will have to remain essentially in the business of new products. *That is where the greatest profit opportunities lie.*"[33] (Emphasis added.) Elsewhere in his article, Mr. Garai was candid enough to explain what the emphasis on new products means:

> No manufacturer of drugs can afford to restrict his production to genuinely significant pharmaceutical innovations. There simply aren't enough of these around in any given fiscal year or, for that matter, any dozen fiscal years. It should therefore surprise no one that we find slight modifications of existing pro-

ducts marketed by the bushel, a veritable blizzard of parity products slugging it out as each company strives to extend its share of the market, endless polypharmaceutical combinations of dubious merit, and a steady outpouring of new chemical entities whose advantages, to say the least, remain to be established.[34]

The drug companies argue that they often cannot know which slight changes in existing drugs will yield great therapeutic benefits. That line of reasoning is not generally accepted. Dr. Dale Console, former medical director of Squibb, counters with testimony that "with many of these products, it is clear while they are on the drawing board that they promise no utility. They promise sales. It is not a question of pursuing them because something may come out of it . . . it is pursued simply because there is profit in it."[35] The cost of this kind of research is not light, either in terms of talent or money. Haskell Weinstein, former acting medical director of the J.B. Roerig Division of Pfizer, deplored what he regarded as a waste of scientific talent:

A great many extremely fine scientists are employed by these manufacturers. Their talents should not be expended on patent by-passing chemical manipulations, on ridiculous mixtures of drugs, or inconsequential additives to established drugs. Since the number of well-trained capable scientists is severely limited, their potential should not be wasted.[36]

Dr. Console emphasized before a U.S. Senate Subcommittee what happens once a drug company decides to market a compound that has no significant therapeutic advantage over products already available. The decision sets in motion a cumulative process resulting in further waste in the stages of animal and human evaluation: "This may take one or two years, or more, requiring many man-hours of time contributed by experts in various disciplines. Most if not all of this research is wasted as is the time of scientists who might be better engaged in producing something worthwhile."[37] In 1982, of approximately 800 new molecular entities in the clinical testing process in the U.S., less than 5 percent were judged by scientists in the U.S. Food and Drug Administration to have the potential for important therapeutic gain.[38]

The U.S. Task Force on Prescription Drugs concluded that of all the new products introduced onto the market in any one year, only 10 to 25 percent represent new important chemical entities,[39] and only a fraction of those are important therapeutic advances. According to one estimate, of 1,848 new products marketed in the U.S. between 1959 and 1968, only 30 were important therapeutic advances, about three a year.[40] The New York Academy of Medicine put the figure at about six a year.[41] Of the most recent 112 new molecular entities that had been given U.S. market approval up to March 1981 only 15 percent offered any important therapeutic gain.[42] The Task Force concluded:

> To the extent that an industry devotes a considerable share of its research program to the development of what have been termed duplicative and noncontributory products, there may be a waste of skilled research manpower and research facilities, a waste of clinical facilities needed to test the products, a further confusing proliferation of drug products promoted to physicians, and a further burden on the patient-consumer who, in the long run, must pay the costs.[43]

The Quality of Research

The quality of the research done by the drug companies is often suspect. The MER/29 affair is one reminder that we cannot always trust the results that emerge from the companies' labs. In another example, the pain killer Norgesic was marketed on the basis of tainted data.[44] Newspapers during the mid-1970s frequently featured stories about the falsifying of research results.[45]

Once again, Dr. Console's testimony on the industry's research practices is revealing:

> All along the line of this mis-directed effort the pressure is on to make the compound appear better than it is. This is not conducive to integrity in research. The distortion reaches its peak in the phase of clinical evaluation. Here the criteria are least rigid and there is wide latitude for poor research. To the medical director these mediocre compounds always pose problems, and the diversion of the efforts of his staff is not the greatest. Because they are unimaginative, uninteresting compounds, it is virtually impossible to interest reliable investigators in their

study. They are not motivated to confirm the obvious. Since they are deficient it is safer to subject them to superficial studies rather than critical examination. Claims rather than scientific evidence are the primary objective. And so, poor research breeds more poor research.[46]

In its brief to the Restrictive Trade Practices Commission, the PMAC pointed out that the clinical investigation stage of research and development comes under the aegis of the company's medical director. This should be reassuring, but Merrell's chief scientist and director of research, Harold W. Werner, was one of the three men from that company indicted in the MER/29 scandal. Sometimes a medical director merely exists to throw a cloak of respectability over what are really business decisions. If enough money has been spent on developing the drug and potential sales are large enough, it will go on the market despite the opinion of the medical director. As Dr. Console says, in the end "he has one vote."[47]

Many other examples show that medical directors either do not know what kind of research is going on or else openly condone false and/or poor research. One physician, on contract to drug companies, received more than $32,000 over a two-year period for results of drug tests praising new remedies. The FDA later produced evidence which showed that these trials involved gross fraud; the physician was convicted in U.S. Federal Court.[48] Dr. Ray Nulsen published a study which "demonstrated" that thalidomide was safe to administer to expectant and nursing mothers. It was later found that the paper was written by an employee of Merrell, the company trying to market the drug. Moreover, Dr. Nulsen had never read the studies that he used as references.[49] These are not just isolated examples. Between 1967 and 1973, the Scientific Investigation Group (SIG) of the FDA investigated 50 physicians who had done studies for drug companies, and found that sixteen had supplied false data. Instances of outright fraud were less common than just plain incompetence, and in most cases of fraud, both the government and the drug companies were being deceived. However, according to Alan Lisock, a medical officer with the SIG, "there are companies who are not above hiring investigators who will give them the results they desire."[50]

In 1982, the Edmonton *Journal* ran a three-part series based on U.S. government documents which detailed numerous instances of questionable drug experiments on humans, fabrication of information and withholding of vital test information by both laboratories and doctors. In the twenty years up to 1982, 43 American doctors were suspended for abuse of experimental drugs, while another 24 are being investigated for serious deficiencies in drug testing. Twenty-seven laboratories were found to have had serious problems with their test procedures and another 100 had committed technical violations of U.S. regulations. Of drug companies and laboratories that supervise doctors in the testing of drugs, 45 percent showed significant deviations from U.S. government testing guidelines.[51]

Before Merck marketed Indocid, it sent the drug to clinicians to be tested. One wrote the following letter back to Dr. Nelson Cantwell of Merck, Sharp and Dohme Laboratories:

> Dear Nelson,
> The enclosed letter is from a very fine patient...I thought you would be very interested in her very vivid and articulate description of the adverse symptoms she encountered with Indomethacin.
> I would emphasize that these do not alarm me nor indicate any evidence of organic damage but *I am afraid they will offer some practical problems in marketing this drug.*
> *Needless to say, I am very grateful for all of your kind efforts in regard to my trip to Japan.*
> I'll look forward to seeing you on my return. I think we *must get together* and plan on publishing some of the data which we have collected. Best regards always.[52] (Emphasis added in Burack.)

Richard Burack, who reprinted this letter in his *New Handbook of Prescription Drugs,* makes the obvious point that the investigator in this case was more than a little biased. As Burack says, it was not the business of the investigator to be concerned with marketing problems, nor had he any business taking favors such as help in arranging Japanese trips. Finally, if he needed help interpreting the data he should have gotten it from outside experts, not from the company. It can hardly be expected that he would produce an unbiased study.

Despite the accumulating evidence of bias and falsification of research data, the Canadian government has no policy for inspecting the drug companies' laboratories or of monitoring their research.

Doctors who conduct therapeutic trials on new drugs were interviewed during a review of the Canadian drug laws in the late 1960s. It was found that although they were competent clinicians, they were not highly qualified in pharmacology and toxicology and depended largely upon the pharmaceutical companies to supply them with information in these areas.[53] Although therapeutic trials are initiated only after it has been established that a drug is safe, it is still disturbing that these clinicians needed to rely on the companies for information, since, as we have seen, the companies are not always completely candid about their products.

At times, drugs which are distributed supposedly for clinical investigation are really intended as just "premarketing softening" as was true with Merrell and MER/29. Merrell used the same tactics in the U.S. with thalidomide (Kevadon), directing its sales staff to persuade the nation's "most influential physicians" to try the drug on their patients. Whether these "studies" were ever published was inconsequential to Merrell, whose major aim was just to make Kevadon widely known among the medical profession. If a physician was hesitant to co-operate, Merrell's salespeople were told to "appeal to the doctor's ego—we think he is important enough to be selected as one of the first to use Kevadon in that section of the country."[54]

These examples point to another disturbing aspect of drug research. Many clinical studies are supported and carried out solely for the purpose of producing allegedly scientific articles at regular intervals. The real purpose is just to keep the name of the drug before physicians. Sometimes, investigators submit sketchy and uncritical observations to the company, leaving the actual writing to a professional medical writer employed by the company. Frequently the article is submitted to one of the journals which look to the company for advertising dollars; rarely is publication refused.[55] A look at the quality of reported drug trials supports the contention that many are unreliable. Of 141 trials published in four British medical journals in the first six months of each of 1966 and 1969, 33 percent were judged unacceptable.[56] Closer to home, there are the drug trials reported in the *Canadian Medical Association Journal* between 1961 and 1967. They were graded on a scale from one to five, five being a completely valid trial according to generally accepted statistical criteria. Of the 264 trials examined, 147, or 55.7

percent, received a score of one, and only 42 a score of five.[57]

Finally, one has to wonder how many studies never see publication. If a company is paying for a drug trial, and their drug is shown to be inferior, it is a good bet that study will never make it out of the laboratory. As one professor of pharmacology put it, "The major pharmaceutical manufacturers do not support comparative studies which might show their product to be inferior. In a sense, they would be foolish if they did so, and their stockholders should correct them, since their object is to sell their drugs."[58]

Ruth Cooperstock, a leading researcher with Ontario's Addiction Research Foundation, raises a series of disturbing questions about a number of aspects of industry-financed research:

> One wonders what the effect of reporting negative findings might be for the researcher under these conditions. How widely are negative findings disseminated? Has any research ever been conducted on the differences between the findings reported by those doing clinical trials supported by industry funds and the results of government or university supported research? Were the research methods employed the same for the two groups? With no knowledge of funding, would judges evaluate the research as of equal substantive and scientific quality, including such matters as the adequacy of the kinds and numbers of subjects and controls used, the appropriateness of dosage, and so forth?[59]

We have already seen some examples of the research conducted by the drug industry, but there is one type that has not yet been mentioned—testing of new drugs on humans. These tests generally occur in four phases. In the first phase, a new compound is tried out for effectiveness and possible toxic properties on a small group of normal, healthy volunteers. If these people have no serious side effects, and the drug appears promising, it is passed into phase two, which consists of short-term trials of the drug in treating the disease process. In this phase, the effectiveness of the drug and the tolerance of the patient to the drug are studied. Phase three involves long-term, broad-scale clinical trials in volunteer patients. If side effects or toxic properties of the drug exist, it is hoped they will show up in phase three testing. Phase four consists of studies submitted to the Health Protection Branch subsequent to approval for marketing.

No phase one testing is done in Canada.

In the U.S., most phase one testing is carried out on prisoners. Why? Well, in the words of one American scientist: "Criminals in our penitentiaries are fine experimental material—and much cheaper than chimpanzees."[60] The drug companies, usually operating through private physicians with access to the prisons, can obtain healthy human subjects living in controlled conditions that are difficult, if not impossible, to duplicate elsewhere. The reports on the experimental findings are not always pleasant. In one such experiment run for Lederle, the following comments from the prisoners were recorded: "Cold chills, sweated, nauseated throughout the night." "Sharp abdominal pains." "I have a headache and my stomach feels terrible." "My body feels weak all over, right arm hurts worse than ever." "My head feels as if it will fall off." "Chilled, feverish, weak and exhausted." "Lost 4 lbs. in three days—Dr. Epstein said it was a natural reaction except it was more severe in my case for some reason but not to worry."[61] An expose in the New York *Times* reported that hundreds of inmates in voluntary programs have been stricken with serious diseases and an undetermined number have died.[62] In the summer of 1980, the FDA in the U.S. announced that as of June 1981, it would no longer accept any data gathered in trials on prisoners. Within a few months of this announcement, there were reports of drug companies advertising in college newspapers for volunteers. The change in experimental subjects represented a blow to the drug companies since the research conducted on prisoners would never have been allowed on college and medical students.

Research in Canada

In 1960, PMAC member companies were spending about $9.5 million a year on research, but only $3.35 million of that was applied to work being done in Canada. The rest was money charged to Canadian subsidiaries by their multinational parents for research done abroad. Based on the amount of money actually spent in Canada, the Royal Commission on Health concluded that expenses for research and development (R&D) did not play a major role in the price of drugs.[63]

By 1982, $75 million was being spent on research by PMAC companies.[64] PMAC publications devote pages to describing the industry's research effort here, but they are also careful to remind readers that "research in the pharmaceutical industry is virtually 'an investment in faith' since there is little tax incentive nor effective patent protection to do so."[65] The PMAC is also careful to boast of the large number of scientists engaged in pharmaceutical research in this country,[66] but compared to other countries in the Organization for Economic Cooperation and Development (OECD), Canadian R&D employment is not very impressive. In 1975, Canadian companies employed 155 full-time workers in research for every $100 million (U.S.) in pharmaceutical production. That level of employment ranked Canada last on a list of nine OECD countries.[67]

Of the 134 companies listed in the 1975 Census of Manufacturers of Pharmaceuticals and Medicines, only 36 carried out any research in Canada in that year, and by 1982 only six companies were doing any significant amount of research in Canada.[68] Canada's share of worldwide pharmaceutical research and development is one of the lowest among industrialized countries. Pharmaceutical research carried out in Canada is only about 40 percent of that which could be expected based on Canada's share of the world market for drugs.[69]

The standard myth propagated by representatives of PMAC and the drug companies is that the 1969 changes to the patent laws are to blame for the low level of research in this country.[70] They begin by claiming that drug research was flourishing in Canada in the 1960s. They cite supporting evidence by the Canadian Medical Association's director of publications,[71] by the head of Canada's Medical Research Council[72] and by various figures in the Canadian scientific community.[73] For the sake of argument, let us ignore the fact that drugs so far affected by the patent law changes account for less than 17 percent of total 1981 drug sales. In the 1960s, before the patent laws were changed, research in the pharmaceutical industry was already growing at a rate slower than that for all industries.[74] The amount spent on drug research did almost triple between 1963 and 1969, from $6.2 million to $17.3 million, but Gorecki and Henderson believe that much of that increase may have been due solely to the increased clinical testing of new drugs that was required by the government after 1963. In other words, most of what was labelled as research and development was not expenditures on new drug innovations, but the satisfying of regulatory requirements for the introduction of new drugs.[75]

As regards the myth that drug research has suffered from the patent law changes, witness the remarks of E.E. Campana, Ayerst's vice-president of marketing. Referring to the effect of the changes, he said, "Anyone thinking of opening a pharmaceutical research and development centre in Canada has rocks in their head."[76] This myth rests on a trio of claims: that the 1969 patent law changes have reduced the profits of the industry to such an extent that there is no money left to invest in research; that drugs developed in other countries are somehow treated differently from drugs developed in Canada; and that economically it really matters to a multinational company if it loses 20 percent of the Canadian market for a particular drug. In Chapter 3 we saw that, if anything, profits in the industry are better now than in the supposed halcyon days of the 1950s and 1960s. If a drug is sold in Canada it does not matter where the research on it was done—in Canada, the U.S. or Switzerland—a compulsory licence can still be issued against it. There is no advantage to be gained, insofar as avoiding compulsory licensing is concerned, by doing research outside of Canada. Finally, as Canada represents only 1.6 percent of the world pharmaceutical market, and less than 10 percent of the North American market, it is obvious that no company would spend $50 to $75 million to develop a drug just to meet Canadian needs. The major incentive to do research and development in Canada lies in the profits to be derived from selling pharmaceuticals in the major world markets, Western Europe, the U.S. and Japan, which represent 33, 25 and 17 percent of world sales respectively. The prospect of losing 20 percent of the small Canadian market to a generic company would not deter a multinational from doing research in Canada if the company truly had any commitment to promoting research here.

The lack of any factual support for these three claims renders this myth just that, a myth. According to Gorecki: "There has *not* been a massive reduction in R&D activity in Canada . . . Indeed, the weaker inference that R&D has declined is not supported."[77] (Emphasis in original.) If account is taken of inflation, then the growth in research spending stopped in 1973, dropped slightly, and subsequently levelled off, before declining somewhat in the late 1970s. However, the amount spent on R&D in 1980, in real terms, was above that spent in 1969. This pattern of spending in fact just mirrors what happened in R&D expenditures in Canadian industry generally.[78]

It is doubtful whether tax incentives play any major role in the level of R&D activity. Indirect evidence makes the authors of a report on Canadian pharmaceutical R&D sceptical about its importance.[79] Their viewpoint is substantiated by the dearth of research activity which still exists despite government incentives to promote commercial research. Amendments to the Income Tax Act passed in 1961 provided for the acceleration of the rate at which capital expenditures on research could be written off as expenses. In 1962, there was a new plan, administered through the National Research Council, providing for financial assistance for applied research and development on a matching basis, with government contributing up to 50 percent of the cost of some projects. Also in 1962, corporate taxpayers undertaking to increase industrial research in Canada were permitted to deduct 150 percent of their increased expenditures on scientific research for industrial purposes. More recently, in 1978, substantial new tax incentives were approved for research done in Canada. In 1979, investment tax credits for research were increased. In all, the federal government has provided assistance through six different programs to firms engaged in industrial research and development over the years.[80] However, the pharmaceutical industry has made relatively limited use of all but one of these programs.[81] Contrary to the PMAC claims about "little tax incentive" for research, the government has been providing substantial research incentives, and for a considerable period of time.[82]

One of the main reasons for the past and present lack of research is the foreign control of the Canadian industry. A 1980 study for the federal Department of Industry, Trade and Commerce reported that the degree of foreign ownership of a country's drug industry exercised a strong negative effect on the R&D intensity in that country.[83] Dr. David Bond of the federal Department of Consumer and Corporate Affairs contends that "where a company does research isn't a function of the patent laws, you can do research anywhere."[84] However, the multinational firms are inclined to maintain strong centralized research establishments. Donald Davies, chairman of Ayerst McKenna and Harrison, agrees: "Virtually all companies do most of their research in their home country...German companies do the bulk of their research in Germany, and French companies do their work in France. That's just the way it is."[85] The reason for this centralization is that substantial scale economies appear to exist in conducting research into new drugs. One estimate suggests that the critical mass for a research facility is between 200 and 300 personnel and that scale economies begin above that level. Including all the drug companies in Canada, only 930 people were employed in research in 1980.[86] Where centralized research activities occur depends on a variety of factors, including: the country of origin of the multinational; in many foreign countries drug prices are controlled and multinationals are offered the ability to charge higher prices only if R&D activities are increased; in some European countries drugs are approved by the health authorities much faster than in North America, that is, with much less documentation, thereby providing a faster return on investment; significant income tax exemptions and tax holidays are offered in countries such as Ireland and Puerto Rico; some countries, such as France, require companies to conduct research within their borders if they wish to market their products there; finally, the technical and educational development of the staff plays a role in the selection of a research site.[87] Since Canada lacks any large indigenous drug companies, research and development allocated to Canadian subsidiaries is generally devoted to product introduction activities, with only limited new product development.

Consider the case of Anturan (sulfinpyrazone), a CIBA-Geigy product, marketed in 1959, for the treatment of gout.[88] In the mid-1960s, Dr. Fraser Mustard, of the Toronto Sunnybrook Medical Centre, began to suspect that this drug might be useful in the prevention of secondary myocardial infarctions in people with arteriosclerotic disease ("hardening of the arteries"). He approached the management of the Canadian subsidiary of CIBA to get funding for clinical trials to test his hypothesis, but neither the Swiss parent company, nor the U.S. subsidiary were interested and consequently there was no money forthcoming.

The Medical Research Council of Canada did finance the studies, and the results showed that the drug would in fact help to prevent strokes, another consequence of arteriosclerosis. At this point, the U.S. subsidiary of CIBA realized the considerable commercial potential of this new use for Anturan, and funded a large international study designed to get U.S. approval to market Anturan for use in cardiovascular diseases due to arteriosclerosis. The final result of this second study showed that if people are given Anturan after a heart attack, their chances of having a second one are cut almost in half. Until this study came in for severe methodological criticism that cast doubts on the validity of its results, CIBA stood to make a huge profit from research initially started in Canada, research which it refused to fund, and which was finally paid for by Canadian taxpayers.

In 1974, the Trial Drug Screening Program was set up by Canadian Patents and Development Limited, a government agency. According to the Department of Industry, Trade and Commerce:

> The underlying concern which prompted this trial program was a perceived lack of interest by Canadian pharmaceutical firms in evaluating chemical compounds produced in Canadian universities and government laboratories for their possible therapeutic and commercial value... The results of the Trial Drug Screening Program tend to support the view that multinational research-based pharmaceutical firms keep fully informed of the basic and applied research done by Canadian government and universities but fail to pursue comprehensive drug development programs from this research in Canada due to the limited R&D role assignments of their Canadian subsidiaries.[89]

It is the larger firms that do the bulk of the research in Canada, but the effects of foreign control still limit their contribution. The proportion of resources a Canadian subsidiary devotes to research and development is inversely related to its sales volume in Canada. Therefore the largest companies in Canada are substantially dependent upon research obtained from their foreign parents.[90]

The former president of Bristol Laboratories, Edward R. Rowe, did not seem to see anything wrong with so little research being done in Canada: "I think we are very fortunate in Canada to have all of these marvellous drugs made available to us through the efforts of people around the world."[91] We may get the benefit, in drugs, of foreign research, but Canada does not get the economic advantages of research. Scientific employment is reduced;[92] there is no impetus for students to pursue careers in pharmacology research; and the industries that are attracted by research do not develop here. Furthermore, we become dependent on the research priorities of another country, priorities which may not coincide with Canada's.

Research and development expenditures have actually been declining in relative terms. As a percentage of total sales of human pharmaceuticals, they went from 8.5 percent in 1969 to 5.7 percent in 1976. During the period 1971 to 1977, research and development expenditures by pharmaceutical firms continued the trend of the previous seven years, and grew at a slower rate than expenditures for all manufacturing industries: 1.6 percent per year versus 2.3.

The little research money that is spent in Canada is divided into three areas. Eight percent goes to basic research which seeks to discover new concepts of drug therapy or totally new drug products; 36 percent is used for applied research which consists of testing potential drugs on animals and humans; and 56 percent is applied to product development, which encompasses areas such as developing new dosage forms or different forms of the drug, such as pills, tablets, creams or solutions.[93] The absence of basic research is apparent when we consider that Canada originated only 0.5 percent of all new chemical entities introduced by the world pharmaceutical community in the period 1958 to 1970. This performance ranked Canada last on a list of nine OECD countries.[94] Much of the applied research and development that is carried out by Canadian companies is done for one of two reasons: either to take advantage of tax concessions, or to satisfy the Health Protection Branch's regulations about clinical testing of new drugs.[95] Applied research and development also assumes a highly routine character, which tends to make these tasks unappealing to university scientists. Furthermore, in a profit motivated firm, there is always a latent conflict between an atmosphere of freedom, which is necessary for good scientific endeavour, and the necessity of direction from those who are responsible for the conduct of the firm. When applied research and product development are the predominant research activities, both the goals and procedures become relatively well defined, and an atmosphere of completely free inquiry is not crucial.[96] These considerations may explain the fact that although the pharmaceutical industry provided approximately 21 percent of the total funds for health care research in 1977, it utilized only 11 percent of the total number of medical researchers in this country in that year.

What can be done to improve the situation for drug research in this country? There are really two issues to be decided: what is the relative importance of pharmaceutical research versus other kinds of health care research, and how can those dollars best be spent that are eventually allocated to pharmaceutical research?

As was mentioned earlier, drug research competes for money with research in other areas such as nutrition, public health and preventive medicine. With limited resources, when one area is emphasized, the others tend to be shunted into the background as far as funding goes. For example, in the "conquering" of infectious diseases such as tuberculosis and diptheria, drugs played a decidedly minor role relative to improvements in nutrition and public health measures.

Currently, in Canada, our major health concerns are with the so-called "diseases of affluence"—cardiovascular disease and cancer being the two dominant ones. Drug therapy for these diseases is essentially curative therapy, that is, it treats people who are already ill. There are good arguments to be made, however, for shifting the focus to various forms of preventive therapy. These may involve drugs but are more likely to involve behavioral changes in areas such as diet and smoking, and environmental changes aimed at reducing stress in the workplace and limiting environmental and industrial pollution.

My concern here is not to assess the relative merits and demerits of various methods of therapeutics, but simply to emphasize that this debate is a necessary step in developing a policy on drug research. Obviously, the debate will not be a static one and needs will change with differing circumstances, both economic and medical.

However the priorities for overall therapeutic research are ordered, it is obvious that the priorities for drug research in Canada, and worldwide, are grossly distorted when left in the hands of private industry. We have seen in this chapter that drugs are developed primarily for their profit potential and only secondarily for their benefit to society. Sometimes, as with the polio vaccine, these two motives may be congruent, but often they are not (witness the proliferation of the minor tranquillizers; see Chapter 12).

It is not sufficient, therefore, to try to expand research activities simply by encouraging the development of large indigenous Canadian companies. There is no guarantee that the research goals of these companies are likely to be any better than those of the foreign multinationals. For the same reason, a satisfactory resolution to the research problem is not to be found in tax incentives or direct subsidies to companies currently operating in Canada, nor in a system such as France uses whereby companies that wish to raise their prices above a certain level are required to increase their research commitment.

The solution has to involve removing profit as a motive for doing research in order to be sure that the research being done is truly worthwhile. I will develop this idea further in Chapter 14.

Chapter 7
Medical Students, Doctors and Organized Medicine

There are many ways of dealing with health problems. If they are prevented in the first place, no treatment is required. If prevention is not attempted, or if it fails, various methods of treatment can be tried. Obviously, it is in the financial interests of the pharmaceutical companies to promote drug therapy for disease. But drugs can be sold only through a prescription, and only doctors can write prescriptions. Therefore, doctors and medical students become prime objects of concern for the drug companies.

The drug industry's ultimate goal is to convince doctors to prescribe an ever-increasing volume of drugs. Advertising is a favorite and very effective method of reaching doctors, but much more is involved than just impersonal ads, as we shall see. Strategically, the industry seeks to convince the medical profession that the interests of doctors are identical to those of drug companies. To the extent that the campaign succeeds in achieving this identification, it ensures that doctors will view pharmaceuticals as the main form of medical treatment and will correspondingly prescribe more and more drugs. But this commonality of interests has a second, equally beneficial, consequence for the drug companies. A threat to the drug industry, be it from government or consumer groups, also becomes a threat to doctors. The industry thereby gains a very powerful ally in its battles.

Medical education indirectly prepares students for this alliance with the drug industry. Diseases are presented as the result of a specific organism—a virus, bacteria, fungus, or a specific biochemical abnormality—which brings about a specific change in the functioning of the human body. Sickness is not taught as also having social, political or economic causes. With the focus on the individual as the locus of disease, the treatment is also naturally focused on the individual. In this context, agents that can kill the offending organism or restore the proper biochemical balance assume the most important role in treatment. These agents are, of course, usually drugs. Medical education creates a bias in students toward drug treatment, and consequently toward drug makers. Once the student has graduated the drug companies need only build on this pre-existing bias.

It should not be surprising that the companies actively seek to influence medical students early in their careers. In 1978, the PMAC chairman was interested in giving medical students summer jobs in pharmaceutical companies and in facilitating student tours of the plants. Lunches, medical literature and assorted gifts are showered upon the students, most of whom claim that they are outwitting the industry, having gotten something for nothing. But in fact these innocent encounters mark the beginning of a slide into a deepening alliance with the industry. Eventually, students come to depend on the drug companies as a source of medical information and passively accept the industry's priorities and directions. The evolution of this partnership is gradual. No single conscious decision needs to be taken. It is often hard to tell at what step in the process the taking of "helpful," "useful" and "objective" materials blends into the taking of the silver hook that is brand name advertising. What is the difference whether you learn about new drugs in a lecture or over a free lunch or even on a short vacation sponsored by a drug company?

Martin Shapiro went to medical school at McGill in the early 1970s, and writes about his experiences in *Getting Doctored*.[1] At the end of the first year, Eli Lilly offered the students a stethoscope, reflex hammer, tuning fork and doctor's bag, all free of charge. Some students made an attempt to have the entire class reject the offer, but in the end most of the students were indifferent, and the boycott effort failed. Dr. Harold Upjohn, the vice-president of Upjohn, bluntly admitted the obvious about bestowing gifts upon medical students: "You know why they give them. No question about it. They want doctors to be interested in prescribing their brands."[2]

Medical schools make little effort to counter the influence of the drug companies or to encourage students to think critically about the industry. At the University of Toronto, where I attended medical school between 1973 and 1977, education about the pharmaceutical industry consisted of twenty pages of readings which were mildly critical of certain aspects of the industry and a one-hour session in the first year. Until I enrolled in 1973, this hour was divided between two speakers, a representative of the PMAC and a government spokesperson who discussed Ontario's Prescriptions at Reasonable Cost (PARCOST) Program. I, along with a few other students, objected that we did not think that this was a well balanced panel, and the lecturer agreed to add me to the panel. The PMAC representative sat through most of the session with a gaze of incredulity on his face, clearly unprepared for the "unfriendly" comments. He answered my points with personal innuendos directed at me. Interestingly, the PMAC did not send a representative the following year.

The ritualistic giving of gifts does not stop when medical students graduate. Some companies donate a supply of calling cards.[3] In one case, a Canadian doctor was given an all-expense-paid trip to a U.S. drug factory. The trip included expensive entertainment and X-rated films.[4] Doctors who become drinking buddies with detail men often get free supplies of drugs for their families, with the cocktails thrown in for good measure.[5] There are always rulers, paper weights, note pads, paintings, photographs, books and a variety of other little trinkets available to doctors free for the asking. At medical conventions and conferences, the companies often have hospitality suites where free liquor is supplied. During one conference I was attending, a heavyweight championship fight was being staged. One company booked a room in which a large closed-circuit screen had been set up to show the fight. Philip Berger described his experiences at conferences he attended.[6] At one jellybeans were given away to promote tranquillizers and at another freshly cooked boeuf bourguignon was doled out free to eager doctors. At a Toronto conference of family physicians in October 1983, the participants were issued lottery cards. If doctors spent their time "usefully," as judged by detail men, they received a red dot for good performance. Twenty-five red dots on your lottery card made it eligible for a draw; the winners received $100 from the participating companies. At the same conference, a sleeping-pill manufacturer challenged doctors to press a button in the shortest time possible after the detail man said "go." The leaders' scores and names were posted prominently and at the convention's end a winner was declared.

The thought of doctors lining up for free jellybeans or receiving red dots for "being good" evokes memories of children lining up to ask Santa Claus for toys. The difference is that children eventually stop believing in Santa Claus. As Dr. Dale Console, former medical director for Squibb, observed: "It seems impossible to convince my medical brethren that drug company executives and detailmen are either shrewd businessmen or shrewd salesmen, never philanthropists. They make investments, not gifts."[7]

Drug companies pay handsomely for the right to set up booths at conferences. Their fees provide a considerable chunk of the financing for these meetings, thus keeping down the cost to the individual doctor.

Read part of the report by Dr. Charles Godfrey, of the Wellesley Hospital in Toronto, about the 1982 conference of the Pan-American League Against Rheumatism:

> Many resident rheumatologists had their trip to the event sponsored by pharmaceutical companies. In addition, it was possible during the five-day seance to avoid spending a penny of your own money to buy food or drink. The mountains of gustatory goodies made it possible to freebie the week, and still take home something in a doggy bag. This was in addition to the normal give-aways of pens and glossy brochures.[8]

Doctors might maintain that despite accepting all these blandishments from the drug industry they can retain an intellectual detachment. The response from *The Lancet*, one of the world's leading medical journals, was that "such a belief may preserve self-respect, but it is a delusion."[9]

In fact, the drug industry's "investments" spoken of by Dr. Console have borne fruit, for the industry does not lack for defenders among doctors. In 1971, Dr. D.L. Kippen, the president of the Canadian Medical Association, said: "We see a deliberate threat to your industry by government 'acting on behalf of society,' enacting legislation which threatens your autonomy, and reduces your profit potential."[10] Six years later, Dr. E.W. Barootes, a deputy-president of the CMA, concluded that the pharmaceutical industry was gradually being nationalized by an exclusive franchise system, by manipulation and price and market controls.[11] In 1983, Dr. William Goodman, an associate professor in the Department of Medicine at the University of Toronto and a vice-president of the

Association of Independent Physicians, a right wing group that advocates opting out of medicare, said that "civil conscription of. . .drug companies has already occurred" in Canada.[12]

One growing area of interaction between drug companies and doctors is pharmaceutical industry sponsorship of continuing medical education (CME). In an interview in the *Canadian Family Physician* in 1977, Mr. Guy Beauchemin, the PMAC's executive vice-president, admitted to being "extremely interested in this aspect."[13] The topic of CME is not being considered in the next chapter on advertising because the drug industry consistently maintains that sponsorship of CME is not advertising. "We believe [it] must be entirely divorced from marketing," said Mr. Beauchemin. Dr. Richard Crout, director of the U.S. Food and Drug Aministration Bureau of Drugs had a somewhat different attitude toward company-financed CME. Speaking in 1976 he said: "The growing influence of the pharmaceutical industry on medical education is a long-term threat to the integrity of the medical profession. . .It is inevitable that the educational materials produced by and for an industry with an interest in increasing sales of drugs will, on balance, be biased in a direction intended to promote drug use."[14] Dr. Crout's cautionary note is reinforced by a further quote from Dr. Godfrey's report: "At this particular conference pharmaceutically-sponsored symposia were interspersed in the scientific program, lending the blessing of the Pan-American League to all activities. While some of the symposia were top grade, others were simply peddling pills."[15] Mr. Beauchemin implicitly seemed to be agreeing with Dr. Crout's fears of bias, when he replied to a question on the industry's position on speakers who may not be favorable to the sponsor's products: "We're interested in sponsoring speakers of renown in the field of our products."

Mr. Beauchemin felt that sponsoring companies should identify themselves "in a restrained way." Just nine months before he made that statement the *Canadian Family Physician* had received a letter from Dr. D.G. Bates about drug company sponsored CME. Dr. Bates was disturbed about the identification of the company involved: "Prominently displayed on various parts of the brochure was the name of the Pfizer pharmaceutical company. . .an application form, attached to the brochure was self-addressed to Pfizer."[16] Dr. Bates also questioned the involvement of the College of Family Physicians with drug industry supported CME and concluded his letter by urging "the College to re-examine its policy regarding continuing education programs and their relation to the promotional activities of pharmaceutical companies." This same issue was raised again in 1982 by Dr. Christine Bourbonniere in a letter to the *CMAJ*. She was commenting on the First National Gynaecologic Grand Rounds held in London, Ontario, in May 1982. These rounds, discussing metabolic effects of oral contraceptives, were available to thousands of physicians across Canada through satellite hook-up. Ortho Pharmaceuticals was one of the sponsoring companies and the rounds were approved for study credits by various medical bodies. Dr. Bourbonniere reviewed the research upon which these rounds were based and found "that the data were less significant than was suggested by the grand rounds." Her final concerns were that:

> We [the medical profession] are left with a subtle and compli-cated ethical issue. The ethics to be examined are not those of Ortho but, rather, those of our professional bodies and univer-sity faculties collectively. In this case their fault was one of omis-sion—they were not sufficiently critical of the data they chose to endorse or support. This would not be a major issue if it were not for its impact. Many busy clinicians will presume that the conclusions of the national grand rounds are valid simply because they appeared to be supported by the academic estab-lishment.[17]

Some company sponsored symposia appear to have purely commercial motives. McNeil Pharmaceutical took out a full page ad in *The Medical Post*, a biweekly publication sent free to all doctors in Canada. The ad reported on the results of a McNeil sponsored symposium on pain.[18]

The support for the drug industry is not just confined to individual doctors, but extends to the organizational level. Alberta passed a law in the early 1960s allowing pharmacists to substitute one brand of a drug for another. The PMAC was bitterly opposed to such laws. The Executive Committee of the CMA passed a resolution deploring legislation, and the Quebec division of the CMA did the same. Editorials have appeared in the *CMAJ* defending patents[19] and brand names,[20] and in both the *CMAJ* and the *Canadian Family Physician* in defence of drug advertising.[21] In the 1982 and 1983 pages of the *CMAJ*, David Woods, the CMA's director of publications, three times supported the drug industry's claims about research in Canada.[22] When the *CMAJ* received a letter critical of Mr. Woods' comments, Mr. Woods, instead of replying personally, let Gordon Postlewaite, the director of communications for the PMAC, give the rebuttal.[23]

In 1983, the same Mr. Woods toured the facilities of Hoffman LaRoche in Switzerland, England and the United States, and published his observations in a laudatory article in the *CMAJ*.[24] The piece contained the obligatory attack on Canada's system of compulsory licensing with the lament that companies have been forced to close down their Canadian research facilities. The article concluded that "the industry as a whole has a good story to tell and, indeed, individual employees tell it with pride and enthusiasm." Evidently the Roche employees had forgotten to tell certain stories: about the two officials in the Kenyan Ministry of Health who were convicted of accepting $14,000 bribes to purchase enough of Roche's Valium to last the country for ten years and enough of Roche's antibiotic Bactrim (trimethoprim-sulfamethoxazole) to last for thirteen years;[25] or about the $50,000 fine Roche had to pay in 1980 following its Canadian conviction for violating the Combines Investigation Act.

Dr. Alan Klass, who in the early 1970s authored a report for the Manitoba government on drug costs, has on at least two occasions characterized the relationship between the principal drug manufacturers and the *CMAJ* as an "unholy alliance."[26] Dr. Norman Eade of the Montreal Children's Hospital echoed Dr. Klass: "The CMA is in bed with the industry."[27]

The first president of the PMAC was Dr. William Wigle, a past president of the CMA. By virtue of his past position with the CMA, Dr. Wigle had a permanent seat on the general council of the CMA. The result, at that time, was an interlocking directorship between the decision making bodies of both associations. Even after Dr. Wigle was succeeded in the PMAC job the links between the CMA and the PMAC were preserved. The Medical Section of the PMAC, composed of physicians employed in the industry, is an affiliated society of the CMA, and sends a representative to the CMA's general council. In addition, in the 1960s, the two groups had a liaison committee that met whenever submissions were to be made to royal commissions or government committees concerning interests that affected both groups.[28]

This collusion of interests sufficiently alarmed one Canadian doctor, Dr. A.D. Davidson, who expressed his fears:

> ...what makes it all the more upsetting is the fact that Academic and Official Medical Bodies don't appear concerned. I can assure you that I made repeated efforts to interest the CMA, the University of Toronto Faculty of Medicine and individual colleagues in this subject, but was rather consistently reassured or discouraged. You cannot avoid a feeling of intense indignation and betrayal.[29]

As Dr. Davidson said, not many doctors seemed to share his concern. At the same time as the battle between the federal government and the PMAC over patents was just starting to heat up, the CMA Committee on Pharmacy, following the opinions of the CMA-PMAC liaison committee, passed a series of resolutions supporting the PMAC's position.[30] (See Chapter 11 for more details on the fight to change Canadian patent laws.)

The pro-PMAC attitude of the CMA never changed during the entire struggle over patents. In 1966, the PMAC asked the Committee on Pharmacy to reiterate its support for the PMAC's "Principles Governing the Provision of Drugs to Canadians." The committee generally agreed with the principles, but had trouble with one item which stated that "the respect of industrial property rights as represented by patents and trade marks is the essential foundation for progress in research and therapeutics."[31] The cause of this reservation was that the committee had no "proof" that this respect was "the essential foundation" even though it was convinced that the "protection of the innovator of a new drug was important as a continuing stimulus to the development and introduction of new drugs."[32] However, the needed "proof" must have been forthcoming, for the CMA's brief to the government supported the PMAC's position to the last detail, as Lang recounts in his book *The Politics of Drugs*. As if to confirm Dr. Klass' characterization of an unholy alliance between the *CMAJ* and the PMAC, the *CMAJ* published an editorial opposing the patent law changes.[33]

The alliance between the CMA and the PMAC during the fight over the patent law changes shows just how successful the drug industry has been in convincing doctors that the interests of the industry are also those of the medical profession. Furthermore, with government sponsored medicare on the horizon, the CMA saw itself as having a common enemy with the PMAC in the form of the federal government.[34] But there also appears to have been a financial incentive for the CMA to support the PMAC. Lang analysed the financial relationship between the CMA and the *CMAJ*. In 1957, all advertising in the *CMAJ*, not just for drugs, accounted for $317,000 of the total CMA income of $579,239. Dr. Kelly, general secretary of the CMA, concluded that "we are not quite in the position of being dependent upon advertising revenue for our existence, but its absence would make journal publication very expensive and would result in considerably increased membership fees."[35]

By 1965, the net profit for the *CMAJ* exceeded $100,000 for the first time in its history. The point had now been reached, where, according to Dr. Davidson, "organized medicine is too dependent on Drug Company advertising revenue to maintain a healthy attitude of objectivity."[36] This conclusion was reinforced a few years later. In 1969, the *CMAJ* had lost $101,631, giving the CMA an overall loss of $38,000. But by 1970, the *CMAJ* was budgeting for a loss of only $43,271, and expected it could be lower.[37] The reason for this turn around in the *CMAJ*'s fortunes can be directly traced to a change in advertising policy commencing with the October 4, 1969, issue. Before that time, advertisements had been grouped either at the front or the back of the *CMAJ*, separate from the scientific and medical articles. Beginning October 4, ads were scattered throughout the body of the journal, at some points interrupting articles. An editorial was run defending the move, stating that "under the present circumstances, there *are* logical reasons why the advertisements cannot be placed at the front and back of the Journal in their entirety."[38] (Emphasis in original.) The editorial never did supply the logical reasons, but it is safe to assume they were economic. Having advertisements on the same page as scientific content made the *CMAJ* unique in comparison to 40 other medical journals.[39] The *CMAJ* published nine letters on the issue of its change in advertising policy; seven of these were critical of the new policy, but the ads remained where they were. And by 1974, according to the CMA president, Bette Stephenson, those ads were worth $1 million a year. In 1980, 1.5 million of the *CMAJ*'s total revenue of $2 million came from pharmaceutical advertising.[40]

Chapter 8
Advertising

*It's like a fad, or fashion, if a name
catches on with doctors, the drug sells.*
—Leonard Mitchell
Vice-president, research
Frank Horner Limited[1]

A Canadian market of over a billion dollars a year is good enough reason to make sure that it is your drug whose name catches on. This simple truth was not lost on the industry, which spent $154.2 million on promotion in 1978.[2]

Because it is the doctors who choose the drug, not the actual consumer, advertising is aimed almost exclusively at doctors, with some reserved for pharmacists. Dr. Dale Console has suggested that an appropriate motto for industry advertising would be, "If you can't convince them, confuse them."[3] Companies spend about $2,900 per doctor per year in their efforts to convince or confuse. As one observer put it, "No other group in the country is so insistently sought after, chased, wooed, pressured and downright importuned as this small group of doctors who are the *de facto* wholesalers of the ethical drug industry."[4]

Who pays the cost of all this advertising directed at the physician? It is the consumer, as the cost of promotion is reflected in the price of drugs. Proposals to curb the amount of money spent on pharmaceutical advertising have foundered on the federal government's reluctance to interfere with the "free enterprise system."[5] Likewise, the Consumers Association of Canada got nowhere with its four-year battle in the late 1970s to have all drug advertising to

112

doctors banned.

The reason for the advertising is, of course, the same as in any industry—to sell the product and increase profits. An analysis of the Canadian pharmaceutical market in the early 1970s showed that the most significant determinant of a drug's sales was the amount of promotion it had; or put more directly, the single best way to increase sales of any drug is to increase its advertising budget.[6] Nordic Biochemicals found this out soon after the company was founded in 1951:

> We approached our responsibilities with what appears in retrospect to be naive idealism. We assumed that all that was necessary to thrive and expand in the Canadian drug manufacturing industry was to offer the best possible product at a reasonable price, in the expectation that within a very short time we would be operating at capacity. It was thought that advertising could be held to simple announcements in one or two of the main medical journals, announcing our products were available. No provisions for direct mail promotion, an army of detail men, or huge sampling programs were envisaged. While this philosophy was operative, the company teetered on the brink of disaster, but only with reluctance and by degrees did we accept the "facts of life", and the company finally began to prosper.[7]

Other companies are not usually as forthcoming as Nordic. They prefer to claim other motives for their promotions. The PMAC, in one instance, says that successful advertising can increase the volume of production and lead to lower manufacturing costs and a decrease or stabilization of prices.[8] However, we have already heard industry representatives admit that there is no relation between manufacturing costs and the selling price (see Chapter 3).

When Stanley Condor appeared before the Restrictive Trade Practices Commission in his capacity as PMAC general manager, he said that the purpose of advertising was to draw new products to the attention of doctors.[9] But very few therapeutically significant new products are introduced each year, usually no more than five or six. These will be brought to the attention of doctors quickly through colleagues or journal articles. Penicillin was not patented, and therefore was not advertised vigorously, but there is no evidence to indicate that doctors adopted it any less quickly than the antibiotics which were patented and heavily pushed.

While advertising often has little beneficial effect on anything but profits, it can sometimes lead to harmful consequences. Ads "alerting" doctors to a new drug frequently emphasize how safe it is. One example is Ortho's four page glossy promotion for a new type of birth control pill which claims a "low incidence of nuisance side effects" and "no significant effect on...blood pressure."[10] Doctors lulled into a sense of complacency by similar statements may prescribe products before all the risks associated with the drugs have come to light. Sometimes serious side effects will show up only once in a thousand or in ten thousand people. That was the case with chloramphenicol and aplastic anaemia; thalidomide produced problems only in pregnant women. *The Medical Letter*, a highly respected journal which accepts no advertising, says, "All promotional statements that a *new* drug has few, mild or no side effects should be ignored."[11] (Emphasis in original.)

What about the educational value of drug advertising? There seems to be some debate about this. Cyanamid of Canada claims that the principal purpose of advertising is to alert doctors to the existence of drugs, not to try to teach them about drugs. [12] But the PMAC tells us that "medical journal advertising is...another important source of information for the doctor."[13] The *Canadian Medical Association Journal* has run editorials asserting that "pharmaceutical advertising has had and will continue to have considerable educational influence on the practising physician."[14] Pierre Garai, the advertising executive who was quoted previously, dismisses educational claims for pharmaceutical advertising, and approvingly quotes Dr. Charles May:

> The goal of promotion even when traveling under a circuitous path under the guise of "education" is to achieve uncritical acceptance of a preconceived message—to captivate the mind; stimulation of skeptical thinking would block the purpose. This is in sharp contrast to the objective of true education, which seeks to cultivate the use of the mind for independent judgments. The success of promotion does not depend on the authenticity of the message but on skill in manipulation of belief.[15]

Contrast the talk of education, information and reducing manufacturing costs with what Guy Beauchemin, executive vice-president of the PMAC, said in 1977: "If advertising doesn't influence doctors then a hell of a lot of people are wasting a lot of money."[16] And it is not just blindly influencing doctors. When thalidomide was introduced, it was advertised as non-addictive and safe during pregnancy. These claims were made not on the basis of careful scientific study, but from careful market analysis. Drug company market researchers knew that physicians were concerned about the use of barbiturates as sedatives and were also worried about the safety of drugs administered during pregnancy. Those were the points emphasized in advertisements for thalidomide, to the misfortune of many people.[17]

A quote from Dr. Ernest Dichter of the Institute for Motivational Research makes the attitude of the industry clear:

> ...medical men are subject to the same kinds of stress, the same emotional influences as affect the laymen. Physicians have, as part of their self-image, a determined feeling that they are rational and logical, particularly in their choice of pharmaceuticals. The advertiser must appeal to this rational self-image, and at the same time make a deeper appeal to the emotional factors which really influence sales.[18]

Advertisements concocted in the 1960s for mood modifying drugs were tailored to fit the stereotypes doctors held about those who would need these products. Ads for Ritalin pictured a housewife tired because of overwork and in need of a "pick-me-up," while those for Valium showed an apparently successful but anxious woman or an executive climbing the ladder of corporate success but unable to relax. According to John Pekkanen, a fellow of the Drug Abuse Council in Washington D.C., these ads deliberately reflected everyday complaints, thereby vastly enlarging their potential target population.[19]

In the late 1960s, one advertising executive became sufficiently aroused about the way mood modifying drugs were being promoted to doctors to voice his apprehensions publicly:

> At the time I finally became concerned about this question, I began to speak to industry groups on the social responsibility of

the pharmaceutical industry. I was then asked to speak before an annual meeting in New York. At the time I was vice-president of the fifth largest advertising agency in the world. And having submitted, as was normal, my speech to the agency's senior executives for clearance, I was told not to make that speech nor any other that was not approved beforehand. I felt I had no choice but to defend my right to freedom of speech, and I resigned.[20]

The prescribing habits of doctors are closely monitored by the industry. Consider what was said at a symposium on pharmaceutical marketing in 1970:

> All of us recognize the end purpose of our efforts in the area of physician typology. It is to identify those segments of the physician population which contain our best customer propects ...By far the most important criterion is estimated or observed prescribing volume...overall prescribing productivity...When we compared prescribers and non-prescribers...it emerged that non-prescribers thought the patient's condition less severe than the prescriber. It is not inconceivable that one could devise a strategy which questioned the doctors' interpretation in these cases.[21]

The language is convoluted, but in simple terms the speaker was saying that a way could be found to convince the doctor who prescribes relatively infrequently to prescribe more and more often. The means to this goal were to question the doctor's judgment on medical issues.

The drug industry makes it its business to find out who the high prescribing doctors are. Through means that are not revealed, the drug companies come into possession of lists with the names of doctors considered to be "high prescribers." One possible source of information might be the *Canadian Medical Directory*, published by Southam Business Publications. It contains the names, addresses, specialty and year of graduation of physicians practising in Canada. But on the form sent to doctors to collect this information, another question is asked: "In an average day I write approximately_____ prescriptions in private practice and approximately _____ prescriptions in hospitals." The purpose given for the question is to validate the complimentary circulation of *Modern Medicine of*

Canada, a medical journal affiliated with the *Canadian Medical Directory*; but is that the only reason for the question?[22] Two other possible sources of prescribing rates are Maclean Hunter's Canadian Mailings, which supplies lists of doctors to companies for promotion purposes, and International Marketing Surveys (IMS), which is supplied information on doctors' prescribing habits on a regular basis by 500 Canadian doctors.[23] IMS also provides companies with prescription statistics based largely on drug store and hospital audits, and tells companies how they and their competitors are benefiting from their sales force, their medical journal advertisements and direct mail campaigns.[24]

One document listed 5,000 doctors in Canada who wrote at least fifteen prescriptions a day. These men and women, who represented about one quarter of the active physicians in Canada, accounted for over three quarters of all the prescriptions issued in the country.[25]

Some journals, sent free to doctors, are specifically targeted at those physicians known to be the most prolific drug prescribers. According to the U.S. Task Force on Drugs:

> The philosophy behind the high-prescribing practitioner [H.P.P.] list is a simple one. It provides the manufacturer with the opportunity to make steady users of any given drug out of the most prolific users of drugs generally. To accomplish this, the "H.P.P." list uses the concept of marketing selectivity: directing promotion to physicians who are proven high-volume prescribers.[26]

Whenever any criticism is directed at the Canadian drug companies for their advertising practices, they are quick to remind critics of all the controls on drug advertising. All ads must be cleared by the Health Protection Branch and by the companies' medical directors. The PMAC has a code of marketing practice. And advertising, to quote the PMAC, *"must be instructive, scientific and detailed to a degree rarely necessary in advertising products to the public."*[27] (Emphasis in original.)

The PMAC marketing code was adopted in 1966, but not on the initiative of the PMAC. The Kefauver Act in the United States provided for the regulation of advertising in that country and Canadian subsidiaries were dragged along, owing to the international nature of the industry. The code has enabled the pharmaceutical manufacturers to say, "we have a code now as of January 1966...are we not nice, we have a code of honour."[28] However, according to testimony before the Special Commons Committee on Drugs, "They [the drug manufacturers] had to have a code of honour because they get their advertising, some of it, from the United States, where it has to meet the Kefauver requirements. So all they are doing (in Canada) is giving in to necessity."[29] Some of the general provisions of this code are:

1. Claims for the usefulness of a product shall be based on acceptable, scientific evidence, and should reflect this evidence accurately and clearly.

2. Prompt, complete, and accurate information concerning therapeutic agents shall be made available to the medical and pharmaceutical professions.

3. Quotations from medical literature...shall not change or distort the true meaning of the author.[30]

The existence of this code, for whatever reasons it was adopted, should provide reassurance as to the good intentions of the industry. But however sincere the industry was in adopting it, the code itself is only voluntary. In the early 1970s, the National Council of Churches of Christ (NCCC) held a series of widely publicized hearings in the U.S. on the impact of advertising on drug usage. One of their conclusions was:

The self-regulatory mechanisms of the pharmaceutical industry, the advertisers and the broadcasing and print media are minimal and ineffective. Where advertising codes exist compliance is voluntary and unenforced; the responsible parties resist establishing sanctions for code violations. The existence of advertising codes without enforcement procedures gives the consumer a false assurance that drug advertisements are true.[31] (Emphasis in original.)

The validity of the NCCC conclusion is reinforced when the facts of the Indocid and Chloromycetin promotions are compared to the principles enunciated in the PMAC code. Many questions are raised. Why, for example, does the code allow companies to say one thing in the U.S. and another in Canada, since the same companies and the same drugs are involved in both cases? Recall the case of Inderal. In the U.S., the company was forced to include a warning about abruptly stopping the drug in its advertisements in U.S. journals, but initially, in Canada, the company did not feel compelled to include a similar warning in ads appearing in Canadian medical journals. In another case, Abbott had to send a corrective letter to every doctor in the U.S. because it could not substantiate its claims that Enduron (methyclothiazide, a drug used in treating high blood pressure) was superior to rival products. A year later, Abbott was making the same unsubstantiated claims to Canadian doctors.[32]

Can we really rely on the HPB's monitoring of advertising after hearing Dr. Albert Liston, director-general of the HPB's Drug Directorate, say that "it's not our policy to treat advertising as the definitive source of information with respect to drugs."[33] Based on this policy, the HPB makes only informal spot checks of drug advertising. There is no program of continuous reviewing of ads to ensure that the prohibition against misleading advertising is observed.

We have had one look at the drug companies' medical directors in a previous chapter, but there is more to the story. According to Dr. H.F. Dowling, medical directors are subject to numerous pressures—from the scientist who devised the drug and takes a personal interest in its success; the director of marketing who wants to put it out yesterday; and the executive who is worried about the red ink on the balance sheet and looks to the new drug for salvation. The medical director can say no to promotional campaigns for only so long. "If he says no once too often, he can be fired in a moment, and what other company will hire a man with the reputation of saying no at the wrong time?" asks Dowling. "As I have said before, the relative position of the medical directors has been downgraded in the hierarchy of the pharmaceutical companies in the past few years."[34]

Martin A. Seidell used to be the medical director of the Roerig Division of Pfizer in the U.S. "My decision to leave Pfizer's employ was longstanding," explained Seidell, "because I had come to realize that the managerial policies in the marketing division were incompatible with both the ethics of my profession and my sense of morality."[35]

There are six ways of promoting drugs; the four major ones are:

detail men, direct mailings to physicians, giving out free samples, known in the trade as "sampling," and journal advertising. These four will be considered shortly. (Currently, there are plans to have drug advertising directed at physicians shown on specially prepared television shows. These shows on various medical topics will be broadcast on television stations across Canada, usually in the early morning weekend hours. A 30-second spot will cost about $2,500.) The fifth promotional method, drug company sponsored continuing medical education, was discussed in Chapter 7. That leaves the newest (until T.V. advertising starts) and perhaps the most dishonest method, which is promoting drugs through the public media. Typically, a drug company calls a press conference to announce a major, or not so major, "breakthrough," the story appears in the newspapers, magazines and on television and radio, and the public demands the new miracle from its doctors. According to the Montreal *Gazette*, which represents one link in this chain, "Montreal and Toronto public relations firms...often hound media medical reporters...with repeat phone calls, heavy information packages about company products and notices of important conferences on new drugs and talks to be given by doctors on a company's payroll."[36]

In 1981, CIBA-Geigy rented a Toronto harbor floating restaurant to launch Transderm-V (scopolamine), an anti-nausea medication absorbed through the skin from a disc placed behind the ear. Because the product had been used by U.S. astronauts, the company decked out young women in yellow space suits to hand out press kits.[37]

Dr. Charles Godfrey of Toronto Wellesley Hospital attended the 1982 Pan-American League Against Rheumatism conference and wrote about the "massive drug promotion program" there for a new anti-arthritic medication:

> The result of the claims made for the medication was that thousands of patients demanded the drug from their physicians. Just how such a campaign is launched was apparent in a press conference at the Washington meeting...a spacious suite was thrown open to the press and associated hangers-on. After being offered the usual liquid refreshments, this reporter was queried whether he was staying for lunch following the conference....
>
> As the TV cameras ground away and editors stop-watched

pertinent seconds for public viewing on the 10 o'clock news, it became obvious that it would be impossible not to piece together a fast moving, hard hitting pitch for the medication...

The skill of the presentation was overwhelming. One TV reporter turned to the public relations representative and asked if a bottle of the medication could be made available for photographing. She was handed a video tape of several clips showing the bottle, the bottle being opened, and a hand taking the pill. In addition, there was, for good measure, some visuals of deformed arthritic hands, complete with X-ray back-up.

When thanks were given for the prefabricated package, it was pointed out the video tape did not have to be returned. It had been prepared for giving away.[38]

In detailing, direct mailing, sampling and journal advertising, testimonials play a major role. Testimonials usually take the form of quotes about how wonderful this or that drug is. Drug companies seek them from reasonably prominent physicians, with the hope of convincing other doctors of the worth of the drug in question. Often these testimonials are genuine expressions of the belief in a drug's value, but not always. Dr. Dale Console testified about testimonials:

Testimonials are used not only to give apparent substance to the promotion and advertising of relatively worthless products, but also to extend the indications of effective drugs beyond the range of their real utility. They appear either as complete reprints or as priceless quotations in advertisements or brochures. They convince too many physicians that they should prescribe the drug.

Now, the true nature of these testimonials is well known to the industry and its own contempt for them is shown by its vernacular for sources from which they are easily obtained. These are called stables. Still it is an important function, usually of the medical division, to send representatives with generous expense accounts to all parts of the country searching out these sources. The burlesque is compounded by calling the drug trials "scientific studies" and by supporting them with grants which are charged to research costs.[39]

Dr. Console goes on to recount how one particular testimonial was obtained:

> Sometime in 1956, when I was still a Medical Director, the
> lagging sales of one of our products led management to decide
> that the product needed a boost. The boost took the form of
> obtaining an endorsement from a physician who was a
> prominent authority in the field. We knew that the particular
> physician was being subsidized by another drug company and
> so management decided that it would be simple for me as
> Medical Director to "buy" him. I objected since I felt the
> product did not deserve endorsement. My business colleagues
> overruled me and I left with a blank check to win his favor. I
> was free to offer him a large grant to support any research of his
> choice "without strings" or to retain him as a consultant with
> generous annual compensation. I was quite certain that the
> doctor would throw me out of his office if I approached him
> with any of the techniques suggested by my colleagues. They all
> had the obvious odor of a bribe. I decided, therefore, to use a
> strategem that was more likely to be effective and that I thought
> (at the time) would be easier on my conscience.
>
> I took the doctor to lunch, and after the usual two Martinis,
> I told him exactly what had been going on and of my disagree-
> ment with my colleagues. In this manner we established a
> physician-to-physician relationship in which we were both
> deploring the questionable tactics used by the drug industry.
> Conversation gradually shifted to the product and, to make a
> long story short, we got our endorsement almost as a personal
> favor.[40]

A more recent example of how testimonials are used is to be found
in the 1982 pages of *The Medical Post*. McNeil Pharmaceutical took
out a full page ad in this tabloid to report on the results of a
symposium the company had held to promote its new pain killer
Zomax (zomepirac sodium). The ad carried photographs of Dr.
Davy Trop, chief anaesthesiologist at the Montreal Neurological
Institute, and two other doctors who had also participated in the
symposium. In one picture, the caption below the three physicians
read: "We believe, along with our Canadian and American
colleagues, that Zomax has added a new dimension to the study of
analgesics."[41] (In 1983, Zomax was temporarily removed from sale

in the U.S. and Canada following reports of fatal reactions associated with it.)

Also in 1982, Miles Pharmaceuticals had Dr. Gilles Pelletier, a physician at the Montreal Heart Institute, travelling the media circuit to promote Adalat (nifedipine), a new heart drug from Miles.[42]

The official attitude towards physicians endorsing products, at least as expressed by Dr. W.G. Henderson, deputy registrar of the College of Physicians and Surgeons of Ontario, is that the practice is "not ordinarily considered good ethical behavior," but there is no legal sanction against testimonials.[43] Obviously some doctors are not deterred by this lukewarm directive.

Detail Men

"The sales representative is the main tool in North America. We have come to the conclusion that it is the best and most efficient system for the next decade." That is the opinion of Percy Skuy, president of Ortho Pharmaceutical (Canada) Limited.[44] This view is supported by Jack Miller of International Marketing Surveys Montreal.[45]

There are about 2,200 detail men in Canada or one for every thirteen physicians. Almost 46 percent of the companies' promotional budgets, or about $70 million in 1980, is allotted to all aspects of detailing.[46] According to Jack Miller of International Marketing, this sum represents "15 percent of a company's total revenue—the single largest expenditure, even more than on raw materials to manufacture drugs. Each call to a doctor in his office or at a hospital costs about $80." Each physician is visited over 200 times a year by detail men, or almost once per working day. Some doctors, the high-prescribing practitioners, get seen by detail men more often than others. The drug companies concentrate on them for obvious reasons. In one study, doctors who wrote one to ten prescriptions a week saw on the average 2.8 detail men per week; doctors who wrote more than 150 prescriptions a week saw 8.0 detail men per week.[47] One goes where the money is.

The Canadian Medical Association seems to view detail men as a benign force. Dr. Norman DaSilva, the CMA's medical director, said that "today the detail men focus more on projecting the corporate image, trying to stimulate interest in the brand or in an old product that's slipping away. There isn't as much of a hard sell."[48]

It is worthwhile to examine the functions of detail men for a number of reasons. One is because of the obvious importance that the industry attaches to their actions. Secondly, the content of their sales message cannot be monitored as can the content of most other forms of advertising, and therefore, detailing represents an almost totally unregulated activity.

In an interview in *Maclean's* in 1980, John MacInnis, a detail man for McNeil Pharmaceutical, candidly acknowledged that his job entailed "perceiving needs, or creating them."[49] McNeil hired MacInnis at the age of 21 when his work experience amounted to three years of driving ambulance. One of the drugs MacInnis sold was Haldol (haloperidol), an antipsychotic medication. However, his company training did not deal with what mental illness is. "Diagnosis is the doctor's job," he believes. "Besides, I can't see how that would help us sell."

It was presumably to give detail men some medical training that the drug industry founded the Council for the Accreditation of Pharmaceutical Manufacturers Representatives of Canada. The Council offers a one-year course of study to detail men (graduates are known as Accredited Pharmaceutical Manufacturer Representatives or APMRs). Final exams are held in a Canadian university setting and the end product is supposed to be better qualified to converse with the physician "in the fields of physiology, pathology, pharmacotherapeutics and other related subjects," as the wording of one ad has it.[50] In the opinion of the director of the Council, John Stewart, the graduates "provide accurate information supported by adequate documentation on all topics of the physician's concern as they relate to drugs."[51] (Mr. Stewart is also associate director of scientific affairs at Purdue Frederick, a PMAC member company.)

In the *CMAJ* of December 9, 1978, Dr. Kenneth O. Wylie, then-president of the Canadian Medical Association, issued a blanket endorsation of detail men who have taken the APMR course. His endorsation is in the form of a letter, written on the official stationary of the president of the CMA, which gives the impression that Dr. Wylie is stating an official CMA position. Although Dr. Wylie describes the Council as "non-profit," he neglects to mention that it is almost totally financed by the drug industry.[52] This action of Dr. Wylie's is another clear example of the collusion between the drug industry and organized medicine that was described in the last chapter.

Dr. Norman Eade investigated the Council and this new breed of detail man. He reports that the Council has no teachers and conducts no classes; all coursework is done by mail. The functional staff consists of one administrator and a secretary. The "Canadian university setting" where the exams were written was a room rented at a university. The Council refused to make a copy of the text or core material available for Dr. Eade's inspection. A representative final exam was largely of the true-false variety, including questions on the rates of profit of various industries and other such matters unrelated to the safety or efficacy of drugs.[53] Dr. Eade concluded: "This program is a ploy to make the detail men more convincing in their presentations. Doctors are often very naive and they don't have much time to review data on drugs."[54]

According to the PMAC "Standards of Conduct for Medical Service Representatives," a detail man should be

> honest in all his dealings and should provide contacts with full and factual information on his products, with no attempt at misrepresentation or exaggeration. His statements must be accurate and complete and must not mislead either directly or by implication . . . His assertions must be scientific and backed up with medical evidence.[55]

That statement can be compared to the actual printed instructions given to detail men in the Los Angeles area during the Indocid campaign:

> It is obvious that Indocid will work in that whole host of rheumatic crocks and cruds which every general practitioner, internist, and orthopedic surgeon sees every day in his practice.
>
> Tell 'em again, and again, and again. Tell 'em until they are sold and stay sold.
>
> You've told this story now, probably 130 times. The physician however, has heard it only once. So, go back, and tell it again and again and again and again, until it is indelibly impressed in his mind and he starts—and continues—to prescribe Indocid. Let's go . . .
>
> Take off the kid gloves . . .
>
> Now every extra bottle of 100 Indocid that you sell is worth an extra $2.80 in incentive payments. Go get it. Pile it in!!![56]

Because the MER/29 story has been so extensively documented, it provides further insights into how detail men operate.[57] When any new product is being introduced, detail men are given a set of instructions and a sales pitch to follow word for word. When introducing MER/29 to physicians, the detail man would begin: "Doctor_____, let us talk about people who have atherosclerosis. Any issue of the A.M.A. *Journal* will indicate how serious this disease can be..." At this point the detail man takes out the latest issue of the *Journal of the American Medical Association*, and turns to the obituary section, where s/he had previously circled the names of those doctors who had died from atherosclerosis. The first objective is to persuade physicians to test MER/29 on at least a few of their patients in order to get them into the habit of using the drug in their practices. Physicians are told they could then use their clinical experience to decide about whether or not to continue using MER/29. (The implication intentionally disregards the fact that it takes experience with thousands of patients over many years to evaluate a drug properly.)

Detail men are reminded to be especially sure to cultivate interns and residents in hospitals, since they "represent considerable future growth to all of us." "The resident or intern who knows Merrell well and Merrell products is the prescribing physician who in the near future will be our most valued Merrell writer [of prescriptions]." To "break the ice," the detail men are to dispense free tie tacks bearing the caduceus medical symbol (snakes intertwined about a staff), in addition to the regular talk on MER/29.

(Detail men are still in the habit of spending a lot of time in hospitals wooing interns and residents. According to Leslie Dan, president of Novopharm Limited, promotion in the hospitals is very effective. Doctors are attached to hospitals, and frequently "develop the habit of prescribing that product [used in the hospital]."[58] Mr. Dan's view is supported by an analysis of the Canadian drug market which showed that a drug's share of the retail market was significantly influenced by how widely it was used inside hospitals.)[59]

Later on in the MER/29 sales campaign, detail men were given a new structured set of instructions to recommend to the physician for the use of MER/29. These recommendations were described in the sales manual as "designed to help the doctor develop a very clear understanding of the steps he should take in using MER/29...Like human beings in general, the physician likes to have his actions spelled out for him. It gives him a feeling of confidence and permits him to act more freely." To assist physicians to "act freely," the detail men were to give them a supply of laboratory request slips inscribed with the MER/29 imprint. The pad was to be introduced in the fifth sentence of the presentation, when the detail men were to say: "...by checking the block marked serum cholesterol every time you [the physician] request laboratory work." At this point, the detail men were told: "Make an actual check-mark in the serum cholesterol block on the first page. It will leave a lasting impression with the doctor of exactly what you are talking about."

When Merrell knew that MER/29 could cause loss of hair and skin changes, detail men were instructed to boast that "MER/29 has demonstrated its safety...no serious toxicity and few side effects in over 3 years' clinical use and in over 400,000 patients." After the September 1961 issue of *McCall's* had reported that MER/29 could cause hair loss and severe skin conditions, Merrell's detail men were told how to "twist" the article into "a positive sales aid" by emphasizing that the side effects were infrequent and were "completely reversible" when MER/29 was discontinued. Cataracts, of course, are not reversible and were not mentioned. When Merrell knew of three cases of cataracts, its detail men were warning doctors that "once a patient is on MER/29 he must stay on MER/29," and that "taking patients off MER/29 is bad medicine."

Direct Mail

Mailing promotional brochures about drugs directly to doctors represented an expenditure of about $6.5 million in 1980.[60] In 1963 Canadian general practitioners were receiving 1,200 to 1,300 pieces of drug company mail a year. The latest estimate is based on a count made by a Hamilton, Ontario, doctor from July 1981 to June 1982.[61] He received almost 200 pieces of direct advertising from the drug companies and about 140 free copies of controlled circulation journals, journals whose main reason for existence is to be a conduit for pharmaceutical advertising. The drop in the volume of mail between 1963 and 1981-82 probably does represent a trend away from the use of direct mail, although it is hard to assess the exact magnitude of the drop since the count for 1981-82 is based on only one physician's experience.

Although 48 percent of a 1963 sampling of 200 Canadian doctors considered this type of mail "unwelcome," 44 percent found it "informative."[62] In the early 1960s, 200 pieces of direct mail were analysed by fourth year medical students at the University of Manitoba. They found 21.5 percent did not state the generic name; 48 percent made no mention of toxicity or side effects; 95 percent did not mention costs; and over 80 percent used irrelevant illustrations or pictures in bad taste.[63]

In 1960, the *Canadian Medical Associaiton Journal* received a letter from Dr. Katherine E. Richter. She wrote that the volume of direct mail she was receiving had "gone beyond the stage of being a nuisance, and has become a molestation."[64] In reply, the editor of the *CMAJ* quoted from the report of the CMA's Committee on Pharmacy: "'Many of the advertising practices of the drug houses appear wasteful and unprofessional. This applies particularly to direct-mail advertising to doctors. This has reached the point where it is nothing more than a nuisance to its recipients and your Committee would recommend that representations be made to the Pharmaceutical Manufacturers Association that it should be discontinued and the savings passed on to our patients.'"[65] This quotation was contained in a letter sent to the PMAC asking it to "take steps among its member companies to curtail or eliminate it [direct mail advertising]."[66] Eighteen years later, in 1978, Dr. Helga Holst sent a letter to the *CMAJ* saying: "...I am distressed and angered by the amount of unsolicited advertising I receive from pharmaceutical companies."[67] Plus ca change...

Why had little changed? Well, as Cyanamid of Canada once said regarding advertising expenditures: "We as a commercial organization are averse to spending money where it is of no avail to do so."[68] Nordic Biochemicals summed things up pretty well:

It was rapidly discovered that although doctors publicly deplore the mass of direct mail literature, a sales volume on practically any product could be created by advertising it by mail providing it is done persistently and massively.[69]

Sampling

The drug companies spent about $13.6 million in 1980 in distributing free samples of drugs to doctors.[70] Nordic said: "A representative [of the company] must usually 'bribe' his way into the doctor's presence by the offer of free samples in generous volume."[71]

But Dr. Nathan Schecter of the Ottawa Civic Hospital claims that the majority of the samples are discarded.[72]

At the same time as Nordic was talking in terms of "bribes," Cyanamid was explaining to the Restrictive Trade Practices Commission why sampling was so important to the medical profession: "In the first place, it is important for a doctor to be personally acquainted with a new drug and its results before he prescribes it with confidence."[73] The PMAC echoed this view.[74] So once again, the industry is trying to convince doctors that the true worth of a new drug can be determined by trying it on a few patients for a few days.

Sometime between 1961 and 1973, the importance of samples must have drastically changed. In the latter year, the PMAC was complimenting itself on instituting a voluntary code of sampling practice to reduce the distribution of unsolicited pharmaceutical samples. This voluntary code was not all that successful. In July of 1973, Dr. Murray Katz wrote in the Montreal *Star* that in one month his mail included twelve different unsolicited samples.[75]

A study of drug sampling was done by some final-year medical students at the University of Western Ontario in 1967.[76] They discovered that about one quarter of all samples received by doctors are unwanted. One doctor who had requested no samples received samples of thirteen different drug preparations with a retail value of $23.05 in the course of one month. The average retail worth of samples received by five doctors, including the one mentioned above, was $255.05 per month. The average value of unrequested samples was $55.20 per doctor for that single month. Assuming that the volume of sampling was constant over the year, then in 1967, the retail value of unwanted drugs given to Canadian doctors would have been about $18.5 million. (The actual cost to the drug companies of these free samples is much less of course, since the retail cost is far above the production cost.)

Journal Advertising

This form of promotion cost an estimated $20 million in 1980,[77] but it is especially important because nearly all physicians read medical journals, and therefore, the advertising is almost impossible to avoid. Drug advertising makes up 45 to 60 percent of the total content of most Canadian medical journals.[78] In fact, according to Dr. Mark Clarfield, a Montreal geriatrics specialist, most medical journals, in Canada and the rest of the world, survive not because they have anything of value to say, but because they are vehicles for drug company advertising. Only a small core of medical journals publish most of the scientifically significant articles. Of the references cited in the scientific literature between 1963 and 1973, 50 percent appeared in just 152 of the 2,400 medical journals available worldwide.[79]

We have already seen how declining advertising revenue caused the *Canadian Medical Association Journal* to alter its format. But there is strong evidence that advertising can also influence editorial policy. In 1969, the *Journal of the American Medical Association* (*JAMA*) was offered a paper endorsed by the heads of all five NAS/NRC panels on drugs. (See Chapter 6 for more information on these panels.) The article was about fixed-dose combination products. The authors' findings indicated serious dangers connected to this class of drugs; they wanted to alert the medical profession and they tried to publish their findings in *JAMA* because of its wide circulation. They had every reason to expect the article to be accepted because the AMA's own Council on Drugs had condemned fixed-dose combination drugs as far back as 1957. However, the request to *JAMA* for publication, made on behalf of the panels by Duke C. Trexler, executive secretary of the National Research Council, was, he said, refused "bluntly, flatly" and without explanation by Dr. John H. Talbot, editor of *JAMA*.[80] This kind of behavior might seem strange until one realizes that *JAMA* had recently run two full page ads for Panalba, one of the best selling fixed-dose combination drugs. These ads appeared despite the assurance given in 1961 to Senator Estes Kefauver that the AMA's Board of Trustees planned to withdraw all ads for drugs such as Panalba from *JAMA* over the following several years. Dr. John Adriani, the head of the AMA's Council on Drugs, said the refusal of the article "boils down to this, they [the AMA] need every dollar they can get."[81] The *New England Journal of Medicine* was offered the paper and published it on May 22, 1969.

It seems, though, that even the *New England Journal of Medicine* (*NEJM*) may not be immune to pressure from the pharmaceutical industry. According to Dr. Martin Rizack, a consulting editor of *The Medical Letter*, one *NEJM* issue ran *The Medical Letter* review of a drug alongside its advertisement. The drug companies ganged up, threatened a withdrawal of all advertisements, and the experiment ended.[82]

Vernon Coleman, former editor of a British monthly medical journal, writes that "most editors would agree that they are under great pressure to provide the drug industry with what it needs. As one editor put it, wanton criticisms of some drug companies is inadvisable."[83] He then goes on to relate an experience of his own:

> Several drug companies told the journal's publisher that they would not consider advertising in the journal while I was editor. In my presence one offered to buy advertising space as long as I promised not to write anything derogatory about the drug industry in the future.[84]

Dr. Alan Klass, in his book *There's Gold in Them Thar Pills*, makes the point that regardless of the content of the advertisements, their mere appearance in prestigious medical journals implies apparent approval. The top people in medicine write in such journals, which lends the journals a special charisma that even extends to the advertising. The implicit approval of the ads is further reinforced by the fact that advertising in journals is generally limited to medical textbook publishers and manufacturers of professional equipment and drugs. There are no ads for T.V. sets, dish detergents and so on. Dr. Klass says:

> In a curious way, therefore, both because of the disciplined habit of obedience to the guidance of leaders, and because no other advertising is permitted, the imprint of the drug manufacturer's advertisement obtains a subtle and persuasive impact on the professional reader. As a result of sophisticated insight by the advertiser, the trick in the advertising message is not only the message itself but the media.[85]

Dr. Klass' opinion was repeated almost exactly by an advertising director of Smith Kline and French: "The journal advertising takes on a certain psychological aura of authority by running cheek and jowl with the scientific and expert editorial matter."[86]

At first glance, it would appear that there are enough safeguards on journal advertising to obviate any reasonable fears. The PMAC has its own code of marketing practice, and even specific guidelines about journal advertising. The guidelines state:

Promotion should in no way be offensive to the physician and should conform to the high ethical standards of the profession.

Advertising material containing scientific and technical information should give doctors and members of allied professions as complete a picture as possible of the properties of the product, based on current scientific knowledge.[87]

Furthermore, the PMAC emphasizes that prescription drug advertising is also "anti-promotional" because it has to remind physicians of conditions where the drug should not be used, and provide information about potential toxicity and side effects. The layout of ads "must be in extremely good taste," and if a photo is used, it "invariably is intended to depict in some form the medical problem involved."[88]

Finally, since 1976, the Pharmaceutical Advertising Advisory Board (PAAB) has been screening drug ads prior to their publication.[89] The Board includes representatives from the Canadian Medical Association, the Canadian Pharmaceutical Association, the Consumers Association of Canada, the Canadian Drug Manufacturers Association, the PMAC, the Canadian Advertising Advisory Board, l'Association des fabricants du Quebec de produits pharmaceutique, l'Association des medecins de langue francaise du Canada and the Association of Medical Media. The PAAB has also received the endorsation of the executive director of the College of Family Physicians.[90] As its name implies, the PAAB is only an advisory body, and its evaluations of journal ads can be ignored by both the manufacturer and the journal. (To the best of my knowledge, the PAAB's rulings have so far been followed by all parties.) Furthermore, the PAAB's Code of Advertising Acceptance so closely resembles the PMAC's Code of Marketing Practice that it is hard to see how the PAAB would make much of a difference in screening journal advertising. Dr. Warren Bell provides one example of the PAAB's powerlessness. He wrote to the PAAB complaining that certain irrational combination drugs were being advertised in Canadian medical journals. Although the PAAB agreed that pharmacologically the drugs did not make sense, the PAAB said that it could do nothing about the advertising, since the advertisements conformed to the PAAB's Code.[91]

In one attempt to evaluate journal advertising, medical students read advertisements and then scientific articles about the same drugs.

Seventy-four percent of the students concluded that manufacturers tried to exaggerate the value of their drug between 80 and 100 percent of the time. Seventy percent believed that an attempt was made to minimize the undesirable effects of the drug at the same rate, 80 to 100 percent of the time.[92]

One of the major drug companies advertised an antibiotic named Sigamycin by giving the names and the city of residence of doctors approving of the drug. It was later discovered that those doctors did not exist.[93]

Pierre Garai reports on the introduction of buffered tetracyclines. They were heavily promoted in journals in the 1950s, claiming the virtues of faster absorption and higher blood levels than the unbuffered variety. The result was that the older unbuffered products were driven out of the market. This marketing triumph occurred even though there was never any sound evidence produced that the levels and speed of absorption claimed for the buffered tetracyclines offered any clinical advantage or therapeutic superiority. More disturbing still, the evidence on which these claims depended was shown to be totally specious shortly after the start of the promotion.

Independent researchers repeatedly pointed out that the various buffering agents merely neutralized the retardant effect of the calcium salts originally used as fillers in tetracycline capsules. (Calcium binds to the tetracycline and prevents its absorption into the body.) But, in journal ad after journal ad, buffered tetracyclines were typically described as allowing "more competent control of the disease under treatment" and as introducing "an entirely new concept in broad-spectrum therapy;" in short, as a major medical breakthrough.[94] However, The Medical Letter saw the "breakthrough" somewhat differently. The overenthusiastic promotion of the buffered tetracyclines was resulting in doctors using them instead of other more appropriate antibiotics. This kind of practice was causing the appearance of bacteria which were immune to all types of tetracyclines and was bringing "closer the time when this drug [tetracycline] will have relatively little usefulness as an anti-infective agent."[95]

An advertisement for the use of Librium advocated its use "when anxiety and tension create major discord in parent-child relationships." This ad appeared in 1963 accompanied by an impressive list of 188 references to the medical literature. The Medical Letter

evaluated 177 of these (11 could not be traced) and found that only
three or four clearly had anything to do with young children and
their parents. In another ten or so, the "children" were adults whose
parents were still living. *The Medical Letter* commented:

> Advertisements for other drugs have contained lists of pub-
> lished reports which, on examination, were found to be devoted
> to animal studies, pharmacology and chemistry, and to back-
> ground material having nothing to do with the drug, with no
> references to published clinical studies. When reports on clinical
> studies are listed in drug advertisements, it is not uncommon for
> them to be entirely of the testimonial type, and of little value as
> evidence.[96]

What happened to the PMAC promise that "advertising material
containing scientific and technical information should give
doctors. . . as complete a picture as possible of the properties of the
product"?

A more accurate assessment of journal advertising, in the 1960s
and early 1970s, can be found elsewhere than in the PMAC's
pronouncements. Ruth Hargreaves, the director of the (U.S.)
National Council of Churches' Project on Drug Advertising, wrote
in 1976: "Less than ten years ago, medical journals carried drug
advertisements that were both deceptive and deliberately misleading. Advertising agencies, not research scientists, were discovering
such new diseases as 'environmental depression' and 'behavioral
drift.'"[97] In writing this, Ms. Hargreaves was repeating some of the
conclusions from the hearings held by the Council in 1972:

> *Drugs have been extensively promoted. . . for uses beyond those
> that are medically indicated and, furthermore, a wide range of
> behavior, which would ordinarily be considered the normal
> stresses of everyday living, has been redefined by advertising as
> symptomatic or indicative of medical problems. . .*
>
> *A significant amount of misleading and deceptive advertising
> has been produced by significant portions of the pharmaceutical
> industry. . .*Instances of misleading and deceptive advertising
> appear to be intentional. . .
>
> *Comparison of advertising claims with independent evalua-
> tions reveal numerous and serious descrepancies.*[98] (Emphasis in
> original.)

But the studies and cases of misleading advertising previously mentioned and these statements from the National Council of Churches are somewhat old. Things are better now, are they not? Let us examine more current evidence as it applies to the use of references. Thirty-seven issues of nineteen different periodicals sent to general practitioners in Britain were monitored in 1974. Nine percent of the references cited were unavailable because they were unpublished. A further 18 percent of the published references were not available in any of four libraries, including ones in medical schools and postgraduate centres. Even a request to the advertising company for copies of the references yielded only 80 percent of those cited. Of those received only 29 percent were reports of adequate clinical trials of the drug. In almost 40 percent of the clinical trials, the authors had received help from the drug company in the form of finances, organizing the trial, statistical analysis, supply of data forms or the involvement of a drug company medical adviser in the conduct and authorship of the study. Finally, in some cases there were discrepancies between claims in advertisements and the original text of the references, and quotations in advertisements were occasionally presented in a manner which tended to change the meaning of the original text.[99]

For an even more recent example of the abuse of references, look at the ad for Tantum Oral Rince, from Riker, in the December 1982 issue of *Modern Medicine of Canada*.[100] Eleven references are given. Only one comes from an English language publication; one is from a German journal; and the remaining nine are based on "data on file" at Riker. All of these nine appear to be testimonials and therefore of very questionable clinical value. A highly motivated physician could write to Riker for the data on file in support of the references, but few will. It seems clear that the long list of references is simply designed to impress the doctors by puffing up the ad. This ad is by no means atypical in its use of references.

I went through ads placed in various Canadian medical journals during the 1970s and early 1980s to see whether advertising has improved.

By 1976, clindamycin, a broad spectrum antibiotic, was known to be associated with an inflammation of the colon called pseudo-membranous enterocolitis. This is a condition in which a plaque-like membrane forms in the intestine, causing severe diarrhoea and loss of blood, electrolytes (minerals) and protein. It can be fatal. Upjohn markets a brand of clindamycin called Dalacin C. In 1974 and 1975, the HPB required Upjohn to send letters to all doctors in Canada warning them about the possibility of pseudomembranous enterocolitis with the use of clindamycin. Normally Upjohn's journal ads for Dalacin C would also have had to include this warning, but by 1976 Upjohn was just putting "reminder ads" in journals. These were just full page ads with the name "Dalacin C" and Upjohn's name. (For the first two years after a new drug is on the market all ads must be accompanied by full prescribing information somewhere in the same issue of the journal carrying the ad. After that initial period the ad can consist of simply a picture and a brand name.) A few years before that, Dalacin C's marketing slant was that since penicillin could cause an allergic reaction, Dalacin C should be used instead. Upjohn's pitch had nothing to do with the strengths of Dalacin C, just an implied reference to a possible weakness of another medication.[101]

Ads are still misleading today, either by what they say or what they do not say. For instance, the selling point of Merck Sharp and Dohme's Moduret (a fixed combination of the diuretic hydrochlorthiazide and the potassium sparing drug amiloride HCl) is that it controls high blood pressure and "lessens the problem of potassium depletion."[102] However, the ad neglects to mention that nearly all patients who are healthy except for their elevated blood pressure can be treated with just a diuretic without having their potassium levels drop low enough to produce symptoms.[103]

Consider the contents of ads for three different sedatives: Halcion (triazolam) from Upjohn,[104] Mogadon (nitrazepam) from Roche[105] and Dalmane (flurazepam) also from Roche.[106] According to Dr. Edward Sellers, the director of clinical pharmacology at Ontario's Addiction Research Foundation: "The use of hypnotic drugs [for insomnia] may be unnecessary, irrational or contraindicated. Long-standing sleep disorders necessitate full evaluation rather than immediate prescription of a hypnotic."[107] None of the three ads suggests anything remotely resembling Dr. Sellers' warning. Dr. Sellers recommends that sedatives be given for one to two weeks. The ads for Dalmane and Mogadon say they should be used for "short-term" treatment but do not specify what short-term treatment means. The ad for Halcion says it "should not be administered consecutively beyond 21 days." Following the withdrawal of Halcion and Mogadon, sleeping patterns can be even worse than before these drugs were started;[108] the ads contain no mention of rebound insomnia. The ad for Dalmane warns doctors to "caution patients to proceed cautiously whenever mental alertness or physical coordination may be necessary shortly after ingestion of 'Dalmane.'" However, the warning fails to mention that the flurazepam blood level on the eighth morning after a week of consecutive nightly use may be four to six times that found on the first morning and therefore patients should "proceed cautiously" for days after they stop taking the drug.[109]

A special report on sedatives from the Institute of Medicine of the National Academy of Sciences in the U.S. clearly points out that there are many widely varying causes of insomnia and that the approach to treating insomnia needs to be individualized. The ad for Halcion, however, features sixteen different people all apparently suffering from insomnia; and the implied treatment for all of them is, of course, Halcion. The Institute of Medicine says: "Choosing the most appropriate and least hazardous approach to providing relief depends on a thorough medical and psychosocial appraisal of each patient." Casually prescribing a sedative for people with insomnia could result in death if the insomnia is due to a disease known as sleep apnoea.[110]

Another favorite trick in journal advertising is to separate the warning part of the ad from the part praising the drug. In the June 1978 issue of the *Canadian Family Physician* we find an ad for Catapres, Boehringer's brand of clonidine, a drug useful in some people with high blood pressure.[111] The ad is headed: "Lower his blood pressure...not his potency," but turn the page and under adverse effects of the drug, appears "impotence." You have to read the fine print in the ad for the pain killer Talwin (pentazocine hydrochloride), from Winthrop, to find out that people can become addicted to it.[112]

The PMAC code promised that the graphics in drug ads are "invariably intended to depict in some form the medical problem involved." Let us consider some examples. For years, Ayerst told doctors that Orbenin (cloxacillin), an antibiotic, "stands out." These ads were always illustrated with a full page three-dimensional picture of a wolf or a buffalo or a similar wildlife scene. Now, a three-dimensional picture of an eagle informs us that Fluclox (flucloxacillin) "stands out."[113] Vibramycin (doxycycline), an antibiotic from Pfizer, features a picture of a woman playing the flute.[114]

The ad for Geigy's anti-arthritic Voltaren (diclofenac sodium) tells doctors that one way of discerning the effectiveness of the drug is to "write some Voltaren prescriptions and prove it to yourself."[115] This type of statement is clearly unscientific; writing a few prescriptions for a drug simply does not provide a doctor with a true picture of the drug's worth. To adequately evaluate a drug, it has to be prescribed to thousands of patients under a variety of circumstances.

Upjohn promises that Xanax (alprazolam) has "outstanding therapeutic effectiveness" in patients with anxiety and yields a "lower incidence of drowsiness, depression and confusion."[116] Where are the references to judge Xanax's outstanding therapeutic effectiveness? None is given. Relative to what does Xanax have a lower incidence of side effects? We are not told that piece of information.

Boehringer promotes Dixarit (clonidine) as a non-hormonal treatment for menopausal symptoms.[117] The small print in the ad warns that the medication should be discontinued after two to four weeks if it is not working. But the picture of a prescription for Dixarit shows that the patient is to be given 100 pills, enough to last her over seven weeks.

Sinequan is Pfizer's brand of doxepin, an antidepressant. According to the ads, it makes you yourself again. But when a man is "himself again," he is behind a desk ready for work;[118] when a woman is "herself again," she is playing a guitar.[119] Pfizer has discontinued these ads for Sinequan, but similar sex stereotyping continues in other ads. When the female schizophrenic is under control with Orap (pimozide), from McNeil, she is at a children's birthday party. The "controlled" male schizophrenic is at work on a construction site.[120]

Sex stereotyping, although not as blatant as in the 1960s and early 1970s, is still widespread in ads. Women, for example, are only rarely portrayed as doctors. A particularly offensive ad, no longer used, was in the February 1974 issue of the *Canadian Family Physician*.[121] The first page showed a glowering bus driver over the caption: "He is suffering from estrogen deficiency." Turn the page, and you see a distraught middle-aged woman, and "She is the reason why." The text of the ad associated menopause with "irritability, depression, headache, loss of vitality, tension or emotional instability." These claims, made in the absence of any good scientific evidence for them, relied on elaborate assumptions about the roles of men and women.[122]

Ads for oral contraceptives almost consistently feature women in their early to mid-twenties. They are depicted in the sorts of scenes which find them lying on a cloud or staring dreamily off into space. Working women, non-middle class women, older women are almost never seen. Recently the age of women in oral contraceptive ads has appeared to be dropping, as the makers of the "pill" try to increase their market size. The woman in Searle's ad for Demulen 30 looks to be no older than her mid-teens.[123]

Pictures of semiclad and nude women are particularly popular in ads. Male counterparts are almost never used. Parke, Davis publishes ads for Ponstan (mefanamic acid), advertising it for relief of menstrual pain. One ad shows a young woman dressed in a sheer nightie.[124] Surmontil (trimipramine), from Rhone-Poulenc, "helps relieve depression and restores restful sleep." In the case of one ad, restful sleep is restored to a teenage female who is shown sleeping in the nude.[125] Advertising for dermatological products abounds with pictures of various parts of the bare female anatomy. Some examples are: a naked woman looking at herself in a mirror in an advertisement for Topicort (desoximetasone) for Hoechst;[126] a full-length profile of a nude blonde in an advertisement for Uremol HC cream (urea plus hydrocortisone) from Trans-Canada Derma-peutics Limited;[127] and a front view of a nude woman in an advertisment for Florone (diflorasone diacetate) from Upjohn.[128] Often the women in these ads are also shown in provocative postures. One ad, for Neosporin ointment (polymyxin B, bacitracin and neomycin), from Burroughs Wellcome, goes further. A nude woman is shown, the caption says, "for a great performance."[129]

The PMAC may call these ads "in good taste"; others would term them soft-core pornography. It is worth mentioning in passing that all of the ads referred to that appeared after 1976 were approved by the PAAB.

One of the earliest people to write about the sexism in journal advertising was Robert Seidenberg. His initial article came out in 1971. Prior to the appearance of that article he had published almost 75 papers and three books and never had had much trouble getting his material accepted by editors. His paper on sexism was rejected by about twenty journals before being accepted by *Mental Hygiene*, the organ of the National Association of Mental Health.[130] Interestingly, *Mental Hygiene* is one of the few journals that does not accept drug advertising.

In 1976, the sexism involved in journal ads was criticized by the

Canadian Women's Caucus on Alcohol and Legal Drugs. One particularly blatant example of the sexist attitude of drug companies is related in the following incident:

> At a pharmaceutical display during the 1976 Canadian Psychiatric Association meeting, large advertisements for "N" featured a face of a beautiful woman with eyes half closed. After checking with colleagues of both sexes, and finding that almost all immediately associated this picture with orgasm, a young woman psychiatric resident told the salesman that she felt the picture was disgusting in this context. He assumed that she was a psychiatrist's wife, and replied, jokingly, "Well, it's the kind of thing that turns your old man on and sells our products."[131]

In one study of the effects of journal advertising on doctors, 45 percent of the psychiatrists questioned perceived pharmaceutical advertising, in a randomly selected issue of *The American Journal of Psychiatry*, as showing sexual bias that might negatively influence physicians' perceptions of women.[132] In another study, drug advertisements in four leading medical journals were analysed.[133] The authors found that men were portrayed as needing psychoactive drugs because of tension related to physical disability or work, while women required them because of diffuse anxiety, tension or depression. The ads tended to show women between the ages of twenty and 40, in provocative situations or as irritating patients. Ads showing women as patients tended to use attempts at humor or clever wordplay, while those depicting men seemed to be more straightforward. Indirect evidence[134] indicates that the manner in which symptoms are presented in ads is related to the seriousness with which symptoms are perceived by physicians. Fewer symptoms, presented in a stoical fashion, are seen as indicative of more serious illness. Earlier in this chapter Klass and the advertising director of Smith Kline and French suggested that ads may acquire an aura of scientific authority by virtue of the context in which they appear. Similarly, since ads are supposed to conform to not only the HPB guidelines, but also the journals' own standards and the PMAC's code, the different images presented of men and women may be accepted as established scientific fact by the readers of the ads. One of the study's conclusions is that "the advertisements may...encourage physicians to interpret symptoms presented by women as reflecting emotional illness and those of men as reflecting organic illness, even though the actual symptoms and/or illness might be identical for the two patients."[135] This particular conclusion is substantiated by the responses to a questionnaire distributed by the Canadian Migraine Foundation in 1978. According to Foundation director Rosemary Dudley, men who suffer from migraine are "far more likely" to get drugs that are specifically designed to relieve migraines than are women. Women, on the other hand, commonly are given tranquillizers which are of no proven benefit for migraine headaches.[136]

$154.2 million a year for advertising; $2,900 per doctor per year; and from what I have outlined, most of that money would seem to be wasted from the point of view of presenting an accurate image of the value of drugs. The money is certainly not wasted if viewed from the companies' standpoint as we saw when we looked at profits in Chapter 3.

Periodically, doctors have complained about the amount and quality of advertising. In one survey, 35 percent urged that advertising be more scientific, more accurate, more factual and more informative.[137] The drug industry naturally responds that advertising is not excessive, but if doctors find it so, they can just ignore it. But to ignore the visits by detail men, the ads in journals and the deluge of direct mail, doctors would have to be blind, deaf and dumb, and for good measure would have to lock their offices.

However, according to Pierre Garai:

> What these howls of outrage and hurt amount to is that the medical profession is distressed to find its high opinion of itself not shared by writers of ethical drug advertising. It would be a great step forward if doctors stopped bemoaning this attack on their professional maturity, and began recognizing how thoroughly justified it is. As an advertising man, I can assure you that advertising which does not work does not continue to run. If experience did not show beyond doubt that the great majority of doctors are splendidly responsive to current ethical advertising, new techniques would be devised in short order.[139]

The Director of the Office of Health Economics in England captures the ambiguities well: "Are we not generally agreed that the medical profession gets the advertising it deserves?"[140]

The medical profession may be getting what it deserves, but what about the public? The PMAC asks: "If there were no advertising, would drugs be less expensive?"[141] A better question would be: "If there were no advertising, would there be so much misuse of drugs by doctors?" We shall explore that question shortly.

Chapter 9
What Do Doctors Know About Drugs and Who Tells Them?

*To a much greater extent than is commonly
assumed, whether or not a drug is prescribed,
and [in what] dosage are not simply functions
of the patient's symptoms or condition, but
depend frequently on the characteristics of
the physician.*
—H.L. Lennard
Department of Psychiatry
University of California[1]

Many of the practices of the drug industry, with respect to patents, advertising and the use of generics, are justified by the industry's assertion that physicians either possess wide knowledge about the drugs they prescribe, or else have the time and the means to acquire such knowledge. This claim is reflected in the PMAC's "Principles for the Provision of Drugs to Canadians," which states: "It is the right of the physician to prescribe the drug preparation of his choice";[2] and in articles which contain statements like: "The physician, it can be fairly stated, does not merely prescribe a chemical substance, but seeks a specific therapeutic effect, and this is most likely to be obtained with the aid of a specific product."[3]

But the number of available drugs runs well into the tens of thousands. With the time and energy demands of running an office and having a life away from medicine, it seems improbable that any doctor could have more than a passing knowledge of at most a few score of the medications available. Since it is not required that doctors take any continuing medical education, they often get no

143

feedback on their prescribing habits. Even if they practice in groups, there is usually no peer review of the way they use drugs. All but one of the physicians who appeared before the Restrictive Trade Practices Commission, including heads of hospital pharmacy committees, specialists and heads of pharmacology departments, agreed that it was extremely difficult, if not impossible, to keep abreast of new developments in therapeutics. And that was in the early 1960s, when there were far fewer drugs available. Both the Royal Commission on Health Services and the Special Commons Committee on Drugs recognized deficiencies in physicians' knowledge about drugs, and made recommendations about ways to correct them.[4]

Let us examine just how much doctors really do know about the drugs they use. This investigation is not meant as a condemnation of doctors. Because we will be looking at the sources of information doctors use to learn about drugs, it is important to know what base of knowledge they start from.

In the early 1950s, an intensive study was made of the practices of 88 general practitioners in North Carolina.[5] Some of the findings to emerge from this study were: two thirds of the doctors routinely gave antibiotics to patients with the common cold; the usual treatment for obesity was an appetite-depressant drug; only 17 percent recognized and treated emotional problems with sufficient competence to demonstrate a grasp of treatment methods; for the other 83 percent the usual management was vitamins, iron preparations, antacids, sex hormones or antispasmodics; and finally 46 percent of the doctors made no effort to avoid drug reactions or complications.

In the late 1950s, this study was repeated in Nova Scotia and Ontario with a sample of about 45 male general practitioners from each province, chosen to reflect the geographic distribution of doctors in that province.

Approximately 27 percent of the Ontario doctors demonstrated so little knowledge of general principles involved in the use of antibiotics and sulfonamides that they were given 0 (a score representing inadequate procedure), 41 percent were skilled in their use and the remaining 32 percent occupied an intermediate position. The corresponding figures for Nova Scotia were 45 percent, 12 percent and 43 percent...The individual dose seemed generally to be adequate as far as this could be determined by the observers but in respect to duration of therapy, use of combinations of drugs, awareness of the dangers of toxicity and often the emergence of resistant strains to organisms and ability to differentiate between conditions that should not be treated with these drugs, there were frequent departures from generally accepted principles.[6]

In the United States, 4,513 physicians from a variety of specialties and at various levels of training, took the National Antibiotic Therapy Test in 1974. For the 1,500 in private practice, the average score was 66 percent. Commenting on the results in the *New England Journal of Medicine,* one of the organizers of the test said that it was "clear that greater effort should be directed toward educating practising physicians to use antibiotics properly."[7]

There is also the article about doctors' knowledge of the content of fixed-dose combination drugs referred to in Chapter 4. Of the 23 products about which physicians were questioned, a majority of the 60 doctors correctly knew all the contents of only three of these drugs. For the other 20 drugs less than half the doctors could identify their components.

The deficiencies in physicians' pharmaceutical knowledge have continued into the 1980s. As part of its investigation for a four-part series on prescription drugs, the Montreal *Gazette* interviewed federal health officials, doctors and representatives of the drug industry; people in all three groups "were sharply critical of poor prescribing habits by Canada's medical practitioners."[8]

Since doctors have weaknesses in their knowledge about drugs, where do they go for information? *The Medical Letter* is generally recognized as the most authoritative current source of information on pharmaceuticals. Textbooks contain more information, but they become outdated between revisions. However, seven years after *The Medical Letter* began publication, almost a quarter of over 500 doctors in southwestern Ontario had never heard of it, and only 22 percent used it regularly.[9] As late as 1977, it was reported that only one fifth of Canadian doctors were subscribing to *The Medical Letter.*[10]

Then there is the *Compendium of Pharmaceuticals and Specialties (CPS).* Published by the Canadian Pharmaceutical Association, the national pharmacists organization, it is currently an 800 page volume which has entries for over 2,800 brand name prescription drugs sold in Canada, and gives indications for their use, contraindications, dosages, side effects and ingredients. All the information about these brand name drugs is supplied by the pharmaceutical manufacturers, and about half of the cost of the *CPS* is subsidized by the drug industry. There are also about 160 entries for generic drugs as well as 100 entries concerned with non-pharmacological products such as test kits and detergents for instruments. The entries for the generic products are prepared by the *CPS'* editors. The *CPS* is sent free to all doctors in Canada. An editorial in the *Canadian Medical Association Journal* recommended that doctors read the *CPS* to check up on the products they prescribe.[11]

How reliable is the *CPS* as a source of information? Albamycin T, Panalba in the U.S., a drug almost universally condemned by medical experts, is still being listed in the *CPS* as of 1983, without any mention of the widespread criticism of it. Chloramphenicol was listed in the *CPS* as being indicated for urinary and respiratory tract infections until 1968. Sixteen years earlier, recommendations had been made to restrict its use to only a small number of relatively rare diseases. In 1964, it was discovered that phenazopyridine (Pyridium), a drug used to relieve pain associated with urinary tract infections, could cause haemolytic anaemia. (In haemolytic anaemia there is actual destruction of the red blood cells.) Ten years later, there was no mention of this side effect in the *CPS*.

Mefenamic acid is made by Parke, Davis and Company and is sold in the U.S. under the name Ponstel, and in Canada as Ponstan. It is marketed as an oral pain reliever. In 1972, *The Medical Letter* recommended that it not be used at all. (Since *The Medical Letter* article mefenamic acid has been found to be useful in relieving pain associated with menstrual periods. However, at least half a dozen other drugs are equally effective.) It had not been shown to be superior to either aspirin or acetaminophen (Tylenol), but had many more serious side effects.[12] It is still for sale in both Canada and the U.S. The U.S. equivalent of the *CPS* is called the *Physicians' Desk Reference*. Here is what it said about mefenamic acid in 1978: "Ponstel is indicated for the relief of mild to moderate pain when therapy will not exceed one week." Adverse reactions include: "...diarrhea which may be severe and at times associated with inflammation of the bowel or hemorrhage...Severe autoimmune hemolytic anemia may occur in patients given this drug for prolonged periods of time. Leukopenia, eosinophilia, thrombocytopenic purpura, agranulocytosis, pancytopenia and bone marrow hypoplasia have also been reported in association with mefenamic acid therapy."[13] Compare that to what was in the *CPS* in 1978: "Indications: Relief of pain in acute and chronic conditions ordinarily not requiring the use of narcotics...Adverse effects are relatively mild and infrequent..." The summary does mention diarrhoea: "has occurred rarely following recommended dosage," and various haematological (blood related) side effects: "unconfirmed reports...a direct cause and effect relationship has not been established." The dosage recommendations do not include any limitation on the duration of treatment, except to say that "...clinical experience with mefenamic acid has varied from single doses to 84 days of therapy."[14] All of these statements still appeared in the 1983 edition of the *CPS*.

Tardive dyskinesia is a central nervous system disorder whose manifestations include involuntary movements. These can produce seriously affected speech, distortions of the face, uncontrolled facial expressions and an inability to sustain normal posture. Often these are irreversible. Tardive dyskinesia occurs after prolonged use of the phenothiazine group of major tranquillizers. The first of these, and still one of the most popular, is chlorpromazine, marketed in Canada since 1953 as Largactil by Poulenc. Reports of tardive dyskinesia began to accumulate in the early 1960s, and by 1967, hundreds of cases had been described. However, it was not until the ninth edition of the *CPS* in 1974 that the phrase "persistent dyskinesias resistent to treatment have also been reported" appeared under the heading of "Adverse Effects." Even after the long delay in recognition, the wording of that warning is still extremely weak. No cause and effect relationship is implied, although there was clear evidence for one. It would be like saying that lung cancer has been found in people who smoke cigarettes. The statement is true, but grossly understates the significance of the situation. It was not until 1976 that the *CPS* mentioned tardive dyskinesia by name.

One section of the *CPS*, the Therapeutic Index, lists drugs under pharmacological, therapeutic and sometimes chemical headings. Often doctors will consult these "pink pages," so named for their color, in order to select a drug for use in treating a certain condition. The list of drugs, however, is not comprehensive. Only companies that pay have their products listed here. Therefore, the drugs of the smaller generic firms, drugs that are usually cheaper, may not be included in this section because the company cannot afford the cost. Hence, the cheaper drugs tend to be overlooked by the physician. Furthermore, if companies do not pay to have their products listed in the pink pages, the entry for their drugs in the main section of the *CPS*, which lists drugs alphabetically by their trade name, is extremely scanty and may lack even prescribing information.

The overall quality of the information in the *CPS* can be assessed by looking at the results of two studies of its contents. In the first, a survey of 75 general practitioners was undertaken to ascertain which major sources of information were used to assess and treat drug overdoses.[15] The *CPS* was ranked first by 91 percent of the doctors. The author of the study then analysed the information given in the 1977 edition of the *CPS* on antidepressant drug overdoses. (The antidepressant class of drugs was chosen since a rapidly increasing number of people are using drugs from this class in suicide attempts. Also, overdoses from antidepressants are often fatal even when the "correct" treatment for the overdose is given.) The *CPS* monographs of 22 different brand name antidepressants were examined. Overdoses were not even discussed in ten of these. In twelve monographs the information on the signs and symptoms of antidepressant intoxication and potential complications was inadequate. There were also major inconsistencies in the area of treatment procedures. Since 1972, a drug named physostigmine has been generally recognized as a useful antidote for massive overdoses of antidepressants. Five years later, only one monograph mentioned it and twelve specifically stated there was no antidote.

The most comprehensive study of the *CPS* is found in a paper by Bell and Osterman.[16] The authors took a computer-drawn random sample of 230 entries, and using major pharmacology references, classified the drugs as "useful," "probably useful," "probably useless," "obsolete" or "irrational mixtures." The latter three categories accounted for 46.3 percent of the drugs. Less than 15 percent of the brand name drugs had information about their chemistry or pharmacology included in their monographs, and only two thirds listed adverse effects potentially related to the drug under consideration. In more than half of the entries, uses were suggested for which there was no generally accepted clinical, theoretical or experimental support. For over 60 percent of the pharmaceutical preparations, well known risks, dangers or adverse effects were not mentioned; major therapeutic uses were omitted; or information necessary for using a drug correctly was not included. There were errors of fact related to biochemistry, physiology, pharmacology or repeated careful clinical observations in nearly 40 percent of the entries.

Bell and Osterman point out that there is a lack of critical evaluation of brand name preparations. The absence of such comments, which is in fact the policy of the CPS editors, "amounts to tacit approval," according to Bell and Osterman. "Tacit approval, while not as desirable as explicit endorsement, is obviously far more acceptable to the pharmaceutical industry than impartial, critical assessment." Where several drugs are available, the CPS almost completely fails to discuss the order of choice among drugs in a given therapeutic class. Nowhere, for instance, are the different types of antibiotics ever evaluated for their respective merits and demerits. As Bell and Osterman say, "the net effect [of this type of omission,] besides making the CPS less useful as a ready reference, is to bring it very close to the model of pure drug advertising." The authors conclude that the CPS, as it is presently constituted, is basically a tool to promote the interests of the drug companies and not a reliable nor an impartial reference.

Another source of doctors' information (and misinformation) about drugs is advertising. This should not be surprising since, as discussed in the previous chapter, the drug companies spare no expense to reach doctors through ads and related promotional means. In fact, commercial sources are usually cited more often than non-commercial or professional sources when doctors are asked where they got the information that led them to prescribe a new drug. It has also been shown that physicians preferring professional sources are significantly more likely to express conservative attitudes about drug use than physicians preferring commercial sources.[17]

In one nationwide U.S. study of a representative sample of doctors, 48 percent listed detail men, 20 percent direct mail advertisements and only 17 percent medical journals (medical journals included both advertisements and articles) when asked what information source led them to prescribe new drugs.[18] In the same study, the physicians were asked which two or three sources they considered most important for familiarizing themselves with new drugs. Sixty-eight percent specified detail men, 32 percent journal advertisements, 25 percent direct mail and 22 percent drug samples. In comparison, 35 percent named medical meetings, 24 percent cited conversations with colleagues and 20 percent said journal articles.[19] (The numbers add to more than 100 percent since each doctor named more than one source.) Previous U.S. studies yielded similar results: drug industry sources outweighed professional sources, and detail men usually ranked first.[20]

The most recent American study of this type, published in 1982, deserves some comment, because on first appearance it would seem to show that commercial sources of information are declining in their influence on physicians' prescribing habits.[21] A random sample of primary care physicians in the Boston area was asked what factors influenced their choice of drugs. Drug advertisements were said to have "minimal importance" by 68 percent of the sample; 28 percent described such influence as "moderately important"; and only 3 percent as "very important." Detail men were likewise perceived as minimally, moderately and very important by 54, 26 and 20 percent of doctors respectively. In terms of the influence of scientific papers on drug choice, the numbers were: 4 percent "minimally," 34 percent "moderately" and 62 percent "very important." These same doctors were also asked their opinion about two classes of drugs—cerebral and peripheral vasodilators (drugs that dilate blood vessels in the brain and the extremities) and the propoxyphene analgesics, which include Darvon. The vasodilators are widely promoted as being useful for the treatment of senile dementia and insufficient blood flow to the legs. Most scientific evidence shows that for both conditions the vasodilators are useless. In the case of senile dementia, advertising campaigns for these drugs have promoted the idea that dementia is caused by an inadequate blood flow to the brain—an idea now known to be completely invalid. However, 71 percent of the doctors questioned believed that "impaired cerebral blood flow is a major cause of senile dementia" and 32 percent found "cerebral vasodilators useful in managing confused geriatric patients." Darvon is heavily advertised as being effective for moderately severe pain such as that from fractures or major surgery, but the weight of evidence is that it is, at best, no better than aspirin. Of the sample group of doctors, 49 percent believed Darvon to be stronger than aspirin while only 31 percent thought it was equivalent to aspirin, and 20 percent ranked it as less potent. The authors of the article point out that "physicians who held advertising-oriented beliefs" about vasodilators and Darvon "were generally unaware that they were strongly influenced by non-scientific sources."

The study concludes:

> Rather than coming as a surprise, the predominance of nonscientific rather than scientific sources of drug information is consistent with what would be predicted from communications theory and marketing research data. Drug advertisements are simply more visually arresting and conceptually accessible than are papers in the medical literature, and physicians appear to respond to this difference.

The more prescriptions doctors write a day, the more likely they are to be influenced by industry sources. In one report, of those writing under 30 prescriptions a week, two thirds gave professional sources as their most important sources of information about new drugs. Only 25 percent of doctors writing 100 to 150 prescriptions a week listed non-commercial sources first. No doctors writing more than 150 prescriptions a week gave professional sources as their most important.[22] Only when it comes to using drugs for difficult chronic diseases does a majority of doctors prefer non-commercial sources, and then only by a margin of 54 to 43 percent.[23] However, when doctors do choose a particular company's brand for a severe disease, that preference is based on a perception of the company and/or the detail man as being reliable and scientific.[24] But reliability and scientific accuracy are not always the fortes of either detail men or their companies, as we have seen.

Doctors' reliance on detail men is reflected in their opinion of them. When physicians in southwestern Ontario were asked about their perceptions of detail men, 65 percent rated them good or excellent for reliability and 69 percent said the same for honesty. The ratings were not as good for knowledge of drugs, but still 37 percent of doctors thought that they were good or excellent in this respect. In the same study, 56 percent of doctors gave professional sources as their preferred source of information about new drugs, higher than in most studies. But 48 percent still thought that the methods of promoting drugs were beneficial and 62 percent thought they were ethical.[25] Somewhat different results emerged when the same group was asked about the major influence that led them to prescribe three different drugs—an antibiotic, an appetite suppressant and a tranquillizer. Of general practitioners, 48 percent prescribed the appetite suppressant on the basis of the manufacturer's promotion, versus 5 percent who based their prescriptions either on a colleague's or consultant's recommendation or on post-graduate education. The comparable figures for the antibiotic were 23 and 19 percent. Only for the tranquillizer did professional sources outweigh manufacturer's promotion as the reason for trying the drug. In addition, the doctors were asked if they felt that they had sufficient knowledge of indications, mechanisms of action and side effects to prescribe the drugs. The percentage answering yes for the antibiotic was 68.6; for the appetite suppressant, 53.0; and for the tranquillizer, 71.7. However, 85.4 percent had already prescribed the antibiotic, 68.7 percent the appetite suppressant and 97.1 percent the tranquillizer.[26] It is clear that, of the doctors surveyed, a large number had prescribed the three drugs in question even though they admitted not being adequately informed about the products.

Not all is bleak and dark. The prescribing habits of 29 general practitioners and three internists in one country of an eastern U.S. state were carefully studied in 1970.[27] The appropriateness of their prescribing practices was evaluated in two ways: by a panel of experts and by the frequency of their use of chloramphenicol. (Because of the potentially fatal complications of chloramphenicol and the limited indications for using it, those using less chloramphenicol were judged to be better prescribers.) The ones who were the superior prescribers in this sample tended to be disdainful of journal advertising and detail men as sources of drug information, they wrote fewer prescriptions while seeing more patients, perceived generic drugs as being as efficacious as brand names, and told their patients of possible side effects of the drugs they were prescribing. They consistently agreed with the following kinds of statements: "There are too many drugs on the market for the same indications"; "Contributions of the pharmaceutical houses to research and development are not very great"; and "Drug firms have an unsatisfactory public image." Similarly, these superior prescribers also reported that they received too many visits from detail men, they believed that detail men sometimes de-emphasized the side effects of a drug to a greater extent than could be substantiated clinically, and they felt that they would not lose an important source of prescribing information if they did not receive visits from detail

07-15-93   #476612

NT TRADE   8.98 T
GST   0.63
TOTAL   9.61
CATEND   10.00
CHANGE   0.39

ITEM   1
1CL   4338 13:04TM

men. Significantly, these superior prescribers were also consulted more often by their colleagues on matters concerning therapeutics than were the poorer prescribers in the group.

Unfortunately, most doctors do not seem to agree with the attitude of these superior prescribers towards detail men. In one of the studies previously referred to, it was found that 80 percent of doctors disapproved of their colleagues who might depend heavily upon advertising for their information about new drugs. But doctors who refused to read any pharmaceutcial advertising were condemned by 75 percent of physicians. Doctors who would refuse to see detail men were criticized by 95 percent of their profession.[28]

On the basis of the evidence presented in this chapter we can see that many physicians have large gaps in their knowledge of pharmacological therapy. Sometimes these gaps exist because doctors have naively accepted the claims of the drug companies, but whatever the reasons for their ignorance, it is obvious that the continuing reliance on commercial sources of drug information will not correct it. In the next chapter we will see some of the consequences resulting from this unhealthy state of affairs.

Chapter 10
Prescribing and Problems

Thalidomide gave us deformed babies, chloramphenicol deaths from aplastic anaemia, and MER/29 people blinded from cataracts. But these are only the most visible results of a prescribing system characterized by heavy advertising, physicians' lack of adequate knowledge and the "pill for every ill" philosophy. This latter point will be explored in Chapter 13, but there is one aspect of this issue that deserves comment now. It is generally assumed that patients always expect prescriptions when they see a doctor. But this may be a case of doctors' projecting their own expectations onto patients. Eighty percent of British physicians estimated that patients expect a prescription in 80 percent of consultations. Twenty-two percent felt that patients wished a prescription in 99 percent of visits. However, in a national survey in England, patients indicated that they expected a prescription in only 43 to 52 percent of visits.[1]

Newspaper articles appear periodically with headlines like, "Half drugs, medications useless, Montreal pharmacist complains," or "Controls urged on some doctors' prescribing practices."[2] Are things really that bad? There is some evidence that they may be.

There are two commonly misprescribed groups of drugs. The first of these is the psychotropics or mood modifying drugs. In 1966, enough amphetamines were imported into this country for every person to have received five pills that year. Although at that time there were no legal restrictions on the use of amphetamines, it was generally accepted by medical experts that they were really useful in only a few rare conditions.

A 1977 door-to-door survey in the Borough of Etobicoke, Toronto, found that almost 15 percent of women aged eighteen and over had used a mood modifying drug in the previous 48 hours.[3] For the twelve-month period ending March 1978, over 9.25 million prescriptions had been written in Canada for psychotropic drugs. That is just less than one prescription for every two Canadians.[4] In Saskatchewan, in the nineteen-month period ending March 1977, 22 percent of adults aged 30 and over were prescribed tranquillizers. One in every seven people over age nineteen received a prescription for diazepam alone.[5] High school guidance counsellors in Toronto claimed that doctors were needlessly prescribing tranquillizers for female teen-agers to treat "emotional" problems, rather than referring them for counselling.[6] Drug use in five centres for the mentally retarded in eastern Ontario was studied in the late 1970s. Forty-two percent of the residents were receiving psychotropic medications. The author concluded: "It is quite clear that at least half of the subjects on psychotropics were given those agents unnecessarily."[7]

Of doctors surveyed in Los Angeles, 80 percent agreed that "certain medications are often very helpful in handling the special demands and stresses of everyday living."[8] One third of doctors accepted daily use of chlordiazepoxide (Librium) for a middle-aged housewife having marital troubles as "very legitimate." The more doctors preferred detail men as their source of information about drugs, the more likely they were to accept the use of medication for the relief of normal daily stress.[9]

From March 1977 to March 1978 almost 2.25 million prescriptions were written in Canada for all the various brands of diazepam.[10] In 1971, diazepam was responsible for the appearance of more patients in poison control centres across Canada than any other product—prescription or non-prescription.[11] Alcohol and the benzodiazepines, the class of drugs that includes chlordiazepoxide and diazepam, are the second most frequent combination for overdoses in Canada.[12] Dependence on benzodiazepines is becoming recognized as a serious and growing problem.[13]

Of course, the problem of over-prescribing or misprescribing is not just confined to mood modifying drugs. For example, Vitamin B_{12} is effective for only one condition, pernicious anaemia. In the late 1960s in the U.S., enough of the injectable form of B_{12} was prescribed annually to adequately treat one thousand times the number of patients who actually had the disease. Reasons for using it ranged from "placebo" to "stimulant" to "sedative."[14] Cimetidine is a relatively new drug, marketed by Smith Kline and French under the brand name Tagamet in 1977. It has proved quite beneficial in treating people with duodenal ulcers; however physicians have also been using it to treat a wide range of other conditions. The actual use of cimetidine was monitored in a study conducted between September 1981 and March 1982 in the only hospital in Powell River, British Columbia. The authors found that "physicians prescribe cimetidine for diverse purposes, most of which have not been validated."[15] In 1977, there were 116 deaths in Canada associated with the painkiller Darvon (propoxyphene), marketed by Eli Lilly Canada. Darvon is available only by prescription. Seventy-one of the deaths were ruled suicide and 35 accidental. The chief coroner for Ontario, H.B. Cotnam, had this to say about Darvon: "I don't see much use for it at all. I think you could use aspirin and codeine and get the same effect without having to worry about the suicides and overdoses."[16]

The study of Ontario and Nova Scotia general practitioners referred to in the last chapter found that while 85 percent prescribed rationally for heart failure, only 45 percent did so for infections and a dismal 25 percent were correct when it came to blood pressure. Aspirin is generally considered to be the drug of first choice for people with rheumatoid arthritis, but only 25 percent of 5,000 physicians surveyed in the U.S. in 1966 started with aspirin.[17] The common cold is not commonly treated very well. It is caused by one of a number of viruses, and antibiotics are completely useless against viral infections. This commonplace piece of medical knowledge did not stop American doctors, in 1974, from giving 51 percent of people with a cold a prescription for an antibiotic.[18] Another third got a prescription for an antihistamine and decongestant combination, and 6 percent got just an antihistamine. Neither oral decongestants nor antihistamines have ever been proved to be of any value in treating the common cold. Upper respiratory infections (URIs), most of which are nothing more than the common cold, were treated equally poorly by Canadian physicians. Two hundred and nine members of the College of Family Physicians practising in eastern and northern Ontario and the city of Hamilton responded to a 1973 survey dealing with the treatment of URIs. Fifteen percent said they "usually" prescribed antibiotics and 43 percent said they prescribed them "about half the time."[19]

These studies on the treatment of colds bring us to the other major category of misprescribed drugs—antibiotics. The medical literature is full of reports about the misuse of antibiotics. In 1977, an article appeared in the *Canadian Medical Association Journal* reporting on the use of antibiotics in three Vancouver area hospitals.[20] Appearing in the article were such comments as: "There are numerous examples . . . of chemotherapeutic practices that are difficult to justify from present pharmacologic and bacteriologic practices," and "Unnecessary toxic antimicrobial agents were used in the three general hospitals." Right beside that paper was another on the same topic, based on research done in Hamilton. There, the use of four different kinds of intravenous antibiotics on patients on surgical, gynecological and medical wards was studied.[21] The study concluded, "Overall therapy was assessed to be irrational in 42.0, 50.0, and 12.0% of the surgical, gynecologic and medical patients, respectively." In 1979, antibiotic therapy was evaluated in the Children's Hospital in Winnipeg. Errors in therapy were noted in 30 percent of the medical orders and 63 percent of surgical orders.[22]

These kinds of studies have been reported in the U.S. with the same results, widespread irrational use of antibiotics.[23] The conclusions of one of those studies bears quoting:

> If the antimicrobials were completely innocuous drugs with a potential only for doing good, the sole objection to their irrational use shown in this study would be cost—an important consideration in some instances . . . Unfortunately, cost is not the sole objection, nor the most significant one, to the irrational use of antimicrobials. There are several ways in which the unnecessary or inappropriate use of these agents can be harmful to the individual patient, or to the population in general. Antimicrobials may harm the patient by giving rise to undesirable side effects; they may harm by sensitizing the patient to an antibiotic so that at some future time when he really does need the agent he experiences an unpleasant reaction—if this results in discontinuation of the antimicrobial, the infection may advance to life-threatening proportions. From the point of view of the population as a whole, the widespread and unnecessary use of antimicrobials is most undesirable because it encourages the emergence of resistant strains.[24]

While the financial cost of adverse drug reactions is obviously secondary to the health aspect, it is not trivial. In 1973, Dr. William

McLean, director of drug information and education at Ottawa General Hospital, estimated the cost at $300 million a year for all of Canada.[25]

The true number of adverse drug reactions has only recently begun to be appreciated. It was difficult for physicians to accept a link between a drug applied to the skin and rare damage showing up in the kidney, or to relate a drug taken to control a kidney infection to an uncommon but severe rash. If it was easy to see a sharp drop in blood sugar as a result of too much insulin, it was much harder to believe that an oral antidiabetic drug could cause an increase in deaths from heart disease.[26] Also, when the average hospital patient receives seven drugs during his or her stay, it is often impossible to decide which drug was the culprit. Commonly, two drugs which are safe when given alone can interact to create a problem when given together.

H.L. Lennard and A. Bernstein cite tardive dyskinesia, caused by the phenothiazine class of tranquillizers, as one example of this delay in recognizing and accepting the fact of drug reactions. The first of the phenothiazines was introduced into Canada in 1953. Even in the initial period of enthusiasm over these drugs, some people were worried about the long-term consequences, but because early uncontrolled studies produced seemingly dramatic results, the concerns were not given a great deal of attention. Though hundreds of cases of tardive dyskinesia had been described by 1967, especially in Western Europe, where the drugs were first used, psychiatrists were slow to acknowledge its existence. It was not until 1972, after having settled a lawsuit for damages brought by a patient with tardive dyskinesia, that a major drug manufacturer felt it necessary to include a detailed description of this condition in the labelling of phenothiazines.[27] In 1968, a workshop on tardive dyskinesia was sponsored by the Psychopharmacology Research Branch of the American National Institute of Mental Health. The meeting concluded with these remarks:

> During the last fifteen years, drugs have been given to a large portion of psychiatric patients with little thought of what the risks are. The films of this workshop have shown a number of fairly severe cases of dyskinesia. But many such cases can be seen if one takes the trouble of walking through the wards of mental hospitals. I feel that we should revise our therapeutic

approach with drugs as the risk seems to be considerable. Twenty to twenty-five per cent of the patients are afflicted by this disorder according to our observations; the disorder may last for many years or perhaps indefinitely in the more severe cases. Even if symptoms persist only for months or a few years in the milder cases, the problem still is of considerable clinical importance.[28]

From March 1977 to March 1978, almost 1.2 million prescriptions for phenothiazines were written in Canada, so the problem of tardive dyskinesia is very much present here. Unfortunately, it is also one that is often ignored, with the grave consequences outlined in the preceding quotation.

Poor prescribing leads directly to hospital admissions. The Quebec Order of Pharmacists estimated that 4 to 10 percent of the over 3.5 million yearly hospital admissions in Canada arise from wrong drug dosages, wrong drugs prescribed and adverse drug reactions.[29] Dr. Murray Herst, the senior doctor at the Toronto Baycrest Centre for Geriatrics, estimated that drug reactions were responsible for one fifth of hospital admissions for the elderly.[30]

Once in hospital, for whatever reason, people are still not immune from the adverse effects of misprescribing. A range of drug reactions has been studied at a number of Canadian hospitals. In one Ontario hospital, 100 autopsies done between 1970 and 1972 were examined by the pathology department. It was felt that adverse drug reactions contributed to 36 of the 100 deaths. Twenty-six other adverse reactions were classified as direct but non-fatal complications of therapy.[31]

In the second study, all the patients admitted to the public medical wards of the Montreal General Hospital between July 1, 1965, and June 30, 1966, were monitored.[32] Of the total of 731 patients, 132, or 18 percent, had one or more reactions to drugs, for a total of 193 reactions. And 53 of the 731 patients were initially admitted to hospital because of a drug reaction. Of the 67 patients who died, it was believed that seventeen had suffered a fatal drug reaction. Most of the reactions the patients suffered either prolonged their stay in hospital, required specific treatment, were life-threatening, or caused continuing effects at the time of discharge. Patients who experienced drug reactions were in hospital almost twice as long as those who did not.

A third study was done at St. Joseph's Hospital in London, from June 1969 to June 1972.[33] Among 936 monitored patients, adverse reactions occurred 535 times out of a total of 6,565 drug exposures. In 22 cases, the patients suffered transient or permanent damage. The reaction was life threatening 33 times, although there were no actual deaths attributed to drug reactions. These reactions involved commonly used drugs: five from digitalis (a drug used to strengthen the heart's action), five from heparin (a "blood thinner") and three from antibiotics. If life-threatening reactions occur nationally in 0.5 percent of all drug exposures, as they did in this study, then across Canada, there could be more than 100,000 life-threatening reactions a year. This study also demonstrated the problem with a system of voluntary reporting of drug reactions. Although there were 535 reactions among 936 monitored patients, only 350 adverse reaction reports were received for the other 75,373 non-monitored patients admitted to the rest of the hospital over the same three-year period.

In another Canadian report, 30 percent of 104 patients suffered from either an adverse drug reaction or an error in drug administration.[34] From four other Canadian sources, estimates of drug reactions range as high as three of every ten hospitalized patients. These sources are: Dr. McLean of the Ottawa General Hospital, J.L. Mann, education supervisor for the Toronto General Hospital's pharmacy department,[35] Dr. James Campbell, professor of pathology at the University of Toronto[36] and Dr. Michael Sarin, an internist at Toronto's Wellesley Hospital.[37] When Dr. A.B. Morrison was head of the Health Protection Branch, he estimated that one in three gravely ill people dies in hospital sooner than necessary because of adverse reactions to the very drugs administered to restore health. In testimony given to the House of Commons health committee, he charged that the hard-sell tactics used by drug companies to "flog" their products was a major reason for the medical complications and deaths related to drug overuse and adverse reactions.[38]

Drugs can interact with one another to produce potentially dangerous complications. Some idea of the extent of this problem can be gained from an analysis of 420,000 prescriptions issued in California in a one year period in the early 1970s. Of the 42,000 patients involved, potentially interacting prescriptions had been dispensed to nearly 8 percent.[39] A trade journal commented:

What is most surprising and most alarming is the fact that the more serious the interaction, the more likely seemed its chances of occurring...If nothing else, these figures indicate a threshold of risk that would seem to be clearly unacceptable. More important, they suggest that the interaction problem is at least as severe as some people have been warning.[40]

Not everybody is equally at risk to suffer an adverse drug reaction. The more drugs that one is exposed to, the greater the problem. For a hospitalized patient exposed to more than twenty drugs, there is at least a 40 percent chance of having one or more reactions. Caught in a Catch-22 situation, the sicker the patient, the more drugs s/he is likely to get, and the greater the chance of a drug interaction.

Not all drug reactions can be predicted, but a 1971 American report suggested that between 70 and 80 percent could be avoided without compromising any therapeutic benefits.[41] Elina Hemminki, using 1976 U.S. data on out of hospital patients, analysed the prescribing of antbiotics. Given the then-current prescribing habits of U.S. physicians, she estimated that almost 14,000,000 fatal, serious and minor adverse reactions could be expected annually from antibiotics. But if antibiotics were used only when called for and if the correct drug were used, Hemminki calculated that the total number of adverse reactions would drop to just over 3,000,000 yearly, a reduction of 78 percent.[42]

Not all drug reactions are serious; about 86 percent in the London study ended without permanent damage. But on a national scale there could still be as many as 222,000 serious drug reactions annually.[43] In the U.S., the estimates of the number of deaths attributable to adverse drug reactions range from 30,000 to 140,000 annually.[44]

Chapter 11
Patents

The respect of industrial property rights as represented by patents and trade marks is the essential foundation for progress in research and therapeutics in the pharmaceutical industry.
— PMAC Principles and Code of Marketing Practice[1]

The pharmaceutical industry regards patents as sacrosanct. As previous chapters have shown, patents can keep drugs at artificially high prices, thereby keeping profits high. The Canadian Drug Manufacturers Association has calculated that the 1969 changes to the Patent Act, which facilitated the entry of generic products into the Canadian market, has reduced Canada's 1982 drug bill by between $85 and $165 million.[2] This money would have wound up in the coffers of the multinationals but for the presence of generic drugs. It should come as no surprise that the pharmaceutical industry chose the issue of patents over which to wage its first, and to date biggest, battle with the federal government.

A patent is defined under the Patent Act as a letters patent for an "invention" which is said to be, ". . . any new and useful art, process, machine, manufacture or composition of matter, or any new and useful improvement in any art process, machine, manufacture or composition of matter . . ." The Patent Act gives the owner of the patent "the exclusive right, privilege and liberty of making, constructing, using and vending to others" goods and services embodying the invention. This right is limited to a seventeen-year period from the date the application of the patent is allowed. In Canada, the Commissioner of Patents, presently under the Department of Consumer and Corporate Affairs, is charged with the issuance of patents.

There are two different types of patents respecting pharmaceuticals. When the actual drug itself is patented, that is known as a "product patent." When the process by which the drug is made is patented, that is called a "process patent." Some countries issue both types of patents, some just the latter kind and some issue no patents at all. Canada falls into the second category. (Drugs produced under patents should not be confused with "patent medicines," that is, drugs available without a prescription.)

During the lifespan of the patent, companies have a monopoly on the product and can modify the dosage forms of the drug; combine it with other drugs; and make up special preparations like liquids, sprays, creams, ointments, capsules and intravenous solutions. By covering all bases, even if a new drug comes along to supplant the initial basic drug, the manufacturer continues to profit from the modified forms of the drug.[3] The patent life of a drug can be extended by taking out additional process patents at a later date. For example, Hoechst received its first Canadian patent on Lasix (furosemide), a diuretic, in 1962. The patent was to expire in 1979, but because further patents were granted in 1967, the expiry date was extended to 1984.[4] Large firms can patent everything in sight, thereby not only monopolizing the best products and processes for their own use, but also precluding the use of second-best products and processes by potential competitors.[5]

A former director of research for an American multinational, Dr. Calvin Kunin, enlightened a United States Senate committee on methods by which companies can exploit patents to their advantage: "If I were in the industry, and I were in danger of losing my patent with which I have reaped my fortune over many, many years and I wanted to retain that patent then I would combine that drug with something else so that I have a new proprietary agent. This is the way of keeping this within one's own pocket."[6]

Of course, these are not the reasons that the industry gives for wanting patents retained and strengthened. Drug companies claim that they need exclusive rights to a drug in order to recover the enormous development costs.[7] However, that claim is open to attack on at least three different grounds. First, when the drug companies say that it costs, for example, $50 to $75 million to develop and market a drug, they are not referring just to Canadian costs, but worldwide costs. Since Canada represents about 2 percent of the world market, the Canadian share of development costs that needs to be recouped is $1.0 to $1.5 million, not the full $50 to $75 million. The second point that needs to be examined is the extent to which development costs can actually be attributed to any particular drug. According to at least one expert observer, Paul Talalay, professor of pharmacology at the Johns Hopkins University School of Medicine, "It's naive to accept what the large-scale drug companies say regarding the cost of any given drug. On the whole, because most firms are involved in so many different investments and products, and because, as a result, their bookkeeping is so complex, no drug can be clearly defined as profitable or nonprofitable."[8] To put it another way, almost any drug can be arbitrarily defined as profitable or non-profitable. Surprisingly, this viewpoint is backed up in a PMAC sponsored study:

> The unusually high proportion of unallocable common costs in the total structure of pharmaceutical costs makes it impossible for prices charged for individual drugs to be directly related to costs of producing those specific drugs. Common costs, such as outlays for research and development or similar overhead activities, are applicable to all products in their totality but not traceable to any product individually and can not be allocated to individual products except in the most arbitrary manner.[9]

In other words, drug companies cannot reasonably claim that they need a certain period of time to recover the costs of developing a new drug because these costs cannot be determined. But it would be wrong to mystify the pharmaceutical companies' finances. If their bookkeeping makes it difficult to assign specific figures to specific drugs, overall figures can be applied to the range of drugs; and that leads to the final basis for challenging the industry's contention that patents are necessary for the recovery of development costs of a drug. Research by the Center for the Study of Drug Development at Rochester, New Mexico, calculated that on the average it takes about 8.8 years to recoup development costs.[10] Under the current patent laws the average time that a company has a monopoly on a drug in Canada is about 8.5 years.[11] In Chapter 3 it was pointed out that drugs stay on the Canadian market for at least fifteen years and that even after competitors bring out their own brands the original drug still retains the lion's share of the market. Therefore, even granting the big assumption that costs are allottable, an individual drug company is still in a monopoly position long enough to recover development costs and then to go on making a profit on the drug for many years.

According to the PMAC, patents are one of the most important incentives for research and are "an internationally accepted instrument for the transfer and sharing of technology."[12] But Alan Klass in his book *There's Gold in Them Thar Pills* argues that from the point of view of scientists, patents are a foreign concept. They developed not because of anything within the nature of science, but purely for commercial reasons. Patents impede the free flow of ideas, which is the life blood of science. Once a discovery is patented, other scientists can use it only with the permission of the patent holder. However, no scientific discovery stands by itself, but is built upon the work of other researchers. If the man who discovered the method of growing polio virus had patented his idea instead of freely publishing it, the polio vaccine might never have been developed. As Klass says: "It was only when corporate interest became dominant that the right of a party claiming a patent for the discovery became prominent. Patents serve the industry much more than the individual discoverer and certainly much more than society."[13]

Canada issues only process patents and not product patents. This means that two companies could produce exactly the same drug and not infringe on each other's patent as long as they use different processes. In practice, however, there is little incentive to do research to develop alternative methods for producing a patented pharmaceutical since the Canadian market is too small to justify the expense. Since 1923, Canada has also had a system of compulsory licensing, by which a company may apply to the Commissioner of Patents for a licence to manufacture a particular drug by the patentee's process, upon payment to the patentee of a royalty. Under Section 41(3) of the Patent Act, the Commissioner "shall, unless he sees good reason to the contrary," grant the licence. The onus is on the patentee to show "good reason" why the licence should not be awarded, and over the period 1923 to 1969 only four licences of a total of 49 applied for were refused. The royalty payable has been traditionally set at 15 percent of the net selling price of the bulk material made by the licensee. Compulsory licences are never applied for until a drug has lost its "new drug" status, a process that usually takes about five years. Before that time a company wishing to market the drug would have to repeat all the studies of the originating company.

Theoretically, the right to manufacture afforded by compulsory licences should have had a tendency to reduce the monopolistic situation in the drug industry. It gives companies the opportunity to market drugs which are enjoying substantial sales. Unfortunately, that is only the theory. Between 1923 and 1949, there were no applications for a compulsory licence. The lack of applications up to this time probably reflected the absence of any drug "winners," that is drugs which were major advances and which forecast volume sales with record profits. But after 1949, there were significant developments in a number of therapeutic fields—antibiotics, corticosteroids and tranquillizers being three prime examples. However, from 1949 until 1966, there were only 34 applications made, an increase which the Restrictive Trade Practices Commission did not consider significant in light of the potential.[14]

The drug industry claimed that their willingness to issue licences voluntarily accounted for the paucity of applications for compulsory licences. The Director of Investigation and Research for the Combines Investigation Act, however, did not accept this claim. But he did offer a more plausible explanation. Companies may be reluctant to apply for compulsory licences because a licenser who has been forced to grant a licence may withhold technical knowledge acquired in developing and marketing the drug in question.[15] The Commissioner of Patents, Mr. J.W.T. Michel, pointed out one of the economic realities involved with patents: "The reason why the foreign patentees don't want to grant licences voluntarily [is] because they make much more profit by selling themselves than by just collecting a royalty."[16]

Most of the applications for compulsory licences were made by small Canadian firms turning out products under generic names. These companies were among the few which could benefit from acquiring licences. Their size prevented them from advertising to the extent of the major companies. Consequently, the only sector in which they could compete was in supplying drugs to hospitals and institutions where purchases were made under a tender system.

Licence applicants were further deterred by the requirement that the drug must be manufactured in Canada, with all the costs inherent in manufacturing and quality control. The patent holder, on the other hand, typically imported the raw material in bulk form and then simply prepared the dosage form in Canada.[17]

The Commissioner of Patents emphasized to the Restrictive Trade Practices Commission that foreign companies holding Canadian patents objected very strongly to the granting of licences.[18] In fact, over the years, it was a well established policy among the large companies to delay applications as long as they could, to the point where it was hardly worth the trouble and barely within the capabilities of most of the existing small manufacturers to successfully undertake an application. The large companies never went after one another's patents for fear of the free-for-all that could have developed.[19]

The Director of Investigation and Research summed up the situation:

> At the manufacturer's level, prices of certain drugs are affected by the control over the manufacture, distribution and sale of such drugs exercised through patents. The provisions of the Patent Act relating to compulsory licences appear to have proved ineffectual to combat this situation and the clear intent of the Act has been frustrated.[20]

The Canadian patent laws were inoperative because the industry was, and still is, almost totally controlled from outside the country. The dominance of branches and subsidiaries of multinational companies, chiefly American, and the widespread use of drugs developed in the U.S. meant that the drug trade in Canada operated under the American patent system. There, companies could obtain product, as well as process, patents, and there were no provisions for compulsory licensing. As a result, the prices of products patented in that country were determined by the fact that patent holders held a monopoly. Corresponding Canadian patents were obtained and then the drug was marketed in Canada, either directly, or through a Canadian subsidiary, at a price at least as high as that charged in the U.S. The Canadian public, therefore, was paying prices set by the laws of the U.S.

The Restrictive Trade Practices Commission argued that patents were keeping Canadian drug prices higher than they should be, distorting research efforts and not contributing substantially to Canadian scientific advancement. It therefore recommended in 1963 that Canada should abolish all patents on pharmaceuticals.[21] The Royal Commission on Health hemmed and hawed and, unable to take a position, suggested that the federal government delay abolishing patents for a five-year period.[22]

With this looming threat to the patent laws, the PMAC marshalled its forces to ensure the survival of patents. In 1962, the House of Commons had established a special standing committee (the Harley Committee) to examine the various aspects of prescription drugs. By 1965, it began to consider the relative quality of brand name drugs and their generic equivalents; from there it was a logical step to the question of patents. The PMAC had already relocated in Ottawa and mounted a campaign to preserve the existing patent system. The cost of that campaign is estimated to have been between $200,000 and $250,000 annually. This figure does not take into account expenses incurred by individual PMAC members.[23] Lang believes that the PMAC's main concern was to stop the Canadian government from setting any precedent on patents and compulsory licences that would have been an example for other countries, particularly those with large domestic markets for pharmaceuticals.[24]

The Conservatives were in opposition at the time, and the PMAC supplied the Tory members of the committee with the ammunition to use against anti-industry witnesses. Three members in particular, Dr. L. Brand, Dr. P.B. Rynard and Mr. M. Forrestal, received a continuous flow of materials and pre-briefing sessions from the PMAC and their attorneys. At least one representative of the PMAC was present at all meetings of the committee to relay further questions and facts to these men. The Harley Committee reported in April 1967. While it stopped short of recommending the abolition of patents, it did recommend that the government allow compulsory licences to be issued to enable firms to import drugs into Canada which were already manufactured here under patent.

Having a compulsory licence to import a drug into the country would be a major boon for small companies since they would be able to forgo the major expenses involved in establishing manufacturing facilities. Such a change to the patent laws was anticipated to introduce substantial competition into sectors of the drug market and as such brought about vigorous denunciation from the drug industry. The president of the PMAC, Dr. William Wigle, a past president of the Canadian Medical Association, wrote to the *Canadian Medical Association Journal* threatening that if this recommendation was acted upon the large companies operating in Canada would close down their plants.[25] While in Florida, Dr. Wigle observed: "The Canadian parliamentary committee was willing to put Canada at the mercy of foreign nations in the event of world wide epidemics."[26] H.C. Balmer, president of Glaxo, warned in an open letter to M.P.s that: "The saving to Canadians won't match the cost to government of controlling the influx of hitherto unknown products...[and] if additional resources to secure such control are not planned, we will have chaos indeed." The letter concluded: "Anyone importing Glaxo products manufactured by a related company... *does so at his own peril, and at the peril of the Canadian public.*"[27] (Emphasis in original.)

To support its cause, the PMAC enlisted the support of: the Canadian Medical Association, the Quebec College of Physicians and Surgeons, the Association of Deans of Pharmacy of Canada, the Canadian Manufacturers Association, the Chamber of Commerce, the Canadian Chemical Producers Association, the Chemical Institute of Canada, the Canadian Pharmaceutical Associations, the Canadian Electrical Manufacturers Association and the Connaught Medical Research Laboratories. Finally, the PMAC organized "Operation 100." Each PMAC official was given a list of the top one hundred companies in Canada, along with the names and curricula vitae of their chief executive officers. The PMAC *Bulletin* which outlined the plan said:

> We suggest that you make every effort to contact these gentlemen at the earliest opportunity and explain to them that the implementation of Harley Recommendations 18 and 21 would mean that the Canadian government has decided to unilaterally abolish protection of industrial property rights owned by foreign companies in Canada. It is conceivable that these companies will reciprocate by refusing to recognize Canadian patents abroad.
>
> You should urge these executives to write to Mr. John M. Turner, Registrar General; Mr. C.M. Drury, Minister of Industry; Mr. Robert H. Winters, Minister of Trade and Commerce with copies to the Prime Minister, expressing their opposition to any legislation which would endanger or weaken

patents or trademarks in Canada for any segment of industry. They may also wish to approach their local MPs.

You may want to stress the present discriminatory nature of sections 41-3 of the Patent Act concerning food and drugs.

Additional arguments and information sheets are enclosed. You may want to leave copies of these on the occasion of your visits.

Please keep us informed of your progress on the attached forms.[28]

However, in spite of this intensive lobbying and propaganda effort by the PMAC, Bill C-190, adding Section 41(4) to the Patent Act, and thereby allowing for compulsory licencing to import drugs already made in Canada, was introduced into the House of Commons on February 12, 1968.

The bill also provided for important amendments to the Trade Marks Act. In many cases, a drug selling at a relatively high price in Canada sells at substantially lower prices in other countries under the same brand name. It would seem an obvious incentive, then, for a company to import these lower priced drugs into Canada and undersell the higher priced Canadian produced drug. However, under the provisions of the Trade Marks Act, as it was then written, the owners of a Canadian trade mark could control the importation and distribution of any product bearing this mark, regardless of whether any actual production was carried on in Canada. Whether or not Canadian drug companies, usually subsidiaries of multinationals, actually used this provision of the act to prohibit importation, the threat to do so probably was enough to discourage the importation of these lower priced drugs. The amendments in Bill C-190 abolished this section of the act.

Raymond Rock, a Liberal MP whose Montreal riding contained a number of pharmaceutical plants, opposed the bill on second reading. A few other Montreal area Liberals, later to become quite prominent in the party, Bryce Mackasey and Warren Allmand, probably supported the bill only because of the penalties involved in breaking party ranks.[29]

During the parliamentary debate on the bill, the PMAC and its supporters were once again active, placing all their resources at the disposal of the Conservatives. Representatives of the PMAC stationed themselves in the Commons gallery and would periodically rush down to pay phones, contact the PMAC office and then forward information or questions to the Tories on the floor of the Commons.[30] In the end, all this was to no avail, and Bill C-190, which had had its number changed to C-102, passed on March 28, 1969. Ronald Lang's book *The Politics of Drugs* provides a thoughtful analysis of the ultimately unsuccessful lobbying efforts of the drug industry. Lang notes that the initial investigations into drug costs in Canada had been begun by the civil service in 1958 with the Restrictive Trade Practices Commission Report and "by 1965 these same civil servants had developed a self-induced commitment to lower the cost of drugs and to defeat what they considered to be an arrogant industry."[31] Lang believes that the determination of the civil service was the prime reason for the government's success in securing the passage of Bill C-102.

When Consumer Affairs Minister Ron Basford introduced Bill C-190 in the Commons, he was quoted as saying: "If I were in the drug industry I would make sure that this bill worked, because if it doesn't, we are obviously going to have to do something else."[32] The PMAC did not take this advice, and American Home Products Ltd. immediately proceeded to oppose the legislation through the courts. At first, the company attempted to prevent the application of the law by seeking an order of prohibition against the Commissioner of Patents. That action delayed the implementation of the legislation for a year. When the case reached the Ontario Court of Appeals in March 1970, it was dismissed within fifteen minutes. Then other companies, such as Roche, started challenging the Commissioner's decisions on the basis of the royalty allowance rewarded. These cases were also decided in favor of the government. By 1971, of the 60 licences issued, there had been 43 appeals before the courts. These court battles acted as a disincentive to companies seeking licences, since they could anticipate up to a two-year court fight and a cost of about $100,000 in court fees.[33] The use of court appeals as a delaying tactic was eventually recognized by judges as the following section from a ruling shows:

> . . . there is . . . some ground for thinking that many appeals under s. 41 of the *Patent Act* are brought regardless of any considered opinion that there is, under the authorities, any valid ground for attacking the Commissioner's decision.[34]

Other methods to forestall or limit competition from licensees were also tried. Hoffman-LaRoche issued statements questioning the quality of the licensee's products. In a letter sent to doctors by the President of Roche, J.S. Fralich, the following section appears:

> To our knowledge none of these imitators had to duplicate the enormous amount of work which is necessary in the compilation of a new drug application. Likewise, no clinical investigation activities of any consequence by these companies have come to our attention.[35]

When this type of approach seemed unsuccessful, Roche switched to price cutting on sales of Valium and Librium to hospitals.[36] (For the consequences of this tactic to Roche, see Chapter 1.) Finally, Roche used a technique known as "filling the pipes": just prior to the entry of the licensee's product, the patentee "floods the market," usually in combination with a price special, so that the licensee cannot establish its product in the market for some time.[37]

In 1982, Ayerst lost a two-year court battle with Apotex, a Canadian generic manufacturer. Ayerst was trying to force Apotex to change the color, shape and size of its propranolol tablets so that patients could clearly distinguish it from the Ayerst tablet. The Supreme Court of Ontario dismissed Ayerst's claims, noting that "there is not even the whisper of a suggestion that the appearance [of Apotex's version of propranolol] has adversely affected the plaintiff company in the slightest degree." Although Apotex won, it had to pay for its victory to the tune of $100,000 in court costs.[38]

Obviously, the multinational drug companies were not interested in making C-102 work. At one time, it seemed as if Mr. Basford's "something else" might develop into a crown corporation to manufacture and distribute drugs.[39] However, accommodations were made and "something else" never materialized.

By 1983, over 290 licences had been granted.[40] Absent from the list of licence holders were any of the companies holding a patent on a drug against which a compulsory licence had been issued. Gorecki explains the reasons for this situation:

> The economic self interest of the patentees explain their absence from the list . . . Should each patentee decide to take out a licence against all the remaining patentees then price competition,

much greater than currently exists between licensee and patentee, would result. Given the extreme insensitivity of the demand for drugs to price changes, the price and profit margins of the patentee would fall. Hence, as a group, patentees would experience considerable adverse economic consequences from a policy of acquiring compulsory patent licences.[41]

What kind of an impact has compulsory licensing had? To begin with, it does not appear to have promoted Canadianization of the drug industry. Of all the licences issued, almost half have gone to non-Canadian firms, or to firms that have been acquired by non-Canadian owners. Five companies that have received licences are owned by four multinational pharmaceutical firms, including licensees ranked first and third (by number of licences owned).[42]

Although the presence of generics may have forced the multinationals to reduce the selling prices of their products to the tune of $85 to $165 million (see endnote 2), it does not seem to have significantly affected their profit levels. In the decade ending in 1980, the average before tax profit on capital employed for the pharmaceutical industry was 22.8 percent or 73 percent higher than that for all manufacturing industries.

Despite all the uproar, compulsory licensing has really affected only a relatively small part of the drug market. Between 1970 and 1978, 142 compulsory licences were issued for 47 prescription drugs. Five drugs alone, chlordiazepoxide (Librium), diazepam (Valium), furosemide (Lasix), ampicillin (Penbritin) and thioridazine (Mellaril), accounted for 48 of these licences. Over 80 percent of all licences granted were for drugs in just three, out of nineteen, therapeutic categories: anti-infectives, cardiovascular and central nervous system drugs. Twelve of the categories contained no drugs against which a compulsory licence was issued.[43] Among others, two factors have combined to restrict the number of drugs susceptible to compulsory licensing: the size of the market, that is, the potential for a large sales volume, and the limited availability of the basic fine chemicals to the companies that may seek licences.[44] Even where there is competition, the companies that have obtained licences have been able to make only minimal inroads into the market. An analysis of twenty drugs against which compulsory licences had been issued showed that the licensees' drugs averaged less than 20 percent of the market share of sales.[45]

The drugs affected by the close to 300 licences that have been granted so far do not begin to account for a majority of the sales dollars in the Candian market. In 1981, total sales of drugs under compulsory licence were $170 million, of which only about $35 million represented sales by firms holding the compulsory licences.[46] In that year the total value of the Canadian human pharmaceutical market was $1.01 billion, meaning that drugs affected by compulsory licensing represented less than 17 percent of the market. Six different studies have appeared analysing the effect of compulsory licensing on drug prices.[47] All have concluded that compulsory licences bring down the price of those drugs affected, and in some cases the reduction is substantial. It must be remembered, though, that the great majority of drug sales ($840 million in 1981) are untouched by compulsory licensing.

However minor the impact of compulsory licensing, the multinationals use it to grind many of their already sharp axes. For instance, the patent law changes are being used as an excuse to keep drugs of questionable medical value on the market. "Why should we take these products off the market since there is no incentive to do research and improve them?" asked a disingenuous Bill Robson, president of Smith Kline and French Canada Limited.[48] Terry Mailloux, a corporate vice-president of Hoechst Canada, bemoans the need to use strategies to counter the impact of generic companies on his company's profits. One way to "let money come in to keep things going," he said, is to keep the company's older and more controversial products on the market.[49] Guy Beauchemin of the PMAC agrees that keeping outdated drugs on the market is "a defence mechanism against unjust laws."[50] Some might call it blackmail, an age-old tactic employed by large corporations to ensure that the free market does not slip from their control. Mr. Beauchemin also admits that the drug companies use the existence of the patent law changes to charge higher prices for some of their products. Claiming that they have lost profits as a result of compulsory licences being issued on some drugs, the multinationals increase their prices on drugs still under their monopoly—older non-copied drugs and their newest products.[51] Mr. Beauchemin's statement illustrates that in spite of government controls, the pharmaceutical companies continue to enjoy substantial freedom to raise prices in order to maintain profit levels. Controls appear to be no more than a minor nuisance, one that can even be used by the multinationals as an excuse for flexing new muscles.

In 1979, CIBA used the existence of compulsory licensing as an excuse to cancel a $500,000 research project in Montreal. The company claimed that it was unprofitable to continue researching a certain drug since other manufacturers could market the drug without the bother of research. The drug in question was Anturan, the same one that CIBA had refused research funds for a few years earlier.[52]

Interestingly, as one observer points out, the companies did not consider compulsory licensing so much of a disincentive as to force their complete withdrawal from the Canadian market: "They went on selling their drugs to us, and they went on making good profits. They wanted to turn the clock back to pre-1968 conditions, sure, but even the tighter conditions of the '70s didn't drive them out of the market."[53]

Friends of the industry were quick to leap to its defence. In June 1970, Dr. Jacques Genest, the director of the Clinical Research Institute of Montreal and a professor of medicine at the Universite de Montreal, gave the welcoming speech at a research symposium held to open the Merck Frosst Laboratories in Montreal. Amid the pleasantries of his address were sprinkled comments such as: "It is deplorable to see committees formed by politicians to establish rules for the licensing and the clinical study of new drugs in man, and this without competence or understanding of the philosophy and the complex problems which govern medical research and clinical pharmacology." His elitism was woven into underhanded attacks on the people who testified in favor of the government during the hearings on C-102: "It is unfortunate that quite often decisions of committees of members of Parliament and of the Senate attach equal value to the testimony of businessmen or men of science of second or third rank as to that of experts recognized by their peers as the greatest in their field."[54]

The PMAC and the multinationals are still fighting to have Bill C-102 modified or repealed. A particular aspect of compulsory licensing that the PMAC has repeatedly attacked is the size of the royalty rate paid to the originating company by the licensee. This rate has been established at 4 percent of the licensee's sales. The 4 percent figure was set by the Commissioner of Patents in 1969 just after the law was changed. It has been subject to attack ever since.[55] The multinationals have argued for a higher rate all the way up to the Supreme Court of Canada, and have lost. Through all of their protestations, the companies have never been able to present persuasive evidence to the Commissioner that the rate is too low. Presumably, if their claim had merit, the multinationals should have been able to prove it by now either to the Commissioner or before the courts.[56]

James Doherty, a previous head of the PMAC, said in a submission to a government committee studying further changes in the patent laws:

> Canada has been viewed by decision makers within transnational companies and a variety of other international sources as a pirate country, the likes of Italy, trying to secure the fruits of research and inventions from other countries without making any contributions to the cost of new drugs. Unless something is done to restore the international pharmaceutical industry's loss of confidence in the investment climate in this country, decisions to place investments elsewhere, other than in Canada, will continue to be made and we will continue to witness a gradual downward slide toward becoming a second-rate status nation in the pharmaceutical area, symbolized by lower levels of research and development and productive capacity.[57]

In 1980, in their lobbying efforts to have Section 41(4) of the Patent Act modified, the PMAC and the multinationals promised that if modifications to the Act were made the industry would be prepared to increase its manufacturing and research activity in Canada. According to the Bureau of Policy Coordination in the Department of Consumer and Corporate Affairs, when the industry's package was analysed by the federal Departments of Industry, Trade and Commerce and Consumer and Corporate Affairs, "it became apparent that most of the new R&D and manufacturing promised by the industry was either already planned or was to be financed through government incentive programs."[58]

The PMAC and the multinationals are still issuing promises and/or threats, depending on what happens to Section 41(4). The promises, consequent to a repeal, include: an increase in local manufacturing and employment, a voluntary sytem of price controls and increased expenditures on research. Among the threats, if the law remains unchanged, are: continued plant closings resulting in a loss of employment, and a further reduction in current levels of research and development. It is difficult to believe the PMAC's promise of increased Canadian manufacturing in light of remarks made by the Pharmaceutical Manufacturers Association in the U.S. in a submission to a Congress committee. Member companies were surveyed regarding the reasons for establishing foreign affiliates. The leading considerations were given as tariff and trade restrictions (listed by 95 percent of respondents as "important"), legal requirements for local production (85 percent) and "better servicing of existing work" (81 percent).[59] Apparently patent protection was not a major factor. This conclusion fits with material presented in Chapter 6, in which we examined the reasons for the multinationals' aversion to doing research in Canada and showed that the 1969 patent law changes had no bearing on decisions pertaining to research. The Canadian Drug Manufacturers Association has studied the other promises and threats.[60] According to the CDMA, voluntary systems of price controls would be ineffective and impossible to monitor, and furthermore, since most companies are branch plant operations, their promises about prices could simply be overridden by their multinational parents.

The PMAC points to the 1982 and 1983 closings of the Quebec facilities of Ayerst and Hoffman-LaRoche, respectively, and the loss of a total of about 350 jobs, as examples of how the patent law changes are eroding, and will continue to erode, pharmaceutical research and manufacturing in Canada. But the CDMA analysis offers a different perspective on these closings. The shutdown of Ayerst's research and development division was a consequence of the corporation's worldwide failure to produce significant innovations. This fundamental deficiency resulted in a corporate reorganization and consolidation of its entire R&D division. The Montreal plant, which lacked the capacity to expand, was only one of many foreign casualties. Donald Davies, chairman of Ayerst, concedes that Canada's patent laws were not among the main reasons for closing their research facilities in Montreal: "It's simply far more efficient to do all our research in one place."[61] Hoffman-LaRoche shut down its manufacturing operation in Quebec because it too was suffering from a lack of new products. Roche apparently made a serious strategic error in overexpanding its Quebec physical plant facilities to 400,000 square feet, well beyond its requirements. Ninety R&D jobs were cut at Roche's corporate headquarters in Basel, Switzerland, in 1981 as part of Roche's retrenchment.

Finally, the CDMA points out that because the pharmaceutical industry is not labor intensive, it is unlikely that employment levels will increase in proportion to future increases in sales. The association concludes that "even in the absence of compulsory licensing it is very unlikely that significant increases in employment...could be expected." Lee McCabe of the federal Department of Consumer and Corporate Affairs reinforces the CDMA's cautionary note about the contributions of the pharmaceutical industry to the overall Canadian economy: "People seem to take it on faith that because this industry has a fairly high level of research and development, it must be a winner...But I have to ask myself whether we wouldn't be better off putting our bucks elsewhere—into the Mitels, the Telidons and so on."[62]

In its persistence, the PMAC does appear to be gaining allies in its campaign to have the patent laws changed in its favor. In 1980, the Department of Industry, Trade and Commerce released a discussion paper on the drug industry.[63] A review of the paper by Gorecki and Henderson pointed out "that the IT&C analysis of the drug industry, the effects of compulsory licensing and its significance for Canadians are presented almost as the exact image of the PMAC's position. The 'industry' becomes synonymous with the PMAC...In sum, the Department's discussion paper is largely a reflection of industry views, and not a critical assessment of them."[64] The PMAC's position has also been bolstered by strong support from seventeen separate health and scientific organizations, including the Canadian Medical Association, the Chemical Institute of Canada, the Federation of Biological Societies and the deans of all eight schools of pharmacy in Canada. In addition, the provincial governments in Saskatchewan, Alberta, Nova Scotia and Quebec have made a commitment to support the pharmaceutical industry over the compulsory licensing issue.[65]

In late 1982, press reports suggested that the industry's representations had convinced Andre Ouellet, then-Minister of Consumer and Corporate Affairs, to appoint a committee to re-examine the issue of compulsory licensing. Mr. Ouellet, in a February 1983 letter to the president of the Consumers Association of Canada, confirmed that something was in the wind:

I have recently set in motion a review of compulsory licensing which will initially focus on a proposal put forward by the pharmaceutical industry. It is my view that these preliminary discussions should be limited to industry representatives and federal government officials. If this portion of the review indicates that amendment to the Act may be desirable, I intend to initiate a widely based consultative process that will include groups such as the Consumers' Association of Canada.[66]

Subsequent correspondence and a meeting between the minister and the CAC confirmed the CAC's belief that the discussions with the industry were preliminary to a full public consultation. As part of the presumed preliminary stages, former federal Liberal cabinet minister Martin O'Connell was hired in January 1983 to advise the Department of Consumer and Corporate Affairs on possible patent law changes. This appointment was greeted with considerable suspicion by the Canadian Drug Manufacturers Association because Mr. O'Connell's consulting work since leaving politics in 1979 involved acting as adviser to two multinational drug companies. Mr. O'Connell, naturally enough, did not see any conflict of interest: "My professional role is to give [Mr. Ouellet] the best advice I can."[67]   George Post, deputy minister of Consumer and Corporate Affairs, was quite pleased with Mr. O'Connell's appointment. The new adviser, he said, "is a man noted for his fairness...The fact he has worked for multinational companies only indicates that his consulting business since he left government has been broad."[68]

On May 27, 1983, at a meeting of the House of Commons Health, Welfare and Social Affairs Committee, Mr. Ouellet announced that the government had definitely decided to change the Patent Act. Instead of the full public discussions that Mr. Ouellet had promised the CAC, it seems that the only ones consulted in making this decision were the multinational companies. Mr. Ouellet is quoted in the minutes of the meeting as saying that "the decision is taken to amend the law in order to create a better climate for investment and research in Canada."[69]

In a letter dated June 21, Mr. Ouellet invited the CAC to submit its views not on whether any changes were needed or desirable, but on which of the options for amendment set out in the government's discussion paper should be adopted.[70] Three options were presented:

1. Variable royalty rates: Licences would continue to be granted, but rates would be set according to the level of research and development activity carried out in Canada by the patentee.

2. Market exclusivity: Compulsory licences to import would be granted only after a specified number of years had elapsed following initial marketing of the drug. This practice would provide patentees with a period of market certainty on which to base future plans.

3. Company-specific exemption from compulsory licences: Firms proposing specific performance and price commitments would qualify for an exemption from licensing to import. Failure to meet the commitments would result in a termination of the exemption for one or more products.

Predictably, the PMAC was enthusiastic about Mr. Ouellet's announcement. "We're absolutely delighted by the Government's new tack," commented PMAC president Guy Beauchemin.[71]

Mr. Ouellet promised to spend the summer consulting with interested parties about the exact form that the amendments would take and to introduce legislation in the fall of 1983. Apparently, however, it is going to take much longer for the government to reach a decision than was originally forecast. A variety of groups, including the National Anti-Poverty Organization, the Consumers Association of Canada and the Medical Reform Group of Ontario (a group of physicians committed to the preservation of medicare), have all made strong representations to the government to maintain the legislation as it stands. As of mid-November 1983, George Post was making no further estimate of how long it would take before legislation was introduced. But he did say that the opposition has not deterred the government from its intention to change the Act. Failing to amend the Act, said the sensitive deputy minister, would leave unresolved the "sense of irritation the multinational drug companies feel towards Canada."[72]

In the cabinet shuffle of August 1983 Mr. Ouellet was replaced as Minister of Consumer and Corporate Affairs by Judy Erola. While Ms. Erola has yet to make any definitive statement on the matter, she has indicated where her sympathies lie. During a House of Commons question period Sven Robinson, an NDP member, proposed that she fire Martin O'Connell as a departmental adviser on the grounds that he was biased in favor of the multinational companies. Ms. Erola demurred, explaining that "Mr. O'Connell has provided a very valuable service to this Department because we must have a very balanced view...I think that that balanced view is being provided to my Department at the moment."[73]

By spring 1984, after months of inaction, Ms. Erola decided that the entire issue of amending the Patent Act was too much of a political "hot potato" in an election year and set up a one-person commission of inquiry under Professor Harry Eastman of the University of Toronto. Professor Eastman is scheduled to report by the end of 1984.

In view of all of the PMAC's machinations to reverse Section 41(4), it seems a bit ironic to read this 1978 statement made by its executive vice-president:

> The association had to build and maintain a reputation as an objective "no-nonsense," highly recognized body. Thus it cannot afford to attempt painting black sheep white. It can only present a well-washed black sheep. This objectivity, and honesty is carefully guarded to preserve the association's ability to operate at the highest government policy-making levels.[74]

From the material presented in this chapter and in Chapters 3 and 6, it should be obvious that tinkering with the Patent Act will not increase the level of either research or manufacturing done in Canada. The only substantial effect that amending the Patent Act is likely to have is a decrease in the already low level of competition and an increase in prices and profits for the multinationals.

It should be remembered that the Restrictive Trade Practices Commission did not see any substantial benefits from the presence of patents in the pharmaceutical field and recommended their abolition. Compulsory licensing was just a compromise position agreeable to the Liberal government of the day which ideologically could not accept abandoning the patent system. To compromise further by accepting any of the three proposals put forth by Consumer and Corporate Affairs would simply strengthen the position of the multinationals and bring back the pre-1969 situation.

Chapter 12
The Government:
Actions and Reactions

The last chapter examined one attempt by the federal government to control the cost of drugs. Cost is one of two pharmaceutical areas in which Ottawa has decided to play a role. The other has to do with the effectiveness and safety of the drugs sold in Canada. In only one notable instance has the federal government imposed restrictions on the prescribing of a class of drugs already on the market. The case involved the amphetamines. Otherwise, almost no effort has been made to change the prescribing patterns of doctors. Provincial governments have, so far, confined their activities to the issue of the cost of drugs. This chapter will consider the actions taken by both levels of government and their successes and failures.

Control of Drug Quality

Not until the 1939 amendment to the Food and Drugs Act did the federal government start to play a role in limiting the sale of drugs. That amendment gave the government the authority to make regulations defining the conditions of sale of any drug likely to be injurious to health. Before that, various provincial Pharmacy Acts maintained a list of drugs whose sale was restricted to a prescription from a physician, but these lists lacked uniformity from province to province. At the 1941 meeting of the Dominion Council of Health, an advisory body to the federal Minister of Health, concern was expressed about the over-the-counter sale of a number of dangerous drugs to the general public. The Council recommended that the federal government pass regulations for control and distribution of these drugs and such action was taken in a Cabinet Order in Council in October 1941. In 1944, the powers of the federal government to control the sale and conditions of sale of drugs were enhanced by the addition of the following section to the regulatory authority it already had: "to define the conditions of sale of any drug in the interests of or for the protection of public health."

In 1939, the government had suggested that a cautionary statement appear on the label of prescription drugs. This proposal was discussed with the Canadian Pharmaceutical Manufacturers Association (CPMA, the predecessor of the PMAC), which wished to modify the proposed statement. The CPMA's modification, which would have nullified the intent of the warning, was rejected by the government and the matter was dropped.[1] This attempt to alter the cautionary statement is the first recorded instance of the industry's effort to influence government policy, but far from the last.

Incredibly, it was only in 1951 that it became mandatory that information about new drugs be submitted to the Food and Drug Divisions of the Department of Health and Welfare prior to marketing of the drugs. This revision of the law was provoked by the realization that Canada was being used as a proving ground for foreign, mostly American, manufacturers to test-market their new drugs. In some instances, insufficient clinical experience had been obtained to provide adequate directions for the safe use of the drugs.[2]

The Canadian drug laws were changed again in 1963, following the thalidomide experience. Although the 1951 regulations had forced manufacturers to show that their products were safe, it was not until 1963 that manufacturers had to submit "substantial evidence of the clinical effectiveness of the new drug...under the conditions of use recommended."[3] Unfortunately, neither the 1951 nor the 1963 changes were made retroactive. Therefore, drugs marketed before 1951 have never had either their safety or their efficacy established, and drugs marketed between 1951 and 1963 have never been required to show that they are efficacious. In total, some 1,500 drugs marketed before 1963 and still being sold in Canada have never undergone modern testing. The Health Protection Branch believes that about 450 of the 7,000 prescription drugs available in Canada are either completely worthless or lack meaningful medical benefits. Dr. Ian Henderson, current director of the Health Protection Branch's Bureau of Human Prescription Drugs, cites the continued use of barbiturates as one example of a group of drugs that should no longer be used: "Some of these are 30, 40, 50 years old...there are better drugs for the bulk of patients."[4] Even some people within the drug industry agree with Dr. Henderson. Don Davies, president of Ayerst, admitted in a rare moment that "some drugs [on the market] are crap."[5] But Guy Beauchemin of the PMAC is not given to such lapses. In his opinion the continued use of possibly inferior drugs is the result of fierce competition among drug companies. "This is one of the prices we pay for a capitalistic system," he said.[6] One wonders who the "we" is he refers to.

Dr. Henderson sees the need for a thorough evaluation of drugs put on the Canadian market before 1963. By 1982, the U.S. was finishing just such a ten-year review program; Japan was involved in an eleven-year program; and all member countries of the European Economic Community had agreed to complete reviews by 1990. Dr. Henderson estimates that such a review in Canada would cost about $3 million and take four years. However, since 1977, three requests to the Department of National Health and Welfare for the necessary funds have all been rejected. Nor does it seem likely that the money will be forthcoming. Monique Begin, federal Minister of Health and Welfare, has said that Canada will not follow the U.S.'s lead in reviewing drugs that have never been tested for efficacy or safety.[7]

The drug industry is not particularly upset with Ms. Begin's attitude. According to Mr. Beauchemin, "Some companies are strongly opposed to a review of drugs, for economic reasons...A hell of a lot of products would drop out."[8]

Again, in 1967, the procedures for approving a new drug were changed, but not made retroactive. At that time, the HPB, with the agreement of the drug industry, required the companies to submit a product monograph before approval for marketing would be given. A product monograph is a document containing detailed information about all aspects of a drug. These monographs are now made available, by the drug companies, to physicians on request. Prior to 1967, some companies produced similar documents on some of their drugs, but there was no formal requirement to do so. Since the necessity for product monographs was not made retroactive there may still be drugs around that do not have them. In these cases, doctors are denied potentially vital information.

Under Canadian law, the Health Protection Branch, formerly the Food and Drug Directorate, is the agency responsible for controlling prescription drugs. Before the HPB will grant a manufacturer a

Notice of Compliance, which allows a drug to be marketed, certain tests have to be carried out. A drug must be tested in tissue cultures and in at least three different animal species, one of which should be a non-rodent. This provision is necessary because many drugs behave differently in different species of animals. After the animal studies, the manufacturer applies to the HPB for permission to conduct tests in humans. The kind of information which must be submitted with the application depends upon the phase of human testing for which the manufacturer is seeking approval. (See Chapter 6 for a description of the different phases of human drug testing.) In the final stage, the drug is reviewed by the Bureau of Human Prescription Drugs, a branch of the HPB. The Bureau may require the manufacturer to present new information, even to redo some of the previous tests. If all is in order, a Notice of Compliance is granted, and the drug can be sold on the Canadian market.

Canada's standards for marketing new drugs are among the world's most stringent, judging by the duration of the application process and the volume of information to be submitted.[9] But there are also some glaring deficiencies in the regulations. Canada does not require companies to repeat drug trials done elsewhere if the trials submitted are of good quality. In practice, that means that Canada depends heavily on the U.S. drug testing system for information used to determine drug safety. But testing deficiencies that are uncovered in U.S. laboratories are not communicated to Canadian officials. In 1982, the Edmonton *Journal* reported that investigators with the U.S. Food and Drug Administration found 127 laboratories to be in violation of FDA regulations, and that over the past twenty years 43 doctors had been suspended for abuse of experimental drugs and 24 more were under investigation. U.S. officials cautioned that these doctors may be only the tip of the iceberg. How do these discoveries affect Canadians' health? We do not know because we do not get the information. Dr. Dennis Cook, acting director-general of Health and Welfare Canada's Drug Directorate, told the Edmonton *Journal* that the impact on Canadians could be negligible but it could also be significant.[10]

Canadian regulations are silent on the question of who can and cannot be used as research subjects, and on the necessity of obtaining a subject's informed consent prior to participation in a drug study. The lack of a law requiring patients to give informed consent does not bother Dr. Albert Liston, director-general of the Drug

Directorate of the HPB. "It's intentional," he says. "It's the practice of medicine...how a physician deals with his patients."[11] Drug trials in patients are not started until the HPB has approved the study protocol or design. But the HPB has no legal authority to demand such a protocol. Nor does Canadian law require that the study be monitored to assure that the trial is being carried out according to the terms of the protocol submitted. Legally, drug trials cannot be stopped unless the federal Minister of Health considers the drug to be hazardous. If the drug is proving to be useless or if it is causing disturbing side effects, it is up to either the researcher or the company to call off the trial. Companies do monitor trials of their products but according to Dr. Henderson drug company monitors are mainly concerned with whether or not government forms are being completed properly. In a *Globe and Mail* interview, Dr. Henderson surmised: "There are probably lots of protocol violations we government officials know nothing about...I don't place much faith in drug company monitoring."[12] Referring to the possibility of inaccurate records kept by clinical researchers, to deviations from research plans submitted to the HPB and even to the remote possibility of deliberate fraud, Dr. Henderson said, 'I'm sure there are violations."[13] Dr. John Hamilton, professor of pharmacology and toxicology at the University of Western Ontario and president of the Canadian Federation of Biological Societies, agrees that some sort of check needs to be kept on the results of research done by the drug companies: "Canadians would feel a lot happier if independent laboratories were checking the results of the drug manufacturers in some cases. I think it's important to have some testing done by independent companies that are paid regardless of whether their results are positive or negative."[14] But once again the lack of funding from the federal government has stymied efforts to do the job properly; money has not been made available to Dr. Henderson to hire the staff necessary to monitor drug trials.

Under Canadian regulations, drugs have to be shown to be safe and effective for the uses claimed, but there is no requirement that they be any more effective than drugs already on the market for the same use. This shortcoming in the rules is one of the factors that has allowed a proliferation of what are called "me-too" drugs—drugs that are chemically slightly different from ones already existing, but essentially no better. This situation characterizes the benzodiazepines, the class of drugs that includes chlordiazepoxide (Librium) and diazepam (Valium). Librium, from Hoffman-La Roche, was the first of the class on the market, and was the most popular minor tranquillizer available until Valium came along. By 1975, Valium was the second most widely prescribed drug in Canada, and contributed substantially to the fortunes of Roche.[15] Roche saw that it had a winner in Valium and Librium, so now we also have flurazepam (Dalmane), clonazepam (Rivotril) and bromazepam (Lectopam) from Roche, plus oxazepam (Serax), clorazepate (Tranxene), lorazepam (Ativan), triazolam (Halcion), flurazepam (Somnol), nitrazepam (Mogadon) and temazepam (Restoril) from other companies seeking to cash in on the "benzodiazepine bonanza." Each of these drugs is marketed with claims as to why it is superior to all the others, but according to at least five articles in leading medical journals there are few substantial clinical differences among them.[16]

One of the major reasons for the deficiencies in Canadian drug laws and regulations is the generally comradely relationship between the government and the industry. The legislation setting up the HPB is, according to the Montreal *Gazette*, "Rooted to implicit faith in the drug companies' testing and marketing ethics, and in the free enterprise system."[17] This approach starts right at the top with Monique Begin, who said in a *Globe and Mail* interview that she did not believe that Canada needs detailed regulations to control the drug approval process.[18] She said she prefers that "the players" involved in getting a drug on the market—federal officials, drug manufacturers and physicians conducting clinical trials—"be forced to continue to use their heads and judgement" in carrying out the guidelines. Dr. Liston of the HPB concurs with Ms. Begin's attitude, adding that existing regulations do not have major deficiencies.[19] HPB officials repeatedly told the Montreal *Gazette* that they have opted for a co-operative and "open door policy" with Canadian drug company officials instead of a tough adversarial stance.[20] They were also proud of their cozy relations with representatives of Canadian drug subsidiaries of U.S. companies. "We try to work things out together," said one official. This approach was viewed as "naive and very dangerous" by many American consumer advocates and sources within the U.S. Food and Drug Administration, especially when Canadian branch plant operations are controlled by foreign head offices.[21] One senior FDA source emphasized: "The companies will try to get away with everything they can. None of this nice guy stuff is going to work when millions of dollars in potential profits are involved."[22]

Added to these disturbing inadequacies in Canadian regulations concerning drug testing and approval is the inadequate level of staffing of the Bureau of Human Prescription Drugs. Since 1971 the workload of the Bureau has increased 10 percent annually, but the number of personnel has remained static at 80. Dr. Henderson is perturbed by these facts. "Productivity has increased but people are getting edgy," he says, adding that there is reason to fear that employees "will soon start cutting corners" when evaluating safety and efficacy data on new products.[23]

Drug companies are under no obligation to inform the HPB of adverse drug effects that occur outside Canada, even though the same drugs may be in the testing phase or on the market in this country. In 1970, Upjohn told the U.S. Food and Drug Administration that Dalacin C (Upjohn's brand of the antibiotic clindamycin) was suspected of causing a potentially fatal form of diarrhoea called pseudomembranous enterocolitis. By 1972 Upjohn was warning American doctors of the link between Dalacin C and enterocolitis. Canadian drug officials were not told of this problem until 1974 and Canadian doctors were officially informed only in December of that year, a full two years after their American counterparts. In 1980, Selacryn, a drug marketed by Smith Kline and French for use in treating high blood pressure was withdrawn from the U.S. market eight months after it first appeared. In that time it had caused 510 cases of liver damage and 34 deaths. Fortunately, Selacryn was never marketed in Canada, but it was undergoing premarketing testing here. Canadian officials learned of the cases of liver disease and deaths associated with Selacryn only after the American ban.[24]

The most recent example of non-reporting involved Oraflex (benoxaprofen) an anti-arthritic product from Lilly.[25] In 1980, this drug was marketed in Britain. Shortly after the drug appeared on the shelves of British pharmacies, Lilly's British subsidiary informed British health officials of the first of eight deaths resulting from suspected adverse reactions to Oraflex between May 1, 1981, and January 1982. In February 1982, nine months after the first known British death, Oraflex was evaluated by the HPB as safe for use in Canada. In its submission, Lilly did not mention the eight deaths in Britain connected to Oraflex. Other omissions from Lilly's initial documentation included: suspected adverse drug reaction reports compiled in 1981 by U.S. doctors participating in Lilly sponsored tests with Oraflex; and the results of a Lilly sponsored study presented in Paris in June 1981 showing that dosages of Oraflex had to be modified for elderly patients.

Although Canadian officials approved the drug in February 1982, Lilly decided to delay the marketing until that September. The HPB's first indication of the dangers of Oraflex surfaced in early May 1982. According to Dr. Liston of the HPB, Lilly had told officials "about seven deaths in Britain. It was just before some deaths were described in the British Medical Journal." At the same time, Lilly gave the HPB a summary of the data presented at the June 1981 Paris symposium. (It took the HPB another month to locate the full study in the pages of the *European Journal of Rheumatology and Inflammation*.) The combination of the information in the Paris symposium and the deaths reported in the *British Medical Journal* led to the HPB putting a ban on any promotion or marketing of Oraflex. The drug remained on sale in Britain and the U.S. until August 4, 1982, and by the time it was finally removed from the market it was inconclusively linked to 61 deaths in Britain and 11 in the U.S. Had Oraflex been marketed in Canada it would have required a ministerial order to remove it from sale.

Federal authorities believe that Eli Lilly Canada, the Canadian subsidiary, was kept in the dark by its corporate parent about the problems with Oraflex. Lilly Canada is not saying much. "We've been directed to not talk about it [Oraflex]," said Dr. Robert Dolman, medical director at Lilly Canada. At Lilly corporate headquarters in Indianapolis, Indiana, Robert Culp said: "Until the whole review process [of Oraflex] has been completed, we can't answer specific questions about Canada . . . It is the policy of Eli Lilly and Company worldwide to comply fully with all requirements of the law and applicable regulations."

In late 1982 the U.S. FDA was examining an internal report which recommended that Lilly be prosecuted for failing to report adverse reactions to Oraflex. At the same time in Canada officials at the HPB were refusing to say whether any legal action would be taken against the Canadian subsidiary or its U.S. parent.

In light of what transpired over the years with Dalacin C, Selacryn and Oraflex, it is hard for the public to take Guy Beauchemin of the PMAC seriously when he says that "there should be a moral obligation to report all data."[26]

Once a drug enters the market, it remains classified as a "new drug" at the discretion of the HPB, until it has been in use "for sufficient time and in sufficient quantity" to assure the HPB that it is "safe and effective." Usually this process takes about five years. Once the drug loses its "new drug" status, other companies may produce it without furnishing any further data to the HPB. Should another company wish to produce the drug prior to this time, it would have to repeat all the studies. In effect, the originating company has at least a five year monopoly on the product.

While a drug is still classified as a new drug, the HPB requires manufacturers to monitor the experience with the drug and to report any failures to meet the specifications established in the submission, any unexpected side effects, injury, toxicity or sensitivity reactions, or any unusual failure of the drug to produce its expected pharmacological activity. (This reporting obligation only applies to incidents that occur in Canada.) Any failure on the part of the manufacturer to make such a report can result in the withdrawal of the drug from the market. However, this requirement is dropped once a drug loses its new drug status, that is, once it becomes an "old drug." At that point, the HPB has no authority to prohibit a drug from being sold solely because the manufacturer may have failed to report adverse reactions. It would apear therefore that the practical effect of classifying a drug as "established as safe and effective" is to relieve the manufacturer from the need to report new problems with the drug, and to make official scrutiny of the drug's performance that much more difficult. The result is that the HPB may not be furnished with vital information, in effect allowing the "older established" drugs to go unmonitored.[27] (As of October 1982, Dr. Henderson had not released any drugs from their new drug status since he became director of the Bureau of Human Prescription Drugs in 1977.)

There is a Drug Adverse Reaction Program headed by Dr. Edward Napke, chief of the Product Related Disease Division, Bureau of Epidemiology, in Ottawa, which receives reports of adverse reactions sent in by doctors. However, since the system of reporting is voluntary, the program receives only about 4,000 reports out of an estimated 400,000 annual adverse drug reactions. Since the 1960s Dr. Napke has been calling for a much more exhaustive and active approach to post-marketing surveillance, but as of 1982 he had a staff of five and a total operating budget of $21,000.[28]

The HPB does have other means available to regulate the sale of old drugs. If there is evidence that all brands of a particular drug are dangerous, the HPB can label it a "prohibited drug" and ban it from the market. The most famous example of a banned drug is thalidomide. If evidence suggests that a particular brand of a drug is unsafe, the manufacturing company can be requested to submit proof that its drug is safe. If such proof is not forthcoming within a specified period of time (the amount of time depending upon how dangerous the drug is thought to be) then an order from the Minister of Health can forbid the sale of the drug. In 1977, this provision was used to stop the sale of contaminated batches of Vasodilan made by Canada Packers. Although federal drug inspectors can seize drugs that violate the Food and Drugs Act and regulations, only a ministerial order can force a company to recall a drug. However, the use of these other control mechanisms relies on learning about problems connected with old drugs. Therefore, the absence of a compulsory reporting system for incidents involving these drugs weakens these regulatory powers by limiting the flow of information to the HPB.

The only other control the government has over drugs on the market is found in an article of the Food and Drugs Act forbidding false advertising. Unfortunately, this regulation, in place since July 1, 1954, is very poorly enforced. During the most recent five-year period, ending in 1983, there was not a single conviction for false advertising of prescription drugs. The HPB makes only informal spot checks on advertising rather than continuously reviewing ads to ensure that the prohibition against false and misleading claims is respected. "It's not our policy to treat advertising as the definitive source of information with respect to drugs," said Dr. Liston in 1977 as justification for the loose monitoring of drug ads in medical journals.[29] In the event of convictions, the penalties range from $500 and/or three months in jail for a summary conviction, to $5,000 and/or three years in jail for a conviction upon indictment. In practice, the jail sentences are never imposed and the fines are hardly substantial enough to act as a deterrent.

Had this regulation been better enforced, about 90 Canadian children might have been spared the birth deformities caused by thalidomide. When thalidomide entered the Canadian market on April 1, 1961, it was already known that it could cause polyneuritis, an inflammation of the nervous system which can result in permanent damage to that system of the body. From the beginning, the company marketing thalidomide, the American multinational William S. Merrell Company, included a warning about polyneuritis in the prescribing instructions; the warning, however, was formulated in a misleading way, stating that the symptoms disappeared immediately upon withdrawal of the drug. This misrepresentation of the facts was retained in all instructions for the eleven months the drug was on the market.[30] If Canadian doctors had known that the effects could be permanent, the use of thalidomide would almost certainly have been curtailed.

The thalidomide experience also provides an example of government reluctance to remove a drug once it is on the market. By the end of November 1961, Merrell had learned that thalidomide could cause malformations in foetuses (a condition called phocomelia) and communicated this finding to the Food and Drug Directorate (FDD). On December 5, under FDD direction, Merrell sent out a letter to all physicians in Canada warning against the use of thalidomide by pregnant women and women who might become pregnant. As more information came in about cases of phocomelia, the FDD requested that a second letter be sent to doctors, and this was done on February 21, 1962. In some countries this letter would have been superfluous. The drug had already been removed from the market in West Germany at the end of November 1961, and by mid-December in Britain. Why was it still being sold in Canada? According to Dr. C.A. Morrell, head of the FDD, Canada "had no cases yet" of phocomelia, and the evidence for a connection between thalidomide and phocomelia "is only statistical." Dr. Morrell was able to make this statement despite mounting evidence of the connection. An article documenting the relationship had recently appeared in *The Lancet*, a major British medical journal.

It took Dr. Morrell until March 2, 1962, to order the complete withdrawal of thalidomide from the Canadian market. At the end of August of that year the Rokeah Pharmaceutical Association in Toronto sent Dr. Morrell a letter expressing concern over the laxity of his department in taking action with regard to thalidomide. Dr. Morrell's reply was: "Existing regulations do not authorize us to prohibit the sale of a drug in Canada." Even after he did act, Dr. Morrell was not truly convinced that thalidomide was dangerous. After receiving letters from physicians who were upset about the withdrawal, Dr. Morrell responded on April 27, 1962:

I think if the medical profession would take a stand, such as you have taken, that there is every possibility that thalidomide could indeed be reinstated on the Canadian market and to this end I would encourage you to urge strongly your colleagues to express themselves to us on this question.

In conclusion I feel certain that if the majority of Canadian physicians want to have this drug, it will make a strong case for its reinstatement.[31]

Five months after thalidomide was removed from the market, F. Hugh Wadey, the Canadian managing director of Merrell, claimed in a letter addressed to doctors: "At no time did Kevadon [the company's name for thalidomide] literature suggest usage of the drug for nauseas of pregnancy." However, in a brochure called "Kevadon-Merrell safe, sound sleep," we find the following claim under the heading "Safety Data": "Nulsen [Dr. Ray O. Nulsen] administered 100 mg. Kevadon to 81 expectant mothers and [Dr. A.P.] Blasiu to 160 nursing mothers. In both instances all of the babies were born or nursed without any abnormalities or harmful effects from the medication."[32] There can be no doubt, based on that quote, that Merrell not only knew that thalidomide was being used in pregnant women, but that Merrell was also, at least implicitly, encouraging such usage. It was later learned that Dr. Nulsen's study was highly flawed;[33] here again is evidence that lax enforcement by the HPB of advertising claims contributed to the thalidomide tragedy.

If any more proof of government inaction is needed, consider the cases of Albamycin T, sold in Canada by Upjohn, and Entero-Vioform, made by CIBA. Albamycin T used to be available in the United States under the name Panalba. It is a combination of two antibiotics, tetracycline and novobiocin. When it was sold in the U.S., it was one of Upjohn's most popular items. Panalba was one of more than 4,000 drugs evaluated by the National Academy of Sciences and National Research Council panels in the U.S. In their report on Panalba, and similar fixed-dose combination drugs, the members concluded unanimously that these products "no longer belong in the therapeutic armamentarium." According to the panels, about one in every five patients who receives the novobiocin component of Panalba would be expected to have an allergic or hypersensitivity type of reaction. Also, a smaller proportion of patients "experience temporary but very severe liver damage as a result of the novobiocin component," and a "still smaller number" suffer blood disorders. On the question of whether drugs such as Panalba should be removed from the market, the head of the panel, Dr. Heinz F. Eichenwald of the University of Texas, said: "There are few instances in medicine when so many experts have agreed unanimously and without reservation."[34] Upjohn launched a fierce battle in the U.S. to save Panalba, but was eventually forced to withdraw the drug in 1970. In Canada, in 1984, Albamycin T is still being sold.

In Japan, Entero-Vioform, marketed there under the name Ouiform, has caused thousands of cases of a nerve-paralysing disease which can result in blindness and paralysis of the arms and legs. The drug, used to treat diarrhoea, is banned in Norway and Sweden, and was "voluntarily" withdrawn from the American market by CIBA. The voluntary withdrawal from the U.S. came about because the U.S. government had decided that the drug was, in fact, not useful for treating diarrhoea. The Department of Health and Welfare in Canada, however, could see no reason to ban Entero-Vioform. In defence of the drug, CIBA representatives said: "We remain convinced that it is safe and effective when used in accordance with our recommendations."[35] (In November 1982, as a result of intense worldwide pressure, CIBA-Geigy announced that it was progressively withdrawing Entero-Vioform from world markets. Canadian stocks of the drug should be exhausted by the end of 1983.)

The one major exception to the government's general timidity in imposing restrictions on drugs already on the market involves the amphetamines.[36] In the late 1960s there was increasing concern over the widespread prescribing of amphetamines,[37] and "speed freaks" were well known and all too common.[38] All the amphetamines used in Canada were, and still are, imported from the U.S. Even before the government acted, however, the amount entering the country had dropped from 1055.2 kilograms in 1966 to 283.7 kilograms in 1970 and 95.0 kilograms in 1972. However, in 1972, there were still 1.92 million prescriptions filled for amphetamines, representing a retail value of $1.8 million.[39]

On January 1, 1973, it became illegal to prescribe amphetamines as "pep pills" and diet pills, leaving only six medical conditions for which the drug could legally be used.[40] But even before this ban became effective, the drug companies were up in arms. One company sent a telegram to then-Health and Welfare Minister Marc

Lalonde protesting the "undue haste and implementation of unwarranted and harmful legislation." Not surprisingly, the telegram came from Smith Kline and French, the company most directly involved in Canada in the research and development of amphetamines. William Robson, vice-president of the company, said: "If a doctor feels a drug should be of some benefit to a patient, he should be able to prescribe it. Don't put it in a straitjacket."[41] Mr. Robson claimed he was not concerned with protection of the amphetamine market but with the "principles involved." In this case, he was probably being honest. While $1.8 million in retail sales is nothing to be ignored, Mr. Robson was probably genuinely worried that the government might become more aggressive in regulating the uses of prescription drugs. But, as we can see from the Albamycin T and Entero-Vioform stories, he need not have been worried.

Control of Prices

The earliest attempts by the federal government to lower drug prices involved abolishing the 12 percent sales tax at the manufacturers' level and reducing the tariff on imported drugs from 20 to 15 percent. Neither of these steps, taken in 1967, had any substantial effect on prices. Since then, the effort to reduce prices has been limited to an attempt to increase price competition within the industry. Compulsory licensing was one step in this direction, while another was the Pharmaceutical Industry Development Assistance Program (PIDA). (In 1977, PIDA was replaced by the Enterprise Development Program.) Under PIDA, a $2 million fund was established for issuing low interest loans to assist smaller Canadian drug manufacturers in reorganizing their manufacturing, marketing, distributing and research operations. The stated aim of the program was to enable Canadian firms to compete more successfully with the multinational giants.

Perhaps the federal government's most ambitious project to reduce costs has been the drug quality assurance program, known as QUAD. (When the program's name was subsequently changed, the "A" in QUAD came to stand for assessment rather than assurance.) Started in 1971, this was a four-fold program involving: drug analysis; inspection of manufacturers' plants; efficacy tests and assessment of manufacturers' claims; and an information system to advise pharmacists, doctors and the public of test results. Generic and brand name drugs were to be compared for quality and effectiveness and the results published in a periodical sent free to all physicians. The government seemed to be taking a no-nonsense approach. Ron Basford, the Minister of Consumer Affairs, issued pugnacious resolutions: "I don't mind at all a good knock-down drag-out political fight," he said.[42] "One way or another, we'll get them [high drug prices] down."[43] The PMAC companies' initial response to the QUAD program was to boycott it and refuse to submit to voluntary intensive examination.[44]

Rx Bulletin, the journal which published the results of the QUAD testing, was generally well received by doctors. It also published objective evaluations of new drugs, thereby giving physicians a critical and unbiased opinion as a counterweight to the advertising of the companies. In October 1973, the government claimed that the journal's rising costs necessitated a switch from monthly to bimonthly publication, and in June 1975, again under the claim of rising costs, publication was abruptly terminated. It is disturbing that the passing of *Rx Bulletin* seemed to go unmourned by organized medicine. Neither the editorial pages nor the correspondence section of either the *Canadian Medical Association Journal* or the *Canadian Family Physician* made any mention of the event.

Federal programs like QUAD have usually provoked a hostile reaction from the pharmaceutical industry. In 1972, Dr. William Wigle, president of the PMAC, was decrying "discriminatory actions" by the federal government against the industry, in this case the introduction of compulsory licensing, which, in his words, had created in international circles "an atmosphere of insecurity and lack of confidence in further investments in Canada."[45]

The various cost-control schemes originated by the provinces have all shared basically the same direction as those by the federal government. That is, they are aimed either at stimulating price competition, or at taking better advantage of the price competition that already exists. In addition, there have been direct subsidy programs to help reduce drug costs to different sections of the population. (See Table 12-1.)

In 1962, Alberta became the first province to allow a pharmacist to substitute a generic or name brand equivalent for the drug named in the prescription. In practice, this meant that a pharmacist could give a patient a drug costing less than the one prescribed by the physician. The PMAC replied by having an article published in the

Canadian Medical Association Journal disparaging the quality of generic drugs.[46] CIBA unsuccessfully challenged the legislation in the courts.

In 1970, the Ontario government, under public pressure to do something about drug prices, and with a provincial election on the horizon, announced its first program aimed at lowering drug costs, PARCOST (Prescriptions At Reasonable COST). There were two basic ingredients in the program. The first was the *PARCOST Comparative Drug Index*, supplied free to all doctors and pharmacists, which listed comparable drugs, in order of price, according to generic name and supplier or manufacturer. The second component was an agreement by participating pharmacists (participation was voluntary) not to charge more than $2.00 for filling a prescription. (By 1983, the maximum dispensing fee had risen to $4.65.) In 1972, the government added a provision allowing substitution of an equivalent drug for the one prescribed, unless the doctor specifically prohibited substitution.[47] The government was hoping that doctors and pharmacists would consult the index and use the lowest priced brand of whatever drug was necessary for that particular patient.

PARCOST was not a particularly aggressive scheme, since nothing was compulsory. Nevertheless, the drug industry felt threatened, and the marketing director of Lilly predicted that the end result of the program would be "minimum acceptable quality, reliability and service."[48] Some drug companies were reportedly supplying doctors with rubber stamps and labels saying "no substitution" to use on their prescriptions. In 1975, the *PARCOST Comparative Drug Index* was combined with the *Drug Benefit Formulary* into a publication which listed about 1,200 drugs. Drugs for the old, poor and disabled were now paid for by a second provincial program, the Drug Benefit Plan, provided that the drugs were in the *Formulary*. However, there was a catch: if the *Drug Benefit Formulary* also listed equivalents to the drug prescribed, then the government would only reimburse the pharmacist for the value of the least expensive drug included in the listing. The PMAC claimed that the *Drug Benefit Formulary* was "a possible threat to a viable drug manufacturing industry," and recommended to the government that it abandon the *Formulary*.[49] Such a move would not have been politically possible, and was never taken seriously by the Conservative government.

As of 1983, PARCOST was almost a dead program, with only 9 percent of the province's pharmacies participating, compared to a high of nearly 60 percent in 1972, soon after the program was launched. The main reason for the exodus from PARCOST appears to be the maximum allowable prescribing fee of $4.65, which is seen by pharmacists as being too low to be economically viable. Pharmacists who are not in PARCOST generally charge a dispensing fee of about $5.00. However, the $4.65 maximum dispensing fee has further implications. Under the terms of the legislation governing PARCOST, any pharmacist who substitutes a generic drug for a brand name drug, regardless of voluntary participation in PARCOST, *must* do so under the rules of PARCOST and that means that the dispensing fee of $4.65 applies. Therefore, to escape the restriction on the size of the dispensing fee, pharmacists are avoiding substitution wherever possible.[50] (Substitution is never mandatory under the scheme, but for people covered by the Drug Benefit Plan pharmacists are paid only the cost of the least expensive equivalent listed in the *Formulary* and therefore have no reason not to substitute the equivalent that they can purchase the cheapest.) Without substitution by pharmacists, consumers do not necessarily receive the cheapest drugs and end up suffering financially. Also, prescriptions are still generally written using the trade names of the products of the large multinationals. Without substitution the fortunes of the smaller, generally Canadian-owned, companies will suffer since their brands will not be dispensed. If these companies, which sell the generic products, go under, there will be less competition for the multinationals and drug prices may begin to rise.

In 1972 the Klass Report was published in Manitoba.[51] The New Democratic Party government of the time was embarking on a series of social welfare reforms and had come out with a study highly critical of many aspects of the drug industry. Some reasonably progressive recommendations were included on methods for controlling the prices of drugs. Highlighted in the report was a recommendation to set up a committee to prepare a Manitoba *Formulary* of equivalent brand name drugs along with the respective prices of these medications (similar in effect to Ontario's *Drug Benefit Formulary*). A Crown corporation was to have been established for the purpose of province-wide central purchasing, and distribution to pharmacies, of the most widely used drugs on this list. Pharmacists would have been required to use these centrally purchased drugs instead of more costly equivalents. In the end, the government did not go ahead with bulk purchasing, but did pass a law making it mandatory for pharmacists to substitute cheaper drugs for those named on prescriptions, unless prohibited by the physician. Furthermore, the substitute could not be sold at a price higher than that of the lowest priced equivalent drug. After this legislation passed, the president of the PMAC made a thinly veiled threat to the Manitoba government:

> It will remain to be seen how much value would be put on the Manitoba market by research-oriented companies. It is each company's decision whether the size of their Manitoba market will merit the cost of properly servicing that market. If they can't meet the prices they could be forced out of business. In the long run, the patients of the future will suffer since the research-oriented firms have been responsible for about 90 per cent of the new drug discoveries made in the last 35 years.[52]

During the 1970s, other provinces initiated programs to control drug costs to the consumer. Saskatchewan introduced North America's first universal drug coverage program guaranteeing that the cost to the consumer of any prescribed drug on a government approved list of about 1,200 would be no more than $2.00. (By 1983, this co-payment fee had risen to $3.75.)[53] Saskatchewan also picked up on the recommendation in the Klass Report and implemented a scheme of province-wide purchasing for over 100 high volume drugs. Manitoba brought in a plan to pay 80 percent of the cost of prescription drugs after the first $50. (By 1980, the deductible was $75.) British Columbia enacted legislation similar to Manitoba's, but with a $100 deductible (increased to $125 in 1983 and $175 in 1984).

By mid-1983, all provinces except Prince Edward Island allowed voluntary substitution by pharmacists. Most provinces also have plans which pay part or all of the cost of prescription drugs for people over 65 years of age. By October 1975, 88 percent of the elderly in Canada were protected against major drug purchases under provincial programs. Overall, by 1979, almost 44 percent of prescriptions filled in Canada were covered under a government plan, and almost 20 percent more were paid for by private, third party insurance plans.[54] (See Table 12-1.)

The PMAC's response to government plans for price reduction (as opposed to insurance plans that would cover drug costs) has been typical and predictable:

> Such well-intentioned policies presented disincentives to the further extension of an industry oriented towards innovation, investigation and development in Canada...It is an unfortunate observation that many were, and continue to be based as much on emotional or political factors as on a careful consideration of objective evidence and we have consequently witnessed the "stretching of the skin of science to fit the drum of political necessity."[55]

Representatives of some PMAC member companies have admitted that questionable drugs are being promoted harder in Canada than elsewhere to make up for profits they perceive to be lost as a result of current federal and provincial laws designed to reduce drug prices.[56]

In the last chapter the effects of compulsory licensing on drug prices were examined and found to be at best limited. While it is obvious that certain provincial plans have reduced or eliminated out-of-pocket expenses to consumers, especially the elderly and those on welfare, the cost has merely been shifted from the individual to all taxpayers. The question remains as to whether or not provincial programs have succeeded in significantly lowering the cost of drugs to society as a whole.

There have been two attempts to examine the impact of PARCOST on drug prices. The first, in 1973, concluded that an overall savings to the consumer of $5 to $8 million had been realized for the preceding year as a result of the program.[57] A second report appeared in 1981 and examined the movement of prices on 41 drugs over the period 1970 to 1977. Of the 41 drugs, 36 were interchangeable, meaning that they were manufactured by more than one company; for the remaining five drugs, only one brand was available. The average price decreased for 27 of the 36 interchangeable drugs and the decrease was statistically significant in 22 cases. In five of the nine cases where the average price rose, the change was also significant. For the five non-interchangeable drugs the average prices all increased. The authors of the study concluded that "the PARCOST program helped bring about a decrease in average drug prices in Ontario."[58] Encouraging as these results may be, remember that there is effective price competition for only 138 of the 1,335 products listed in Ontario's *Drug Benefit Formulary*, and with PARCOST in decline it seems questionable whether even these savings will continue.

Since 1980 most provincial governments have knowingly allowed their efforts to reduce drug costs to be undermined through a process known in the trade as "discount pricing" or "discount competition."[59] Under a provincial drug plan, drug "A" will be listed in the provincial formulary as selling for, say $10.00 per 100 pills. That is the amount that the pharmacist is supposed to have paid the drug company for 100 pills and that is the amount the pharmacist will be reimbursed by the government if the pharmacist dispenses the 100 pills to someone covered by the province's drug program. The pharmacist's profit theoretically derives from the dispensing fee.

Under discount pricing, the drug company will sell its product for say $2.00 per 100 instead of the listed price of $10.00. The government still pays the pharmacist $10.00 and the pharmacist pockets the extra $8.00 as pure profit. The drug companies are willing to discount their drugs because the bigger the pharmacists' profit margin, the more likely they are to dispense that particular company's brand of drug "A," thereby increasing the company's market share. In fact, it is even in the interests of the drug companies to inflate the prices for their products listed in the provincial formularies because the larger the profit margin for the pharmacist the greater the incentive to use the company's brand. Meanwhile the companies continue to lobby against government intervention.

Ontario officials admit that discount pricing is costing the provincial drug plan at least $10 million a year and the total over-charging across Canada is estimated at between $40 and $60 million annually. (A 1983 study done by Winnipeg's Associated Health Planners for the Saskatchewan government concluded that inefficiently run provincial drug plans have boosted the drug bill across Canada by $200 million annually.)[60] Consumers not covered by government drug plans also suffer financially because the inflated prices in the provincial formularies effectively set the price charged to cash customers and to private drug insurance plans.

The practice of discount pricing is not just confined to the multinationals but is actively engaged in by generic companies. Earl Coulson, head of Ontario's drug benefit plan, says, "The company with the lowest price in the formulary doesn't get any business... The generics use this approach as a marketing tool; if

Table 12-1: Provincial Drug Plans

PROVINCE	PLAN AND COVERAGE
Alberta	No official drug reimbursement program, but drug benefits for the elderly, social assistance beneficiaries and those receiving widow's/widower's pensions are administered through the provincial Blue Cross Plan. There are no user fees for welfare recipients, but those 65 and over pay a minimum of $1.00 or 20 percent of the cost of the prescription, whichever is more.
British Columbia	Pharmacare Plan. It covers all the residents of the province. The elderly, welfare recipients and residents of nursing homes do not pay anything, but for all others, individuals or families, there is a $175 deductible in addition to a 20 percent co-payment of costs above this amount.
Manitoba	Pharmacare Plan. It covers all the residents of the province. Social assistance recipients and nursing home residents make no contributions. Those under 65, individuals or families, have a $75 deductible plus a 20 percent co-payment of drug costs above this amount. Those over 65 have a $50 deductible plus the 20 percent co-payment.
Newfoundland	Indigent Drug Program. It covers all those receiving social assistance benefits and those over 65 on full or partial guaranteed income supplement—38,000 people in 1977-78. There are no user fees for those on welfare but seniors pay the pharmacist's dispensing fee.
New Brunswick	Prescription Drug Program consisting of the Health Services Program for social assistance

Table 12-1: Provincial Drug Plans

PROVINCE	PLAN AND COVERAGE
	recipients and the Prescription Drug Program for people 65 and older, people with cystic fibrosis and nursing home residents. In 1976-77, 383,082 prescriptions were dispensed under the Health Services Program. Drugs are dispensed without cost but there is a user charge of $1.00 for those under eighteen and $2.00 for everyone else. There were 815,534 prescriptions dispensed in 1976-77 under the Prescription Drug Program to those over 65. Seniors pay a $3.00 dispensing fee for each of the first ten prescriptions per year. Nursing home residents pay nothing.
Nova Scotia	Pharmacare. In 1976-77, it covered 73,731 people 65 years or older and those classified as disabled. Drugs are dispensed free of cost and there are no user charges.
Ontario	Drug Benefit Plan. It covers people 65 or over, or recipients of family benefits assistance, general welfare assistance, extended care benefits, home care benefits, vocational rehabilitation assistance and homes for special care services — a total of 1.35 million eligible people in 1982-83. There are no user charges, but the drugs must be listed on the government formulary in order to be covered.
Prince Edward Island	No official drug reimbursement program, but prescriptions dispensed by the government's central pharmacy are free to diabetics and people receiving social assistance.

Table 12-1: Provincial Drug Plans

PROVINCE	PLAN AND COVERAGE
Quebec	Le Programme de Medicaments. In 1977 it covered 963,018 people 65 or over or receiving social assistance. (Some people 60 to 64 are also now covered.) The drugs are free and there are no user charges, but the drugs have to be included in the government formulary in order to be covered.
Saskatchewan	Prescription Drug Plan. It covers all residents of the province, but the only drugs paid for are those included in the government formulary. In 1983, for drugs in the formulary, the average cost to the consumer was $3.75. There is no cost to welfare recipients in nursing homes or to those with chronic illnesses.

Adapted from: R.F. Badgley and R.D. Smith, *User Charges for Health Services,* Ontario Council of Health, Toronto, 1979; M. Gerson, G. Gougeon and J. Barolet, "The Price of Prescription Drugs," *Protect Yourself,* June 1984, p. 12.

they can get a high price in the formulary, they can use the price margin as a selling point to the pharmacists."

Saskatchewan and British Columbia are the two provinces that have escaped discount pricing. In both places the pharmacists are only reimbursed for their actual acquisition costs rather than the artificial prices listed in formularies. In addition, in Saskatchewan, high volume drugs are purchased centrally on a tender system which eliminates the possibility of discount pricing on these medicines. The 1983 survey by Associated Health Planners documented the disparity in prices different provinces paid for their drugs. Saskatchewan and British Columbia had the lowest costs while Alberta consistently paid the most.

Some provinces are planning to move to the system used in B.C.

and Saskatchewan. According to Jack Hare, executive director of the Nova Scotia Health Services Commission, by 1984 the 200 pharmacists in Nova Scotia will be paid only their acquisition costs. Ontario is also going to restrict payments to pharmacists, but only on the products of generic manufacturers, not on the products of the multinational that initially introduced the drug. One example of this discrimination between manufacturers is the case of cimetidine. At present, pharmacists pay $9.00 per 100 tablets from generic manufacturers but receive $19.95 from the government. Under Ontario's proposed reforms the pharmacists would receive only $9.50. Tagamet, the original brand of cimetidine from Smith Kline and French, lists in Ontario's formulary for $26.54 per 100, but pharmacists can purchase Tagamet for $13.00 from the company. Even after the payment for generic cimetidine drops to $9.50, Tagamet will continue to list for $26.54. The price margin on generic cimetidine will be $0.50 versus $13.54 on Tagamet. It is obvious which company's brand pharmacists will be dispensing. This discrimination among manufacturers is intentional. "The originator, in our view, deserves special consideration. They did develop the product, test it and market it," said Ron LeNeveu, assistant deputy minister of health in Ontario.

The federal government has failed to ensure that the drugs used by Canadians are safe and effective. Hundreds of products on the market have never been tested for safety or efficacy; drugs such as Albamycin T, banned or withdrawn in other countries, continue to be sold here; research is not monitored and as a result the government has no way of knowing whether the results reported are valid. The basic deficiency in Canada's regulations seems to be, to repeat the words of the Montreal *Gazette*, the "implicit faith in the drug companies' testing and marketing ethics, and in the free enterprise system." It is this faith which underlies the legislation setting up the Health Protection Branch.

Federal and provincial efforts to lower the cost of drugs have been only marginally successful. Manipulation of many provincial drug plans cost Canadians tens of millions of dollars annually. In order to achieve significant reductions in the prices of drugs, we must have programs that directly challenge the power of the multinationals.

Proposals to place the HPB in a more adversarial postion with respect to the companies and to challenge the market power of the multinationals will be found in Chapter 14.

Chapter 13
Medicalization:
The Ideology of Drug Use

Controlling the quality and the cost of drugs are both important goals, but even safe cheap drugs still have to be used properly. The use, or misuse, of drugs is an issue on which the medical establishment—doctors, organized medicine and the drug companies—hold strong views. They assert that the way to control the misuse of drugs is to let individual physicians be free to use whatever drug they think is best for their patient. Therefore, the control of physicians' prescribing habits is left in the hands of medical institutions or medical societies, those groups deemed knowledgeable enough to pronounce on what is or is not proper prescribing practice.

Hospitals usually operate their pharmacies on a formulary system. A committee of doctors and pharmacists draws up a list of drugs which constitutes the stock of the pharmacy. All doctors working in the hospital automatically agree that if they write an order for a drug, the hospital pharmacist will dispense whatever brand of that particular drug the hospital is using. This system is essentially a form of mandatory substitution. In order to establish and update a formulary, the merits and demerits of drugs have to be studied. This serves as a method of continuing medical education in therapeutics for those involved. By its nature, a formulary restricts the range of drugs available to a physician, and usually excludes drugs that are of questionable value. Doctors can have drugs administered that are not included in the formulary, but they have to justify the need for them. The system tends to ensure that doctors are knowledgeable about drugs they wish added to the formulary.

Hospitals have other methods available for controlling indiscriminate prescribing. For example, widespread use of certain potent antibiotics can lead to the development of bacteria that are resistant to these drugs. Some hospitals, therefore, try to control their use by limiting prescribing privileges to certain senior physicians.

While provincial formularies exist, such as those in Saskatchewan and Ontario, they generally use less rigorous criteria for including drugs than do hospital formularies. Furthermore, not all provinces have formularies and even in those that do doctors are not limited to prescribing from drugs listed in the formulary. In fact, doctors in office practice are free to prescribe whatever they want, although narcotic prescribing is monitored. And doctors receive a lifetime licence to practice. There are no formal requirements for them to keep their drug knowledge up to date. If things degenerate badly enough, doctors can be charged with malpractice, or have their licences suspended, but these are rare occurrences. Many conscientious doctors recognize the need to stay current with drug therapy, and there are many ways of doing that. Hospitals and medical schools run seminars; there are continuing medical education courses; hospital pharmacies publish bulletins about drugs; there are journal articles; and there is *The Medical Letter*. Medical associations encourage their members to take advantage of these educational opportunities. It is also common to find talks or workshops on drug therapy at the meetings of these groups. But neither the courses sponsored by organized medicine, nor the articles read by individual doctors in *The Medical Letter*, nor the formularies used by hospitals and provinces are ultimately going to control the misuse of drugs. There is much more involved than just keeping doctors informed.

By confining the problem of drug misuse to the question of the knowledge of the physician, a second, and more complex aspect of the problem is ignored. In a deliberate effort to expand the market for their products, drug companies are literally creating new diseases. In the opening chapter on Valium and Ritalin, we saw how the industry tries, with a good deal of success, to redefine societal problems as medical diseases, thus rendering them treatable with drug therapy. Advertisements advise a doctor to prescribe Vistaril (hydroxyzine pamoate) for a young child who is anxious about going to school or to the dentist; or encourage Tofranil (imipramine hydrochloride) for parents who are depressed because their daughter has run away from home.[1] In this chapter, we will also see how medical diseases, such as hypertension (high blood pressure), are being treated with drugs although the root cause of hypertension seems to be the social, political and economic factors associated with modern industrial society, factors which are left entirely untouched. The process of redefining the nature and/or cause of a problem to bring it under the umbrella of medicine is what is meant by the term "medicalization."

Medicalization is not just a ploy of the drug industry. It is, in fact, just a specific example of a more general trend in capitalist countries. Modern capitalist society is increasingly creating a spectrum of problems that it cannot solve. Partly to obscure the fact that the present economic system cannot solve these problems and partly because central to capitalism is the axiom that individuals are the authors of their own fortunes, problems tend to become "individualized." For instance, individualized solutions to the energy crisis require each of us to insulate our homes, turn down the thermostat and buy small cars. Inflation is running high, so we must cut down on consumption, reduce our expectations and ask for smaller wage increases. In medicine, we do not seem to be able to do anything about the high rates of heart disease and cancer, and therefore people are told to start jogging and stop smoking.[2]

These approaches all have some value, but at the same time they ignore essential structural problems in society. In fact, by redirecting the focus onto the individual, they ensure that these problems are never seriously addressed. Certain questions never get asked: Why do we even need private cars? Do monopoly conditions in our present economy have anything to do with inflation? What is it about our society that causes people to smoke and to be physically inactive? Turning the problems back on the individual is just another example of the classic practice of "blaming the victim," a point of view which has soared in popularity over the past decade, as bestselling books by pop psychologists demonstrate. Medicalization is another way of blaming the victim for his or her problems, problems that are socially created.

Medicalizing problems, or removing them from their societal roots, is a process that has its origins in the paradigm of the "specific aetiology" of diseases. This theory developed from the work of Pasteur and Koch, who discovered that disease could be produced by introducing a single specific factor, a virulent microorganism, into a healthy body. From this observation in the field of infectious diseases, the doctrine of specific aetiology spread to all other areas of medicine. As Marc Renaud argues, in this paradigm all diseases are assumed to have a specific cause which can be found by examining the body's biochemical and physiological workings.[3] The insights gained from this theory have substantially contributed to the control of many infectious diseases. But the widespread acceptance of this paradigm in the late nineteenth and early twentieth centuries as "the" approach to illness was at the expense of another, broader theory. The "ecological" view of disease, which was largely forgotten, held that disease was the result of an interplay of forces in the environment and in the individual. "Germs" were only one factor leading to disease. Nutrition could influence an individual's resistance to germs, poor working or housing conditions were also encompassed as causes of sickness in the ecological approach.

Class interest on the part of physicians (that is, identifying with the interests of certain classes and not of others) helped to suppress the ecological paradigm. According to John Powles:

> While the well-to-do physicians proffered their clinical skills to the rich, it was social and preventive medicine that was needed most urgently for the poor. Unfortunately, the prestigious physicians dominated the teaching hospitals and medical education and, therefore, the theoretical and practical development of public health and preventive medicine received little encouragement.[4]

These same physicians enthusiastically received the 1910 Report on Medical Education in the United States and Canada (commonly called the Flexner Report) which secured the triumph of the specific aetiology paradigm. The report advocated making the cornerstone of medical education scientific medicine, one of whose products was the specific aetiology theory.

The Flexner Report was commissioned by the Carnegie Foundation, and the Rockefeller Foundation was responsible for its implementation. It was decidedly in the interests of the capitalist class to back scientific medicine, with all its consequences. A social theory of disease might focus attention on factory conditions and other characteristics of working class life that produce disease. Scientific medicine taught that each disease had a single well defined cause, and that control of the disease could best be achieved by attacking the causative organism or by correcting the function of the diseased part of the body. Medicine was thereby turned into a primarily curative science focusing on the health of individuals. Most forms of preventive medicine that survived, such as immunization, were also individually oriented. Mass public health measures such as a clean water supply and sewage disposal were championed by middle-class reformers, often out of self-interest. As the germ theory of disease gained wide acceptance, they became increasingly aware of how easily disease could be transmitted to them and their children. The domination of curative medicine, fostered by the specific aetiology theory, stimulates the consumption by physicians of increasingly complex equipment and the prescription of an ever-widening number of drugs. In effect, health needs become commodities that can be profitably supplied by capitalist enterprises like the drug industry.[5]

Renaud summarizes the historical process:

> It [the specific aetiology paradigm] transforms the potentially explosive social problems that are diseases and death into discrete and isolable commodities that can be incorporated into the capitalist organization of the economy in the same way as any other commodity on the economic market. In an incredible *tour de force*, it succeeds in providing culturally valued solutions to problems largely created by economic growth, and even makes these solutions to a certain extent profitable for capital accumulation and thus for more economic growth. With scientific medicine, health care has grown into an industry which helps maintain the legitimacy of the social order, and which, in part, creates new sectors of production. With such a paradigm, "society" is epistemologically eliminated as an important element in the etiology of disease, therefore impeding the growth of a consciousness of the harmfulness of economic growth...thus obscuring the extent to which illness depends on socially determined ways of life and on the damaged natural environment—an enlightened consciousness of which would be potentially threatening to the social order.[6]

One example of this process is the disease called hypertension. High blood pressure, either alone, or accompanied by arteriosclerosis, leads to strokes and heart attacks, two major "diseases of civilization." Recent epidemiological studies have shown that in primitive societies, such as that of the Australian bushpeople, blood pressure does not rise with age, contrary to the experience in Western industrialized societies.[7] The problem then becomes one of identifying which of the many differences between these two societies has caused the change in blood pressure patterns. Strong evidence has been gathered implicating the stresses of modern industrial capitalist society as a major contributing factor.[8] According to one researcher, "Our earlier evolution has left us genetically unsuited for life in an industrialized society."[9]

Stress producing mechanisms are integral to a class society.[10] Two primary features of such a society which contribute to stress, and ultimately to hypertension, are community disruption and increased work pressure. Capitalist society uproots people from a rural, extended family and village community. It thrusts them into a hostile, competitive urban environment in which their previous social institutions and reaction patterns make no sense. Adoption of new forms of social organization, such as the nuclear family, help to alleviate some of the stress. But modernization is also characterized by increased breakdown of even the nuclear family through separation, divorce and the practice of placing elderly people in institutions.

Mass unemployment also contributes substantially to community disruption. The worker loses the community of the work environment, and new stresses are placed on the family. Workers can be forced to relocate, either to get a new job or because, with a downturn in the economy, they can no longer afford their current housing.

The continual development of new technology and work organization necessitates multiple work role adjustments. These in turn mean that a high proportion of people experience a lack of fit between their skills and the work position they find themselves in. People who do not have the correct qualifications for their job, or who experience conflicting demands within the job, have been shown to have higher blood pressure than those who do not. Piecework pressure and working to time deadlines both result in elevated blood pressure.

Although stress plays such a key role in the generation of hypertension, most doctors, while acknowledging it as a factor, usually ignore it when it actually comes to treating a patient. Even doctors who do recognize the importance of stress can do no more than try to alter it at the individual level through techniques such as meditation, yoga or self-hypnosis. Furthermore, these methods are often possible only for middle and upper class people. A worker on an assembly line or a clerical worker in an office could hardly find the opportunity during the day to meditate.

Besides stress reduction, it is known that many cases of mild and even moderate hypertension can often be treated successfully by other non-drug methods. These include weight reduction, muscle relaxation and yoga, among others.[11] Unsurprisingly, drug ads never mention these other forms of therapy. But most research, too, ignores them. Instead large amounts of money and scientific talent are devoted to discovering newer and, sometimes, more effective drugs. Concentrating time, money and scientific expertise on drug therapy is done at the expense of other modes of treatment. The other therapies outlined here are less costly to the patient and do not carry the side effects of drugs. However, research into new antihypertensives is a good investment for the drug industry. About 11 percent of the Canadian population over twenty years of age has high blood pressure, by commonly accepted criteria.[12] High blood pressure is a life-long disease and that means life-long pill taking. Also the drug companies know the economics of a physician's practice. With visits lasting an average of ten to fifteen minutes, it is much easier to write a prescription than to start enquiring into a patient's dietary habits or to set up a physical fitness program. Consequently, for the majority of doctors, the treatment of hypertension begins and ends with drugs. By 1977, four of the 25 most frequently prescribed brand name drugs in Canada were those used in the therapy of high blood pressure. (Some of the four are also used in treating other diseases, and their frequent prescribing may, in part, be due to these other uses.)

Clearly, there is a choice to be made in dealing with hypertension: try to change the mechanisms in our society that lead to stress or rely on society to give us a technological solution to the disease. So far, the latter option, in the form of pharmaceuticals, has been chosen. Attempting to treat stress-caused hypertension on an individual basis with drugs is equivalent to giving Valium to women who are upset because their husbands beat them.

By looking at stress in the context of Western capitalist society, I do not mean to imply that stress is non-existent in socialist countries. It is present, and at least in Eastern Europe, results in the same types of problems as in the West.[13] And doctors in socialist countries treat the problems the same as their Western counterparts, that is, they usually use pharmaceuticals. These similarities exist because the two types of societies have much in common. Although socialism has meant state ownership of factories and other means of production, technology and factors related to daily working conditions are patterned on models developed in capitalist countries. The existence of a hierarchial organization in factories or a repetitive, boring routine in manufacturing and office jobs cannot be separated from the technology and values that have created the workplace atmosphere. Therefore, it is not surprising that the social stresses in capitalism are reproduced under socialism.

The reliance on drugs in socialist countries can be similarly understood. Although medical care may be more equitably distributed in Eastern Europe than it is in North America, the basis for that care is the same scientific medicine that we know here in the West. If the ideology of scientific medicine is the same in two societies, then the approach to medical problems and to treatment will be the same.[14] Doctors trained in Eastern Europe may be better at dealing with social problems, and the drugs they use are not made for profit, but treatment is still oriented toward the individual and therefore drugs play a primary role.

No drug is completely specific in its actions. The undesirable effects are conventionally labelled "side effects." The non-specificity of drug action applies equally to psychoactive drugs, those used to treat loneliness, social deviance and other ailments that go by the name of mental illness. According to H.L. Lennard, a California psychiatrist:

> Drugs designed to change experience or behavior alter not only internal body processes, as revealed by the range of possible side effects, but also affect the complex of psychological and social processes connecting the individual to his physical and human environment.[15]

These drugs alter an individual's capacity to feel and to perceive. "To the extent that drugs dull the senses, sedate, numb and immobilize they de-differentiate human experience and behavior," says Lennard.[16] At least until the early 1970s, almost no information had been gathered on the effects of the psychoactive drugs on the interpersonal functioning and social behavior of persons who are "on" such drugs—persons who after all live, love, work, play, make decisions, raise children and have to continue to conduct their lives while under the influence of these drugs.[17]

Why are people willing to take these drugs, often specifically requesting them? Why do people go to doctors for problems that have social or economic roots? The answer to both questions is not easy, but the reasons why people act as they do, just as the reasons why people smoke or are sedentary, have to be rooted in the dominant societal ideology. The way people try to regain their health when they are ill will reflect this ideology.

Medical theory used to view disease as a natural phenomenon which existed apart from individuals and which would become apparent only in the human body. This theory developed in precapitalist society and reflected the values of that society. Therapies associated with this model of disease, such as blood-letting, purging and blistering, were supposed to expel the essence of the disease from the human body and to restore the body to a state of natural balance. Not only were such methods widely used by doctors, but patients demanded that they be used.[18]

A similar situation exists today. The dominant medical paradigm, reflecting the society in general, identifies illness as residing in the individual. In the case of organic diseases, there is an organism that has invaded the body or a biochemical mechanism that is malfunctioning. In the case of social problems, redefined as medical ones, there is an inherent personality flaw in individuals which evokes socially unacceptable conduct. Chronic unemployment is known to lead to depression, and eventually to an increase in the suicide rate,[17] but because the disease has been isolated from its social roots, depressed unemployed workers are deemed to have an individual medical problem and are treated with a tricyclic antidepressant.

The limitations imposed on women by the built-in sexism in our society, whether in the home or in the workforce, can produce anxiety and other forms of "neurotic behavior." Because these responses have been labelled diseases, the only available and socially acceptable form of therapy is that delivered by physicians. Jim Harding of the School of Human Justice at the University of Regina explains how drugs are used in managing the socialized contradictions of women:

After being socialized to be passive, helpless, and introverted once the demands of family, life and work are placed on her, a woman may "need" drugs to get and keep her functioning. Helpless and dependent, alienated from her reproductive potentials within a patriarchal society, she may "need" the pharmaceutical industry's drugs to handle menstruation, pregnancy, and later on menopause. When she is rudely awakened from the romanticized image of marriage by the realities of work and parenthood and is isolated in the home with the children, she may indeed "need" drugs to calm her anger and resentment, to keep her from having stronger, possibly more aggressive or depressing feelings and thoughts. Finally, when she is left alone in the "empty nest" after serving her life as a mother and wife, she may "need" drugs to block out her sorrow and confusion about the meaning of it all.[20]

Ruth Cooperstock and Henry Lennard interviewed groups of women who were using benzodiazepines.[21] The study focused on the social and behavioral effects of these drugs as viewed by the user and provides concrete examples of the sorts of issues Harding refers to. According to Cooperstock and Lennard: "Almost all the . . . women described situations of extreme role strain, inability to comply with traditional role expectations, often feeling they lacked the 'right' to express their dissatisfaction and preferences. They see husbands as having other 'escape routes' when marital difficulties or obligations become burdensome."[22] One woman said: "Now I am in a situation I cannot get out of . . . I can't leave them [her husband and children] and because I can't leave them I'm sticking to the Valium. That's my escape."[23] The women in the groups also discussed strains in their family lives and how they cope with these tensions through the use of tranquillizers: "In the summertime I virtually live on them [tranquillizers] because we have a boat. My husband doesn't swim and I am like this (indicating tension) all the time . . . It's the only way I can get to be nice the next day to all those people we have floating around this boat all the time."[24]

The use of tranquillizers as a means of escape is reinforced in the 1979 report from Bryony House, a transition home for women in Halifax: "Women stated they took drugs primarily to cope with the arguments, the beatings, the tension and the very real fear of their mate; to adjust themselves to what was happening at home or to blot it out."[25]

For all these women, tranquillizers were the only socially approved method of coping with their powerlessness. And the only place to get tranquillizers is from a doctor.

As with hypertension, doctors, largely because of their training, are unlikely to see these conditions in a wider social context. This limited perspective of doctors was remarked upon both by an interviewee in Cooperstock and Lennard's study and by Shirley Small of Toronto's Support Services for Assaulted Women:

> I think the thing that upset me most about the way drugs were used with me was that in the early years when I was so obviously unhappy with what was happening in my life the solution to the doctors was so obviously a drug solution.[26]

> I've been working in the area of battered women for a number of years and it's very clear to me that when a woman has been beaten and goes to a doctor she's more often than not given a tranquilizer which tends in fact to make her problem worse. She tends to become more passive and she's more likely to be endangered. This way of treating the problem, as a sort of neurotic problem that these women have is in fact really disgraceful.[27]

Again, as with hypertension, even if doctors do recognize the limitations of drug therapy, they are still powerless to change the social structure. They can, therefore, only attempt to treat the individual. Moreover, the relatively poor preparation that doctors receive in dealing with problems such as depression or anxiety means that the easiest solution is a chemical one. As we have already seen, when it comes to treating women, doctors' attitudes and pharmaceutical advertising reinforce the tendency to reach for the prescription pad.

It is possible to do without drugs, by escaping from the medical model of these diseases. When a sole-support mother at the Opportunity for Advancement program in Toronto announced that the day she got a part-time job she flushed her tranquillizers down the toilet, the program organizers decided to see if this response was atypical. In a follow-up study of more than 300 women who took the fourteen-week life-planning course, they found that there was a 50 percent decline in the use of prescription drugs.[28]

I have tried to outline the effects of psychoactive drugs on the individual, but there exist social implications as well. The social forces that generate the problems discussed here cannot be cured with drugs. But using drug therapy can help to keep them hidden, thereby delaying any possible solutions. The responsibility for dealing with emotions such as anxiety, sadness, grief, rage or hate is removed from society and delegated to doctors and drugs. The use of drugs erodes society's ability, or even need, to develop strategies of human relatedness. According to Lennard, increasing public commitment to the development and employment of drug technology also implies a model of human behavior and behavioral change that in itself generates further use of the very drugs, like heroin, which are disapproved of by the medical community and society at large.[29]

The potential for misuse of psychoactive drugs is considerable, especially against powerless groups such as the elderly, prisoners, children and psychiatric patients. Eleanor McDonald, the director of community education for the Elizabeth Fry Society of Toronto, says that drug over-prescription is one of the most common complaints heard from women while they are in prison. "Women complain that at the first sign of restlessness, doctors prescribe tranquillizers to calm them down," says Ms. McDonald. "These reports are too consistent and general to ignore...When women say they get hooked on tranquillizers while inside, we have to ask pointed questions about the extent to which doctors treat incarcerated women patients as a bunch of troublesome malcontents who simply need to be tranquillized into passivity."[30]

Drugs do make it possible to control people's behavior, without having to resort to physical force. The results are the same, but drugs are the more dangerous of the two alternatives in the long run. Their use is supposedly based on scientific principles which are objective and therefore neutral. Thus, any use of these drugs can be "scientifically" justified as being for the person's "own good." When force was used, at least people knew who was using the force and exactly what was being done to them and why. Drugs blur these distinctions; how can you fight something being done to help you?[31]

I have focused largely on psychoactive drugs because they are the ones that are serving as the new agents of social control. But the philosophy behind their use is the same as that behind the use of drugs to treat hypertension: treat the results of society, not society itself.

Chapter 14
New Directions
for the Future

Ultimately, our concerns about prescription drugs end up being focused on how these products affect the health of individuals and society—economically, physically, psychologically and socially. Any proposals to improve the use of pharmaceuticals must result in benefits in all of these parameters of health. Drugs that are used appropriately and that are inexpensive will have beneficial effects on the individual and on society in general.

In order to remove the profit motive from the field of research and development, and to develop new drugs that will benefit society rather than the pocketbooks of the drug companies, I propose the establishment of a number of independent non-profit research centres across the country. These facilities should probably be affiliated with medical schools to make use of existing resources. Funding for the first few years could be supplied by a combination of direct government subsidies and a special tax on the profits of the drug companies. I estimate that a 10 percent tax on these profits in 1980 would have yielded between $20 and $30 million. Products developed by the research centres would be licensed to any manufacturer interested in marketing them, with the royalties paid to the centres used to sustain ongoing operations. If patents are abolished, as I believe they should be, other sources of operating capital would have to be found.

Challenging the power of the multinational drug companies cannot be done through a patchwork of programs, as has been the case until now. A coordinated set of policies is required if we are to succeed in lowering drug prices and encouraging local manufacturing.

To reduce the cost of manufacturing drugs, I propose the

establishment of a Crown corporation to manufacture drugs which have proven to yield the greatest public benefit. The term "greatest public benefit," rather than "most frequently prescribed," is used for two reasons. First, we have seen that some frequently prescribed drugs, such as diazepam, are, in fact, overprescribed; used properly, they would be used much less. Second, certain potentially life-saving drugs, as we have also seen, are not commercially manufactured because the demand is too low to generate a sufficiently high profit. The total number of drugs that a pharmaceutical Crown corporation would manufacture would depend upon the capital resources that government was willing to invest in it. It would fall obviously to the federal government to set up such an agency, but a group of provinces, or even a single large one such as Ontario or Quebec, could establish a modest company.

Once a Crown corporation existed, sales of its products could be ensured if the provinces instituted a policy of buying the most frequently used drugs on a tender system for the entire province. These drugs would accordingly be distributed to pharmacies in each province. The Crown corporation, operating on a non-profit basis, should be able to enter the lowest bid for the products it makes. Central purchasing, by tender, would also result in substantial savings even for drugs not manufactured by the Crown corporation. This measure would be especially effective if it were combined with the abolition of patent protection. The absence of patents would result in an increase in the number of companies making the more popular products, thus creating a more competitive bidding situation and generally lower prices. Even on a small scale, purchasing drugs by tender results in savings. The Community Health Centre in Saskatoon lowered the average price per prescription by about 25 percent in the first year that the system was in use.

Central purchasing is not a new concept; it was one of the proposals that the Klass Report presented to the Manitoba government in the early 1970s and is already being used in Saskatchewan. The Pharmacare Plan in Saskatchewan is one which should serve as a model for the other provinces (see Table 12-1 for details). In addition, these plans should incorporate mandatory substitution provisions requiring pharmacists to dispense the least expensive equivalent brand of the drug prescribed, unless the physician specifically requests a certain brand. The rest of the provinces should also emulate British Columbia and Saskatchewan, whose drug plans ensure that pharmacists are reimbursed for only the actual amount spent in acquiring the drugs that they sell. All these measures combined should result in significant savings to consumers while keeping government costs to a minimum.

Profits of the private companies in the industry could be controlled as they are in England. There the business operations of pharmaceutical companies are thoroughly scrutinized by public agencies. Special attention is paid to the total return on capital invested in pharmaceutical operations and must not exceed a specific percentage in earnings.

France requires local production of pharmaceuticals and Japan obliges foreign firms to co-venture with domestic firms to market new products. Both of these policies could be adopted by Canada as a means of encouraging more domestic manufacturing.

Lower cost drugs are of little value, of course, if their quality is unknown. To ensure that the drugs that Canadians use are safe and effective, the Health Protection Branch must abandon its "buddy-buddy" relationship with the drug companies. If Dr. Albert Liston, the director-general of the Drug Directorate of the HPB, were more aggressive in his attitude toward the industry, instead of believing that existing regulations have no major deficiencies, perhaps the HPB would be able to get the money it needs to institute a program to evaluate the safety and efficacy of drugs marketed before 1951 and the efficacy of drugs marketed before 1963. If the companies cannot prove, with objective, scientific evidence, that these drugs are safe and efficacious, they should be required to withdraw them from sale.

In order to reduce the number of "me-too" drugs, the HPB should require the manufacturers to prove that any new drug is at least as efficacious as drugs presently available for the same condition or else that the new drug would offer other substantial advantages. "Other substantial advantages" might mean, for example, that although a drug might not work as well as one already being used, it has a significantly lower incidence of side effects. Norway is one example of a country that imposes limitations on "me-too" drugs.

Controls on research need to be tightened up to ensure a high quality of future drugs. Regulations must be established to specify who can and cannot be used as research subjects, and it must be made mandatory to get informed consent before a person can be made a subject in the investigation of a new drug. The HPB should have a budget which enables it to monitor all drug trials; as well, it should have the authority to stop trials in cases of significant deviation from the trial protocol, e.g., if the drug is proving valueless or if there is evidence of disturbing side effects.

Other ways to improve the quality of present and future medicines include:

1. Regular government inspection of the research laboratories of all companies.

2. A requirement that product monographs on all pre-1967 drugs be made available.

3. A system of compulsory reporting by the drug companies of all unusual occurrences involving all drugs they market, no matter how long the drugs have been on the market. Penalties for failing to file a report should include withdrawal of a drug from sale.

4. Staffing at the Bureau of Human Prescription Drugs should be increased to reflect the increased workload of the past decade.

The amount of misinformation conveyed through pharmaceutical advertising, and doctors' reliance on commercial sources for knowledge about drugs, make for strong arguments for major changes in advertising regulations. Limitations should be imposed on the amount of marketing funds that drug companies are allowed to deduct from their gross revenue for income tax purposes. The deduction for each company should be equivalent to the amount of money it commits to research actually conducted in Canada. The HPB should begin a program of strict monitoring of all journal and direct mail ads, prior to their use, to check the accuracy of their contents. Personal contact advertising, that is, visits by detail men to doctors' offices, cannot be adequately monitored and therefore the practice of detailing should be stopped. Brand names should be abolished in advertising. Drugs should be advertised by the generic name and the company's name. For example, there would no longer be ads for Valium, but for diazepam-Roche. With a Pharmacare plan in place in all provinces, doctors would no longer need drug samples to give to poor patients. Since none of the other reasons for leaving free samples have any merit, the practice of sampling should be eliminated.

Finally, steps must be undertaken to ensure that physicians use drugs properly. Medical schools must place more emphasis on social, economic and environmental causes of disease to help doctors to break free of the specific aetiology method of viewing disease.

NEW DIRECTIONS FOR THE FUTURE 223

Learning an ecological model of health and illness should also help doctors to recognize that there are non-pharmacological methods of therapy. Licensed doctors should be required to update their knowledge of therapeutics annually. (Compulsory post-graduate medical education almost became a reality in 1980 in Manitoba.) The Health Protection Branch should reinstate publication of the *Rx Bulletin*, or a similar journal, to be distributed free to all doctors, pharmacists and any other interested people. Such a publication would provide an unbiased source of information about pharmaceuticals. In conjunction with this journal, a committee should be established by the HPB to develop a replacement for the *Compendium of Pharmaceuticals and Specialties*, the deficiencies of which were described in Chapter 9. Information in the new publication would be based on scientific research and clinical observations, not manufacturers' claims. In New Zealand, the prescribing of certain drugs is limited to certified specialists; this system of controlled prescribing merits consideration here, especially for new drugs. Specialists, by virtue of their training, are usually better informed about new drugs in their area of expertise, and are better able to decide where their use will be most appropriate. Furthermore, new drugs often have unanticipated side effects. Specialists, who will be prescribing the drug far more frequently than the average general practitioner, will be in a better position to recognize these side effects. Once the drug has been on the market for a sufficient period of time, the restrictions on its prescribing could be removed.

The measures I have outlined are important steps toward resolving the problems with prescription drugs that were stated at the beginning of this chapter. But in order to decide if they are sufficient, we must be able to identify who the real drug pushers are. Are they the greedy drug companies, the doctors who are biased in favor of drug therapy and do not know enough about drugs, the governments that do not exert enough control, the people who actually request certain medications, especially minor tranquillizers? Obviously, all of these groups must bear some responsibility, but we cannot judge their motivations and actions in isolation from the society in which they, and we, all exist.

As I said in Chapter 2, drug companies are no different from any other enterprise in a capitalist economy. Their primary motivation is to make a profit and therefore they are always seeking to expand their sales by whatever methods seem appropriate. Chapter 7 analysed the alliance that has been forged between the medical profession and the drug industry and suggested how that alliance was, to a degree, predetermined by the nature of medical education. Chapters 7 and 13 showed how medical education reflects the predominant theory of disease—the specific aetiology model—and discussed the historical reasons why that model won out over the ecological model. Other chapters explored the ways in which the medical-pharmaceutical alliance leads to an over-reliance on commercial sources of information about drugs, and illustrated the consequences in terms of misprescribing. Government inaction, described in Chapters 11 and 12, is not atypical in a capitalist society, especially when corporate interests may be hurt; witness how long it has taken for governments to respond to problems such as occupational health and safety or to environmental crises like acid rain. Government interference in the drug industry has usually been aroused only in the face of a publicly perceived major health threat, such as thalidomide or the amphetamines. Not until three major reports had identified Canadian drug prices as the highest in the world was the government forced to take note of the scandal and do something about patents.

The last chapter alluded to a feature of a capitalist society by which socially created problems are "individualized"; this was illustrated by examining the process of medicalization. Instead of investigating society's function in generating conflicts for women in areas such as role expectations, the focus is on the individual woman's "neurotic complaints." In too many cases, the only socially legitimate way of seeking relief from such problems is to request medications that allow one to "cope."

So, the behavior of all of the players—the companies, the doctors, the government and the patients—is understandable as a function of the social system in which they all exist. Therefore, in the end, the real pusher has to be defined as the social system responsible for the proliferation of problems, inequities and harm in the pharmaceutical field, namely, capitalism. The way to approach a true solution to the problems involved with prescription drugs is to replace capitalism with a different system. That, of course, is a tall order. In the short run, the many reforms advocated in this book represent attainable goals worth fighting for. Ultimately, a new system can be brought about, one that will generate different ways of analysing health and disease, that will provide a different model of medical education and different motives for producing drugs.

Notes

INTRODUCTION
1. Pharmaceutical Manufacturers Association of Canada, *The Pharmaceutical Industry and Ontario*, Ottawa, 1978, p. 26.
2. Welcoming statement by Consumer and Corporate Affairs Minister Ron Basford to the Federal-Provincial Conference of Officials on the Cost of Drugs and Hearing Aids, Ottawa, June 10-12, 1970, pp. 6-7, (mimeographed); *Globe and Mail*, February 3, 1976, pp. 1, 5; M. Gerson, G. Gougeon and J. Bartolet, "The Price of Prescription Drugs," *Protect Yourself*, June 1984, pp. 6-12.
3. *Globe and Mail*, June 12, 1970, p. 10.

CHAPTER 1. VALIUM FOR THE ADULTS AND RITALIN FOR THE KIDS
1. Pharmaceutical Manufacturers Association of Canada, *The Pharmaceutical Industry and Ontario*, Ottawa, 1978, pp. 32-33.
2. IMS of Canada, *A Drug Profile: Psychotherapeutic Agents*, Dollard-des-Ormeaux, Quebec, 1978, Figure 1.
3. R. Ball, "The Secret Life of Hoffman-La Roche," *Fortune*, August 1971, pp. 130-134, 162-171; N. McInnes, "Tranquilizer Furor," *Baron's*, August 27, 1973, pp. 3, 10.
4. *Globe and Mail*, December 5, 1978, p. 4.
5. J. Pekkanen, *The American Connection*, Follet Publishing Company, Chicago, 1973, p. 81.
6. "Swiss Slowdown," *Forbes*, June 15, 1973, pp. 36-37. Cited in: I. Waldron, "Increased Prescribing of Valium, Librium, and Other Drugs—An Example of the Influence of Economic and Social Factors on the Practice of Medicine," *International Journal of Health Services*, 7:37-62, 1977.
7. *Globe and Mail*, February 7, 1980, pp. 1, 2.
8. *Globe and Mail*, December 5, 1978, p. 4.
9. I. Waldron, *op. cit.*, p. 47.
10. S. Zisook and R.A. DeVaul, "Adverse Behavioral Effects of Benzodiazepines," *Journal of Family Practice*, 5:963-966, 1977.
11. R. Cooperstock and J. Hill, *The Effects of Tranquillization: Benzodiazepine Use in Canada*, Health and Welfare, Ottawa, 1982.
12. P. Tyrer, D. Rutherford and T. Huggett, "Benzodiazepine Withdrawal Symptoms and Propranolol," *The Lancet*, 1:520-522, 1981.
13. L.E. Hollister, F.P. Motzenbecker and R.O. Degan, "Withdrawal Reaction From Chlordiazepoxide (Librium)," *Psychopharmacologia*,

2:63-68, 1961.

14. L. Covi, R.S. Lipman, J.H. Pattison et al., "Length of Treatment With Anxiolytic Sedatives and Response to Their Sudden Withdrawal," Acta Psychiatrica Scandinavia, 49:51-64, 1973.

15. B.M. Maletzky and J. Klotter, "Addiction to Diazepam," International Journal of Addiction, 11:95-115, 1976.

16. R. Cooperstock and J. Hill, op. cit., p. 25.

17. D. Fejer and R. Smart, "The Use of Psychoactive Drugs by Adults," Canadian Psychiatric Association Journal, 18:313-320, 1973.

18. R. Cooperstock and J. Hill, op. cit., p. 28.

19. J. Pekkanen, "The Impact of Promotion on Physicians' Prescribing Patterns," Journal of Drug Issues, 6:13-20, 1976.

20. G. Gardos, A. DiMascio, C. Salzman et al., "Differential Actions of Chlordiazepoxide and Oxazepam on Hostility," Archives of General Psychiatry, 18:757-760, 1968.

21. D.G. Workman and D.G. Cunningham, "Effect of Psychotropic Drugs on Aggression in a Prison Setting," Canadian Family Physician, 21:63-66, 1975.

22. S. Zisook and R.A. DeVaul, op. cit.

23. Ibid., pp. 965-966.

24. R. Cooperstock and J. Hill, op. cit., p. 31.

25. Ibid., p. 30; E.M. Sellers, "Clinical Pharmacology and Therapeutics of Benzodiazepines," Canadian Medical Association Journal, 118:1533-1538, 1978.

26. I. Waldron, op. cit.

27. N.A. Endicott and J. Endicott, "'Improvement' In Untreated Psychiatric Patients," Archives of General Psychiatry, 9:575-585, 1963.

28. Advertisements cited in: I. Waldron, op. cit.

29. Advertisement cited in: I. Waldron, op. cit.

30. T.A. Ban, W.T. Brown, T. DaSilva et al., "Therapeutic Monograph on Anxiolytic-Sedative Drugs," Canadian Pharmaceutical Journal, 114:301-308, 1981.

31. Toronto Star, August 25, 1973, p. B7.

32. R. Cooperstock, "Psychotropic Drug Use Among Women," Canadian Medical Association Journal, 115:760-763, 1976.

33. The same tendency appeared in the other age groups, fifteen to 24 and 45 to 64, but the differences were not significant. J.E. Anderson, "Prescribing of Tranquillizers to Women and Men," Canadian Medical Association Journal, 125:1229-1232, 1981.

34. L.S. Linn, "Physician Characteristics and Attitudes Toward Legitimate Use of Psychotherapeutic Drugs," Journal of Health and Social Behavior, 12:132-140, 1971.

35. I. Waldron, op. cit.

36. E. Hemminki, "Effect of a Doctor's Personal Characteristics and Working Circumstances on the Prescribing of Psychotropic Drugs," Medical Care, 12:351-357, 1974.

37. V. Ross, "Between Bliss and Bedlam," Maclean's, December 8, 1980, pp. 38-44.

38. I. Waldron, op. cit., p. 43.

39. P. Schrag and D. Divoky, The Myth of the Hyperactive Child, Dell, New York, 1976, p. 81.

40. Ibid., p. 55.

41. L.A. Stroufe and M.A. Stewart, "Treating Problem Children With

Stimulant Drugs," *New England Journal of Medicine*, 289:407-414, 1973.
42. *Globe and Mail*, February 20, 1975, p. W7.
43. Leon Oettinger, M.D., California pediatrician. Cited in: P. Schrag and D. Divoky, *op. cit.*, p. 67.
44. Advertisement cited in: R. Rapoport and S. Repo, "The Educator as Pusher: Drug Control in the Classroom," *This Magazine is About Schools*, 5:94-95, Fall/Winter 1971.
45. P. Schrag and D. Divoky, *op. cit.*, p. 97.
46. E. Sleator, H. Neumann and R. Sprague, "Hyperactive Children: A Continuous Long Term Placebo Controlled Follow-Up," *Journal of the American Medical Association*, 229:316-317, 1974; G. Weiss, E. Kruger, U. Danielson *et al.*, "Effect of Long-Term Treatment of Hyperactive Children With Methylphenidate," *Canadian Medical Association Journal*, 112: 159-165, 1975; K. Riddle and J. Rapoport, "A 2-Year Follow-Up of 72 Hyperactive Boys," *Journal of Nervous and Mental Disease*, 162: 126-134, 1976; A. Blouin, R. Bornstein and R. Trites, "Teenage Alcohol Use Among Hyperactive Children: A 5-Year Follow-Up Study," *Journal of Pediatric Psychology*, 3:188-194, 1978.
47. G. Weiss, E. Kruger, U. Danielson *et al.*, *op. cit.*
48. *Globe and Mail*, February 20, 1975, p. W7.
49. P. Schrag and D. Divoky, *op. cit.*, p. 91.
50. R. Rapoport and S. Repo, *op. cit.*, p. 92.
51. P. Schrag and D. Divoky, *op. cit.*, p. 41.

CHAPTER 2. THE INDUSTRY: ETHICS AND ORGANIZATION

1. Pharmaceutical Manufacturers Association of Canada, *Principles and Code of Marketing Practice*, Ottawa, 1972, p. 3.
2. Unpublished letter to the Hamilton *Spectator*, dated May 26, 1980.
3. *Globe and Mail*, October 25, 1982, p. 5.
4. *Globe and Mail*, June 12, 1975, p. F2.
5. Pharmaceutical Manufacturers Association of Canada, *op. cit.*, p. 2.
6. The information about the marketing of Indocid comes from: W.M. O'Brien, "Drug Testing: Is Time Running Out?," *Bulletin of the Atomic Scientists*, 25:8-14, January 1969; M. Silverman and P.R. Lee, *Pills, Profits and Politics*, University of California Press, Berkeley, 1974, pp. 61-62.
7. W.M. O'Brien, *op. cit.*, p. 10.
8. *Ibid.*
9. *Ibid.*
10. *Globe and Mail*, February 2, 1981, p. B3.
11. Information summarized from: M. Gordon and D. Fowler, *The Drug Industry: A Case Study in Foreign Control*, James Lorimer and Company, Toronto, 1981, pp. 33-34.
12. The information on Ayerst's history is taken from: *Ibid.*, p. 35.
13. Pharmaceutical Manufacturers Association of Canada, *A Profile*, Ottawa, 1980, p. 1.
14. S.N. Condor, "Structure and Function of the CMPA," *Canadian Pharmaceutical Journal (Supplement)*, 97:111, August 1964.
15. R.W. Lang, *The Politics of Drugs*, Saxon House, Westmead, England, 1974, p. 57.
16. S.N. Condor, *op. cit.*, pp. III-IV.

CHAPTER 3. PRICES AND PROFITS

1. M. Silverman and P.R. Lee, *Pills, Profits and Politics*, University of California Press, Berkeley, 1974, p. 171.
2. A.P. Ruderman, "The Drug Business in the Context of Canadian Health Care Programs," *International Journal of Health Services*, 4:641-650, 1974.
3. The industry's use of the CPI in defence of drug prices may start to decline. According to Alan Burrows, the chief of pharmaceutical services for the Ontario Health Ministry, from 1980 to 1982, Canadian drug prices rose 15 percent a year above the inflation rate. *Globe and Mail*, January 8, 1982, p. 5.
4. *Canada, Royal Commission on Health Services: Report*, Volume 1, Queen's Printer, Ottawa, 1964, p. 693.
5. Saskatchewan Prescription Drug Plan, *Annual Report 1978-79*, Regina, 1979, p. 18.
6. J. Siemiatychi, "The Distribution of Disease," *Canadian Dimension*, June 1974, pp. 15-25.
7. "Cost Factor in Misuse of Drug Medication," *Drug Merchandising*, 55:12, April 1974.
8. Canada, House of Commons, *Second (Final) Report of the Special Committee of the House of Commons on Drug Costs and Prices*, Queen's Printer, Ottawa, 1967, p. 14; *Globe and Mail*, October 26, 1972, p. W8. In 1971, the president of the Canadian Pharmaceutical Association, the organization representing pharmacists, said that pharmacists would press the drug manufacturers to lower their prices. The response from the head of the PMAC was that the Combines Investigation Act prevented drug companies from setting prices on an association basis. *Globe and Mail*, August 19, 1971, p. 35. A 1978 study by the PMAC compared drug manufacturers' prices in Canada with those in seven other countries—the United States, the United Kingdom, Germany, France, Italy, Switzerland and Sweden—for the nineteen leading drugs sold in Canada. Except for Italy, Canadian prices were generally lower than those in the other countries; Pharmaceutical Manufacturers Association of Canada, *International Price Comparisons of the Top Nineteen Drugs Sold in Canada*, Ottawa, 1979. Given the PMAC's obvious bias to show that drugs are not overpriced in Canada one may be forgiven for wondering why those particular seven countries were used for comparison and what the results would have been if seven other countries had been chosen.
9. Mr. Robson, however, does not think that current Canadian drug prices are too high. L. Reid, "Testing Patent Laws," *Financial Times*, 17:14-15, October 4, 1982.
10. The Special Commons Committee had the following to say about such arguments: "Your Committee cannot accept this argument...In the ascertaining of the price of a product, whether at the manufacturers' level or at the retailers' level, it appears to the Committee that real costs should be looked at, namely, the cost of labour, raw materials, research and the capital required. This is the true comparison, together with demand, when explaining price differentials between one country and another. It is a question of total efficiency of an industry which must be looked at." Canada, House of Commons, *op. cit.*, p. 16.
11. L.G. Schifrin, statement in: J.D. Cooper (editor), *The Economics of Drug Innovation*, The American University, Washington, D.C., 1960, p. 211.

12. A study entitled "An Economic Analysis of the Pharmaceutical Manufacturing Industry in Canada" was prepared for the PMAC by Professor Brian Dixon at Queen's University in Kingston, Ontario. In this paper, he says: "It will be observed that particularly in the early stages there is little if any relation between costs and the price set." Restrictive Trade Practices Commission, *Report Concerning the Manufacture, Distribution and Sale of Drugs*, Queen's Printer, Ottawa, 1963, p. 344.
13. *Ibid.*, p. 342.
14. J.M. Blair, *Economic Concentration*, Harcourt, New York, 1972, p. 497.
15. Director of Investigation and Research, Combines Investigation Act, *Material Collected for Submission to the Restrictive Trade Practices Commission in the Course of an Inquiry Under Section 42 of the Combines Investigation Act Relating to the Manufacture, Distribution and Sale of Drugs*, Queen's Printer, Ottawa, 1961, pp. 167,176.
16. Restrictive Trade Practices Commission, *op. cit.*, p. 512.
17. Pharmaceutical Manufacturers Association of Canada, *The Pharmaceutical Industry and Ontario*, Ottawa, 1978, pp. 32-33. Twenty-five drugs were on the list. There was no change in the price of one drug, and two drugs could not be found in the *Drug Benefit Formulary* (Queen's Printer, Toronto, 1977), which was the source used to determine if price competition existed.
18. L.L. Dan, "The Drug Industry in Canada: A Position Analysis," *Business Quarterly*, 47:62-71, Autumn 1982.
19. P. Tidball, "The Pharmaceutical Industry's Responsibilities in the Prescription Process," *Canadian Pharmaceutical Journal*, 114:177-179, 1981.
20. Pharmaceutical Manufacturers Association of Canada, International Price Comparisons, *op. cit.*
21. J.M. Blair, *op. cit.*, p. 497.
22. B. Pazderka, *Promotion and Competition in the Canadian Prescription Drug Industry*, Unpublished Ph.D. thesis, Queen's University, Kingston, Ontario, 1976, p. 71.
23. Director of Investigation and Research, *op. cit.*, pp. 257-258.
24. B. Pazderka, *op. cit.*, p. 247.
25. W.S. Comanor, "Research and Competitive Product Differentiation in the Pharmaceutical Industry in the United States," *Economics*, 31:372-384, 1964.
26. "Good Foreign Earnings in the Pharmaceutical Industry," *Chemistry and Industry*, Part 1, February 15, 1975, pp. 142-143.
27. D. Orr, "An Index of Entry Barriers and Its Application to the Market Structure Performance Relationship," *Journal of Industrial Economics*, 23:39-49, 1974.
28. L.G. Schifrin, "The Ethical Drug Industry: The Case For Compulsory Patent Licensing," *Antitrust Bulletin*, 12:893-915, 1967.
29. J.J. Friedman & Associates, *Pharmaceutical Prices in Canada: Guiding Principles for Government Policy*, PMAC, Ottawa, 1981, pp. 60-61.
30. Consumer and Corporate Affairs Canada, *Compulsory Licensing of Pharmaceuticals: A Review of Section 41 of the Patent Act*, Ottawa, 1983 p. 10.
31. Restrictive Trade Practices Commission, *op. cit.*, p. 512.
32. Director of Investigation and Research, *op. cit.*, p. 234.
33. J.M. Blair, *op. cit.*, pp. 388-391. Canada grants patents only on the processes used to make drugs, process patents, not on the actual drugs

themselves, product patents.

34. R.S. Bond and D.F. Lean, *Sales, Promotion and Product Differentiation in Two Prescription Drug Markets*, Staff Report to the Federal Trade Commission, Government Printing Office, Washington, D.C., 1977, p. vi. Cited in: M. Gordon and D. Fowler, *The Drug Industry: A Case Study in Foreign Control*, James Lorimer & Company, Toronto, 1981, pp. 59-61.
35. Company size has a significant influence on a drug's share of a therapeutic market. The bigger the company, the bigger the share. B. Pazderka, *op. cit.*, pp. 239-240.
36. Based on quantities, however, multinationals retain about 60 to 70 percent of the market share as most generic products are substantially lower in price. L.L. Dan, *op. cit.*, pp. 70-71.
37. Maclean-Hunter Research Bureau, *A Survey of Prescriptions 1977*, Conducted for Drug Merchandising and Le Pharmacien, Toronto, July 1977, pp. 11-17.
38. Department of Industry, Trade and Commerce, *The Health Care Products Industry in Canada*, Ottawa, 1980, p. 4.
39. G. Postlewaite, "The PMAC Public Relations Program: Patching a Tattered Image," *Canadian Pharmaceutical Journal*, 111:8-11, January 1978. Mr. Postlewaite is director of communications for the PMAC. Elsewhere in his article he comments on people who criticize his industry: "Where genuine issues don't naturally present themselves, a team of aggressive media researchers, composed of journalism graduates in search of that big story, will soon produce one. An unfortunate side-effect of this condition is that the media can unwittingly provide deceiving vocal strength to smaller non-representative groups or individual hucksters of misinformed opinion." p. 8.
40. Canada, Royal Commission, *op. cit.*, p. 681.
41. P.K. Gorecki, *Regulating the Price of Prescription Drugs in Canada: Compulsory Licensing, Product Selection, and Government Reimbursement Programmes*, Technical Report No. 8, Economic Council of Canada, Ottawa, 1981, p. 154; Canadian Drug Manufacturers Association, *Pharmaceutical Patents: Compulsory Licensing. A Case for the Retention of Section 41(4) of the Patent Act*, Toronto, 1983, p. 24.
42. M. Gordon and D. Fowler, *op. cit.*, p. 89.
43. *Globe and Mail*, August 22, 1978, p. B1. The title of the story was "Canada is Considered Paradise for Importers of Pharmaceuticals."
44. P.K. Gorecki, *op. cit.*, p. 155.
45. Bureau of Policy Coordination, *A Policy Analysis of the Compulsory Licensing of Pharmaceutical Patents in Canada*, Department of Consumer and Corporate Affairs, Ottawa, September, 1982, p. 5, (mimeographed).
46. *Ibid.*, pp. 5, 11.
47. M. Gordon and D. Fowler, *op. cit.*, p. 123.
48. A.P. Ruderman, *op. cit.*, p. 647; M. Gordon and D. Fowler, *op. cit.*, p. 29.
49. M. Silverman and P.R Lee, *op. cit.*, p. 31. At least one official in the Department of Industry, Trade and Commerce had visions of Canada competing with Puerto Rico as a tax haven for drug companies. S. Raikes, "Canada's Drug Licensing Law: A Bitter Pill for Big Drug Firms," *Canadian Business*, 51:21, 24, September 1978.
50. M. Gordon and D. Fowler, *op. cit.*, p. 91.

51. *Ibid.*, p. 65. Management responsibilities also moved out of the country. *Ibid.*, p. 82.
52. *Ibid.*, p. 76.
53. H. Steele, "Monopoly and Competition in the Ethical Drug Market," *Journal of Law and Economics*, 5:131-163, October 1962.
54. Canda, House of Commons, *op. cit.*, p. 18.
55. Cited in: *Ibid.*, p. 10.
56. Department of Industry, Trade and Commerce, *op. cit.*, p. 5.
57. J.S. Hammill, "PMAC Wants to Upgrade Pharmaceutical Image," *Drug Merchandising* 59:15-21, May 1978.
58. "A DM Round Table—The Pharmaceutical Industry," *Drug Merchandising*, 59:12-18, April 1978.
59. Department of Industry, Trade and Commerce, *op. cit.*, p. 10.
60. *Investor's Digest*, May 10, 1983, p. 142.
61. Canada, House of Commons, *op. cit.*, p. 67.
62. Restrictive Trade Practices Commission, *op. cit.*, p. 369.
63. Pharmaceutical Manufacturers Association of Canada, *The Performance of the Canadian Pharmaceutical Manufacturing Industry*, Ottawa, 1975, p. 26.
64. In 1977, this represented about 15 percent of sales. Statistics Canada, *Manufacturers of Pharmaceuticals and Medicines, 1977*, Ottawa, 1979, pp. 8-9.
65. Canada, Royal Commission, *op, cit.*, p. 679.
66. Restrictive Trade Practices Commission, *op, cit.*, p. 362.
67. Statistics Canada, "Detailed Income and Retained Earning Statistics for 182 Industries," *Corporation Financial Statistics*, Ottawa, various years. The differences betweeen the American and Canadian profits should be interpreted with some caution since they are after-tax figures and may just reflect different rates of taxation in the two countries.
68. R.C. Kennett, *Profile of the Pharmaceutical Industry in Canada*, Supply and Services Canada, Ottawa, April 1982, p. 16.
69. M. Gordon and D. Fowler, *op. cit.*, pp. 46, 72, 73.
70. Consumer and Corporate Affairs Canada, *op. cit.*, p. 16.
71. *Globe and Mail*, May 5, 1980, p. B1
72. L.L. Dan, *op. cit.*, pp. 64-65.
73. *Globe and Mail*, November 23, 1981, p. B14.
74. Pharmaceutical Manufacturers Association of Canada, *The Performance of the Canadian Pharmaceutical Manufacturing Industry*, Ottawa, 1975, p. 18; J.J. Friedman & Associates, *op. cit.*, p. 167.
75. G. Gereffi, *The Pharmaceutical Industry and Dependency in the Third World*, Princeton University Press, Princeton, 1983, p. 192.
76. T.R. Stauffer, "Profitability Measures in the Pharmaceutical Industry," in: R.B. Helms (editor), *Drug Development and Marketing*, The American Institute for Public Policy Research, Washington, D.C., 1975, pp. 110-113.
77. P. Temin, "Technology, Regulation, and Market Structure in the Modern Pharmaceutical Industry," *Bell Journal of Economics*, 10:429-446, 1979.
78. Restrictive Trade Practices Commission, *op. cit.*, p. 345. A publication from the PMAC in 1973 makes the same claim. Pharmaceutical Manufacturers Association of Canada, *The Pharmaceutical Manufacturing Industry*, Ottawa, 1973, p. 8.
79. Restrictive Trade Practices Commission, *op. cit.*, p. 367.
80. W.W. Wigle, *Canadian Medical Association Journal*, 100:441-442, 1969.

81. The more sophisticated of the PMAC's publications now recognize this contradiction: "In the past, some pharmaceutical industry spokesmen have argued that profits need to be high enough to support the high levels of r&d expenditures which characterize the industry. As frequently set forth, however, the argument is inconsistent because the profit figures cited have been calculated after deduction of r&d expenditures." J.J. Friedman & Associates, *op. cit.*, p. 119.

82. H.F. Dowling, *Medicines for Man*, Alfred A. Knopf, New York, 1970, p. 108.

83. U.S. Senate, Committee on the Judiciary, Subcommittee on Antitrust and Monopoly, *Hearings on Administered Prices in the Drug Industry*, U.S. Government Printing Office, Washington, D.C., Part 22, 1960, pp. 10372-10373. Cited in: H.D. Walker, *Market Power and Price Levels in the Ethical Drug Industry*, Indiana University Press, Bloomington, 1971. p. 88.

84. Restrictive Trade Practices Commission, *op. cit.*, p. 119.

85. *The Medical Post*, April 22, 1980, p. 12. The assumption here, of course, is that it is possible to aportion the development costs for any particular drug. Chapter 11 will deal with this issue.

86. W.M. Garton, President, PMAC, personal communication.

87. J.J. Friedman & Associates, *op. cit.*, p. 163.

88. D. Orr, *op. cit.*,

89. Canada, House of Commons, *op. cit.*, p. 71.

CHAPTER 4. GENERICS: WHAT'S IN A NAME?

1. Pharmaceutical Manufacturers Association of Canada, *Principles and Code of Marketing Practice*, Ottawa, 1972, p. 4.

2. Canada, House of Commons, *Second (Final) Report of the Special Committee of the House of Commons on Drug Costs and Prices*, Queen's Printer, Ottawa, 1967, p. 23.

3. L. Reid, "Testing Patent Laws," *Financial Times*, 17:14-15, October 4, 1982.

4. Canadian Drug Manufacturers Association, *Pharmaceutical Patents: Compulsory Licensing. A Case for the Retention of Section 41(4) of the Patent Act*, Toronto, 1982, pp. 16-18.

5. *Globe and Mail*, August 15, 1983, p. 9.

6. Maclean-Hunter Research Bureau, *A Survey of Prescriptions 1980, Conducted for Drug Merchandising and Le Pharmacien*, Toronto, August 1980, p. 24. In Manitoba, in 1982, just over 20 percent of prescriptions were written generically. J. Davis, "Prescription Cost Margins in Manitoba Pharmacies," *Canadian Pharmaceutical Journal*, 116:419-420, 1983. It is hard to be sure just what percent of prescriptions could be written generically. In 1972, the PMAC was saying that only 43 percent of the drugs on the Canadian market could even be identified by a single generic name. Presumably, the other 57 percent were combinations of more than one active ingredient, and there are no generic equivalents for these combination medications. "PMAC's Case Against Substitution," *Drug Merchandising*, 53: 20-21, March 1972. According to a 1972 report on the effectiveness of the Ontario PARCOST Program, only 34 percent of prescriptions written in Ontario in that year were for drugs that had a generic equivalent. *Globe and Mail*, June 8, 1973, p. 1. This figure is similar to the 35 percent for all of Canada cited in 1963 by the Restrictive Trade Practices Commission, *Report Concerning the Manufacture, Dis-*

tribution and Sale of Drugs, Queen's Printer, Ottawa, 1963, p. 435.
7. Restrictive Trade Practices Commission, *op. cit.*, p. 445.
8. "Manitoba Firm in its Plan to Label Drugs in Generics," *Drug Merchandising*, 63: 17-18, July 1982.
9. Winnipeg *Free Press*, June 21, 1983, p. 21.
10. P. Biron, "A Hopefully Biased Pilot Survey of Physicians' Knowledge of the Content of Drug Combinations," *Canadian Medical Association Journal*, 109:35-39, 1973. The doctors were not meant to be a representative sample of those practising in the Montreal area.
11. Restrictive Trade Practices Commission, *op. cit.*, p. 126.
12. *Ibid.*, p. 152.
13. U.S. Senate, Committee on the Judiciary, Subcommittee on Antitrust and Monopoly, *Hearings on Administered Prices in the Drug Industry*, U.S. Government Printing Office, Washington, D.C., Part 21, 1960, p. 11610. Cited in: H.D. Walker, "Price Levels and Market Power in the Ethical Drug Industry," Presented to the 1967 Annual Meeting of the Econometric Society, December 1967, Washington, D.C., p. 5, (mimeographed).
14. Montreal *Gazette*, October 27, 1982, p. A-6.
15. M. Silverman and P.R. Lee, *Pills, Profits and Politics*, University of California Press, Berkeley, 1974, pp. 148-149. The United States Pharmacopeia and the National Formulary are both official reference books listing certain specifications for drugs, as regards manufacturing conditions and potency.
16. Canada, House of Commons, Special Committee on Drug Costs and Prices, *Minutes of Proceedings and Evidence, No. 30*, Thursday, January 26, 1967, and Tuesday, January 31, 1967, Queen's Printer, Ottawa, 1967, pp. 2101, 2107. Cited in: R.A. Palmer, "When Consumers are Patients," *Canadian Medical Association Journal*, 100: 1101-1102, 1969.
17. W. Bell, personal communication.
18. M. Silverman and P.R. Lee, *op. cit.*, p. 154.
19. Restrictive Trade Practices Commission, *op. cit.*, p. 137.
20. J.B.R. McKendry, D. Bickerton and G. Hancharyk, "A Comparative Study of Some Brands of Tolbutamide Available in Canada: Part I. Clinical Aspects," *Canadian Medical Association Journal*, 92:1106-1109, 1965.
21. E. Clyde Gregory of Ayerst, McKenna and Harrison. *Globe and Mail*, June 7, 1960. Cited in: Director of Investigation and Research, Combines Investigation Act, *Material Collected for Submission to the Restrictive Trade Practices Commission in the Course of an Inquiry Under Section 42 of the Combines Investigation Act Relating to the Manufacture, Distribution and Sale of Drugs*, Queen's Printer, Ottawa, 1961, p. 14.
22. R.W. Lang, *The Politics of Drugs*, Saxon House, Westmead, England, 1974, p. 189.
23. Canada, House of Commons, Special Committee, *op. cit.*, Appendix B, p. 2101. Cited in: R.W. Lang, *op. cit.*, p. 197.
24. "Generic Products as Equivalents," *Canadian Medical Association Journal*, 88:94-95, 1962.
25. D. Woods, "The Pharmaceutical Industry Needs Remedy for MacEachenism," *Canadian Medical Association Journal*, 126:337, 1982.
26. Director of Investigation and Research, *op. cit.*, pp. 15-16.
27. Pharmaceutical Manufacturers Association of Canada, *The Pharmaceutical Manufacturing Industry*, Ottawa, 1973, pp. 23-25.

28. P.A. Brooke, *Resistant Prices*, Council on Economic Priorities, New York, 1975, pp. 41-42.
29. M. Silverman and P.R. Lee., *op, cit.*, p. 155.
30. M. Silverman, letter to P.R. Lee, dated September 13, 1968. Cited in: *Ibid.*, p. 155.
31. P.A. Brooke, *op. cit.*, p. 42.
32. "How To Pay Less For Prescription Drugs," *Consumer Reports*, 40:48-53, January 1975.
33. E.M. Boyd, "The Equivalence of Drug Brands," *Rx Bulletin*, 2:101-102, 120A, July-August 1971.
34. *Modern Medicine of Canada*, 37(Supplement): 214, November 1982.
35. *Modern Medicine of Canada*, 37:1698, 1982.
36. P. Biron, "Dosage, Compliance and Bioavailability in Perspective," *Canadian Medical Association Journal*, 115:102-103, 1976.

CHAPTER 5. CHLORAMPHENICOL AND MER/29

1. Pharmaceutical Manufacturers Association of Canada, *The Pharmaceutical Manufacturing Industry*, Ottawa, 1973, p. 22.
2. W.W. Wigle, "A Pharmaceutical Industry in Canada?", *Canadian Medical Association Journal*, 97:1361, 1967.
3. Restrictive Trade Practices Commission, *Report Concerning the Manufacture, Distribution and Sale of Drugs*, Queen's Printer, Ottawa, 1963, p. 230. The speaker is Mr. R.B. Thompson, Manager of the Medical Products Department of Cyanamid.
4. Royal Commission on Health Services, *Provision, Distribution, and Cost of Drugs in Canada*, Queen's Printer, Ottawa, 1964, p. 47.
5. H.J. Loynd, communication dated March 12, 1952. Cited in: William C. Hewson. U.S. Senate, Select Committee on Small Business, Subcommittee on Monopoly, *Present Status of Competition in the Pharmaceutical Industry*, U.S. Government Printing Office, Washington, D.C., Part 6, 1968, p. 2549. Cited in: M. Silverman and P.R. Lee, *Pills, Profits and Politics*, University of California Press, Berkeley, 1974, p. 60.
6. Parke, Davis & Company, "Suggested Details." Cited in: William C. Hewson. Present Status, *op. cit.*, p. 2551. Cited in: M. Silverman and P.R. Lee, *op. cit.*, p. 60.
7. "The Peculiar Success of Chloromycetin," *Consumer Reports*, 35:616-619, October 1970.
8. Henry Dolger, M.D., Chief of Diabetes and Associated Attending Physician for Metabolic Diseases, Mount Sinai Hospital, New York. Cited in: H.D. Walker, *Market Power and Price Levels in the Ethical Drug Market*, Indiana University Press, Bloomington, 1971, p. 86.
9. *Ibid.*
10. *Ibid.*
11. Parke, Davis & Company, "Ideas and Suggestions." Cited in: William C. Hewson. Present Status, *op. cit.*, p. 2553. Cited in: M. Silverman and P. R. Lee, *op. cit.*, p. 60.
12. American Medical Association, Council on Drugs, "Blood Dyscrasias Associated with Chloramphenicol (Chloromycetin) Therapy," *Journal of the American Medical Association*, 172:2044-2045, 1960.
13. The Peculiar Success, *op. cit.*, p. 617.
14. Director of Investigation and Research, Combines Investigation Act, *Material Collected for Submission to the Restrictive Trade Practices Commission in the Course of an Inquiry under Section 42 of the Com-*

bines *Investigation Act Relating to the Manufacture, Distribution and Sale of Drugs*, Queen's Printer, Ottawa, 1961, p. 17.
15. The Peculiar Success, *op. cit.*, p. 617.
16. L.G. Schifrin, "The Ethical Drug Industry: The Case for Compulsory Licensing," *Antitrust Bulletin*, 12:893-915, 1967.
17. M. Silverman, "The Epidemiology of Drug Promotion," *International Journal of Health Services*, 7:157-166, 1977.
18. R.A. Fine, *The Great Drug Deception*, Stein and Day, New York, 1972. Most of the information on MER/29 is summarized from this book.
19. *Ibid.*, p. 123.
20. Thomas M. Rice. Present Status, *op. cit.*, Part 10, 1969, p. 4233. Cited in: M. Silverman and P.R. Lee, *op. cit.*, p. 90.
21. R.A. Fine, *op. cit.*, p. 48.
22. *Ibid.*, p. 55.
23. *Ibid.*
24. *Ibid.*, pp. 63-64.
25. *Ibid.*, p. 66.
26. *Ibid.*, p. 71.
27. *Ibid.*, p. 72.
28. *Ibid.*
29. *Ibid.*, p. 111.
30. *Ibid.*, p. 89.
31. *Ibid.*, p. 21.
32. Restrictive Trade Practices Commission, *op, cit.*, p. 276.

CHAPTER 6. RESEARCH

1. W.W. Wigle, *Canadian Medical Association Journal*, 100:441-442, 1969.
2. R. Wilkins, *Health Status in Canada, 1926-1976*, Occasional Paper No. 13, Institute for Research on Public Policy, Montreal, May 1980.
3. "Preventive Medicine Lecture Notes," Faculty of Medicine, University of Toronto, Toronto, 1975, p. 27, (mimeographed).
4. J.B. McKinlay and S.M. McKinlay, "The Questionable Contribution of Medical Measures to the Decline of Mortality in the United States in the Twentieth Century," *Milbank Memorial Fund Quarterly*, 55:405-428, 1977.
5. Pharmaceutical Manufacturers Association of Canada, *The Pharmaceutical Industry and Ontario*, Ottawa, 1978, p. 20.
6. J. Marshall, *Madness: An Indictment of the Mental Health Care System in Ontario*, Ontario Public Service Employees Union, Toronto, 1982, p. 40.
7. A. Scull, *Decarceration*, Prentice Hall, Englewood Cliffs, New Jersey, 1977. See especially Chapter 5, "'The Technological Fix'? Psychoactive Drugs and Community Treatment."
8. *Ibid.*, p. 84.
9. *Ibid.*, p. 86.
10. *Ibid.*, p. 85.
11. F.J.J. Letermendia and A.D. Harris, "Chlorpromazine and the Untreated Chronic Schizophrenic," *British Journal of Psychiatry*, 113:950-957, 1967.
12. A. Scull, *op. cit.*, p. 87.
13. *Ibid.*, p. 88.
14. W. McDermott, K.W. Deuschle and C.R. Barnett, "Health Care Experiment at Many Farms: A Technological Misfit of Health Care and Disease

Pattern Existed in This Navaho Community," *Science*, 175:23-31, 1972.
15. *The Selection of Essential Drugs. Report of a WHO Expert Committee*, WHO Technical Report Series, 615, World Health Organization, Geneva, 1977.
16. Since 1962, drugs had to demonstrate their effectiveness before being sold in the United States.
17. M. Novitch, Food and Drug Administration, 1973. Cited in: M. Silverman and P.R. Lee, *Pills, Profits and Politics*, University of California Press, Berkeley, 1974, p. 131. The labelling was particularly criticized for having failed the primary purpose of providing the physician and the pharmacist with balanced, authoritative and objective guides.
18. *Ibid.*, pp. 123-124. In another FDA study of more than 800 drugs introduced in the U.S. between 1960 and 1973, two thirds were found to represent little or no therapeutic gain over existing drugs. "How to Pay Less for Prescription Drugs," *Consumer Reports*, 40:48-53, January 1975.
19. R.K. Cannan, statement in: J.D. Cooper (editor), *The Economics of Drug Innovation*, The American University, Washington, D.C., 1970, p. 87.
20. *The Medical Post*, April 20, 1971, p. 15.
21. Task Force on Prescription Drugs, *The Drug Prescribers*, U.S. Government Printing Office, Washington, D.C., 1968, p. 5.
22. Task Force on Prescription Drugs, *The Drug Makers and the Drug Distributors*, U.S. Government Printing Office, Washington, D.C. 1968, p. 18.
23. Montreal *Gazette*, October 27, 1982, p. A-6.
24. M.H. VanWoert, "Sounding Board: Profitable and Nonprofitable Drugs," *New England Journal of Medicine*, 298:903-905, 1978.
25. C. Gray, "The Pharmaceutical Industry: Promoting Research in the 80's," *Canadian Medical Association Journal*, 124:787-792, 1981.
26. Canada, House of Commons, Special Committee on Drug Costs and Prices, *Minutes of Proceedings and Evidence, No. 7*, Tuesday, July 5, 1966, Queen's Printer, Ottawa, 1966, p. 540.
27. S. Gershon and B. Shopsin, *Lithium: Its Role in Psychiatric Research and Treatment*, Plenum Press, New York, 1973; National Institute of Mental Health, *Lithium in the Treatment of Mood Disorders*, U.S. Government Printing Office, Washington, D.C., 1974.
28. J. Randal, "Up for Adoption: Rare Drugs for Rare Diseases," *Science 82*, 3:31-37, September 1982.
29. Canada, House of Commons, Special Committee on Drug Costs and Prices, *Minutes of Proceedings and Evidence, No. 33*, Tuesday, February 14, 1967, Queen's Printer, Ottawa, 1967, p. 2444.
30. J.M. Blair, *Economic Concentration*, Harcourt, New York, 1972, p. 391.
31. Restrictive Trade Practices Commission, *Report Concerning the Manufacture, Distribution and Sale of Drugs*, Queen's Printer, Ottawa, 1963, p. 521.
32. *Canada, Royal Commission on Health Services: Report*, Volume 1, Queen's Printer, Ottawa, 1964, p. 656.
33. P.R. Garai, "Advertising and Promotion of Drugs," in: P. Talalay (editor), *Drugs in Our Society*, Johns Hopkins Press, Baltimore, 1964, p. 199.
34. *Ibid.*, p. 194.
35. H.I. Forman, "Drug Patents, Compulsory Licences, Prices, and Innovation," in: J.D. Cooper, *op. cit.*, p. 180.
36. U.S. Senate, Committee on the Judiciary, Subcommittee on Antitrust and

Monopoly, *Hearing on Administered Prices in the Drug Industry*, U.S. Government Printing Office, Washington, D.C., Part 18, 1960, p. 10254. Cited in: J.M. Blair, *op. cit.*, p. 242.

37. U.S. Senate, Committee on the Judiciary, Subcommittee on Antitrust and Monopoly, *Hearings on S. 1552*, "To Amend and Supplement the Antitrust Laws with Respect to the Manufacture and Distribution of Drugs," U.S. Government Printing Office, Washington, D.C., Part 3, 1961, p. 1542. Cited in: J.M. Blair, *op. cit.*, p. 243.

38. Montreal *Gazette*, October 23, 1982, pp. A-1, A-4.

39. The Drug Makers, *op. cit.*, p. 21.

40. H.F. Dowling, *Medicines for Man*, Alfred A. Knopf, New York, 1970, p. 98.

41. New York Academy of Medicine, Committee on Public Health, "The Importance of Clinical Testing in Determining the Efficacy and Safety of Drugs," *Bulletin of the New York Academy of Medicine*, 38:417-439, 1962.

42. Montreal *Gazette*, October 23, 1982, pp. A-1, A-4.

43. The Drug Makers, *op. cit.*, p. 21.

44. W.M. O'Brien, "Drug Testing: Is Time Running Out?", *Bulletin of the Atomic Scientists*, 25:8-14, January 1969.

45. "Adverse Drug Reports Supressed—Doctors," Saskatoon *Star-Phoenix*, August 16, 1974, p. 1; "U.S. Drug Firm Lied About Tumors Found in Testing, Senators Told," *Globe and Mail*, July 11, 1975. p. 12; "FDA Calls U.S. Drug Firms Research Sloppy," *Globe and Mail*, January 21, 1976, p. 11; "FDA Suggests Grand Jury Probe Over Drug Firm's Testing Data," *Globe and Mail*, April 9, 1976, p. 14. For a damning indictment of pharmaceutical research in the U.S. see: M. Dowie, D. Foster, C. Marshall *et al.*, "The Illusion of Safety," *Mother Jones*, June 1982, pp. 35-49.

46. Hearings on S. 1552, *op. cit.*, p. 1542. Cited in: J.M. Blair, *op. cit.*, p. 243.

47. Hearings on Administered Prices, *op. cit.*, p. 10379. Cited in: H.D. Walker, *Market Power and Price Levels in the Ethical Drug Market*, Indiana University Press, Bloomington, 1971, p. 87.

48. W.M. O'Brien, *op. cit.*

49. Montreal *Star*, July 24, 1972, p. C1.

50. N. Wade, "Physicians Who Falsify Drug Data," *Science*, 180:1038, 1973.

51. Edmonton *Journal*, April 3, 1982, pp. 1, 3; April 4, 1982, p. 1; April 5, 1982, pp. B1, B2.

52. U.S. Senate, Committee on Small Business, Subcommittee on Monopoly, *Competitive Problems in the Drug Industry*, U.S. Government Printing Office, Washington, D.C., Part 8, 1967, p. 3453. Cited in: R. Burack, *The New Handbook of Prescription Drugs*, Pantheon Books, New York, 1970, pp. 19-20.

53. E.M. Boyd, "Clinical Pharmacology Trials," *Rx Bulletin*, 1:3-4, June 1970.

54. R.A. Fine, *The Great Drug Deception*, Stein and Day, New York, 1972, p. 169.

55. H.J. Weinstein. Hearings on Administered Prices, *op. cit.*, pp. 10244-10245. Cited in: H.D. Walker, *op. cit.*, pp. 88, 238; A.D. Console. Hearings on Administered Prices, *op. cit.*, p. 10379. Cited in: H.D. Walker, *op. cit.*, p. 86.

56. N.D.W. Lionel and A. Herxheimer, "Assessing Reports of Therapeutic Trials," *British Medical Journal*, 3:637-640, 1970.

57. R.J. Reiffenstein, A.J. Schiltroth and D.M. Todd, "Current Standards in Reported Drug Trials," *Canadian Medical Association Journal*, 99:1134-1135, 1968.
58. H.L. Williams. Competitive Problems, *op. cit.*, Part 2, 1967, pp. 460-461. Cited in: The Drug Prescribers, *op. cit.*, p. 9.
59. R. Cooperstock, "Some Factors Involved in the Increased Prescribing of Psychotropic Drugs," in: R. Cooperstock (editor), *Social Aspects of the Medical Use of Psychotropic Drugs*, Addiction Research Foundation, Toronto, 1974, p. 30.
60. M.H. Pappworth, *Human Guinea Pigs*, Beacon Press, Boston, 1967, p. 64.
61. J. Mitford, "Experiments Behind Bars," *Atlantic Monthly*, 231:64-73, January 1973.
62. *Ibid.*, p. 64.
63. Royal Commission on Health Services, *Provision, Distribution and Cost of Drugs in Canada*, Queen's Printer, Ottawa, 1964, p. 38.
64. *Financial Post*, March 5, 1983, pp. 1,2. Of the $42.9 million that was spent on research in 1978, $33.5 million went intramurally, $7 million extramurally and $2.4 million on capital investment. C. Gray, "The Pharmaceutical Industry—Will Canada Become a Major Research Centre?," *Canadian Medical Association Journal*, 124:910-918, 1981.
65. Pharmaceutical Manufacturers Association of Canada, *op. cit.*, p. 18.
66. See for example: Pharmaceutical Manufacturers Association of Canada, *Background Information on the Canadian Pharmaceutical Manufacturing Industry*, Ottawa, 1979, p. 3.
67. The results for the other OECD countries were: Belgium 229, Denmark 433, Finland 529, France 204, Italy 231, Japan 246, Sweden 448, the United Kingdom 661 and the United States 192. Figures calculated from: K.S. Palda and B. Pazderka, *Background to a Target: An International Comparison of the Canadian Pharmaceutical Industry's R&D Intensity*, Department of Industry, Trade and Commerce, Technological Innovation Studies Program, Report No. 71, Ottawa, 1980, p. 35.
68. L.L. Dan, "The Drug Industry in Canada: A Position Analysis," *Business Quarterly*, 42:62-71, Autumn 1982.
69. Department of Industry, Trade and Commerce, *The Health Care Products Industry in Canada*, Ottawa, 1980, p. 18.
70. For varying versions of this myth see: *Globe and Mail*, October 26, 1982, p. 5; *The Medical Post*, August 10, 1982, pp. 8, 58.
71. D. Woods, "The Pharmaceutical Industry Needs Remedy for Mac-Eachenism," *Canadian Medical Association Journal*, 126:337, 1982; D. Woods, "Antibusiness Attitudes Strangling Drug Research," *Canadian Medical Association Journal*, 127:559, 1982.
72. *The Medical Post*, August 10, 1982, pp. 8, 58.
73. *Ibid.*
74. In the period 1964 to 1971, real growth in pharmaceutical research and development expenditures was 7.2 percent a year as against 8.2 percent for all industries. Department of Industry, Trade and Commerce, *The Health Care Products Industry: Research and Development in Canada*, Ottawa, 1979, p. 22.
75. P.K. Gorecki and I. Henderson, "Compulsory Patent Licensing of Drugs in Canada: A Comment on the Debate," *Canadian Public Policy*, 7:559-568, 1981.
76. *Financial Post*, August 7, 1982, p. 3.

77. P.K. Gorecki, *Regulating the Price of Prescription Drugs in Canada: Compulsory Licensing, Product Selection and Government Reimbursement Programmes*, Technical Report No. 8, Economic Council of Canada, Ottawa, 1981, p. 161.
78. P.K. Gorecki and I. Henderson, *op. cit.*
79. K.S. Palda and B. Pazderka, *op. cit.*, pp. 53-54.
80. These programs are: Regional Development Incentive Program (DREE), Program for Export Market Development(PEMD), Pharmaceutical Industry Development Assistance (PIDA), Program for Advancement of Industrial Technology (PAIT), Industrial Research and Development Incentives Act (IRDIA) and Industrial Research Assistance Program (IRAP). IRDIA was terminated in 1975. In 1977, the Enterprise Development Program replaced PIDA and PAIT.
81. The one exception was IRDIA. The Health Care Products Industry: Research, *op. cit.*, p. 24.
82. Even Edward Bembridge, president of Merck Frosst Canada agrees that Canada provides good tax incentives for research. *Financial Post*, August 7, 1982, p. 3.
83. K.S. Palda and B. Pazerdka, *op. cit.*, p. 35.
84. C. Gray, "The Pharmaceutical Industry—Will Canada...," *op. cit.*, p. 915.
85. *Globe and Mail*, July 16, 1983, p. B1.
86. Canadian Drug Manufacturers Association, *Pharmaceutical Patents: Compulsory Licensing. A Case for the Retention of Section 41(4) of the Patent Act*, Toronto, 1983, p. 29.
87. *Ibid.*, p. 34.
88. This account is summarized from: Department of Industry, Trade and Commerce, The Health Care Products Industry: Research, *op. cit.*, pp. 10-11.
89. *Ibid.*, p. 21.
90. *Ibid.*, p. 16.
91. "Report '72—Canada's Pharmaceutical Industry," *Drug Merchandising*, 53:32, April 1972.
92. In Canada 14.14 percent of employees were classified as "engineers, scientists and other technicians" versus 21.16 percent in the United States. M. Gordon and D. Fowler, *The Drug Industry: A Case Study in Foreign Control*, James Lorimer & Company, Toronto, 1981, p. 56.
93. Pharmaceutical Manufacturers Association of Canada, The Pharmaceutical Industry and Ontario, *op. cit.*, p. 18. Apparently the priorities of the industry, as to how the money is spent, must change very rapidly. Three years earlier the PMAC said that 25 percent of the funding was going to basic research. Pharmaceutical Manufacturers Association of Canada, *The Pharmaceutical Manufacturing Industry*, Ottawa, 1972, p. 11.
94. K.S. Palda and B. Pazderka, *op. cit.*, p. 82.
95. Canada, House of Commons, *Second (Final) Report of the Special Committee of the House of Commons on Drug Costs and Prices*, Queen's Printer, Ottawa, 1967, p. 25; Department of Industry, Trade and Commerce, The Health Care Products Industry: Research, *op. cit.*, p. 17.
96. W.S. Comanor, "The Drug Industry and Medical Research: The Economics of the Kefauver Committee Investigations," *The Journal of Business*, 39:12-18, 1966.

CHAPTER 7. MEDICAL STUDENTS, DOCTORS AND ORGANIZED MEDICINE

1. M. Shapiro, *Getting Doctored*, Between The Lines, Kitchener, 1978.
2. J. Pekkanen, "The Impact of Promotion on Physicians' Prescribing Patterns," *Journal of Drug Issues*, 6:13-20, 1976.
3. Director of Investigation and Research, Combines Investigation Act, *Material Collected for Submission to the Restrictive Trade Practices Commission in the Course of an Inquiry Under Section 42 of the Combines Investigation Act Relating to the Manufacture, Distribution and Sale of Drugs*, Queen's Printer, Ottawa, 1961, pp. 111-112.
4. Toronto *Star*, May 16, 1970, p. 5.
5. S. Wolfe and R.F. Badgley, *The Family Doctor*, Macmillan, Toronto, 1973, p. 64.
6. *Globe and Mail*, December 3, 1983, p. 6.
7. U.S. Senate, Committee on Small Business, Subcommittee on Monopoly, *Competitive Problems in the Drug Industry*, U.S. Government Printing Office, Washington, D.C., Part 11, 1967, p. 4880. Cited in: R. Burack, *The New Handbook of Prescription Drugs*, Pantheon Books, New York, 1970, p. 33.
8. *The Medical Post*, August 24, 1982, p. 12.
9. "Opren Scandal," *The Lancet*, 1:219-220, 1983.
10. "Government Involvement in Health Care," *Canadian Pharmaceutical Journal*, 104:26-27, July 1971.
11. "Pharmaceutical Industry Studies Current, Future Trends," *Canadian Pharmaceutical Journal*, 110:27-29, May 1977.
12. W.E. Goodman, "Drug Substitution: Remedy or Rip-off?," *Canadian Medical Association Journal*, 128:198-202, 1983.
13. "Pharmaceutical Industry is 'Reorienting' Its Promotional Activities," *Canadian Family Physician*, 23:262, 1977.
14. N.M. Kaplan, "The Support of Continuing Medical Education by Pharmaceutical Companies," *New England Journal of Medicine*, 300:194-196, 1979.
15. *The Medical Post, op. cit.*
16. D.G. Bates, "Reader Objects to Drug Co. Sponsorship of CME Courses," *Canadian Family Physician*, 22:815, 1976.
17. C. Bourbonniere, "Ethical Issues in Sponsorship of CME," *Canadian Medical Association Journal*, 127:681, 1982.
18. Advertisement cited in: *Globe and Mail*, October 22, 1982, p. 5.
19. "Patent Protection in Drug Manufacture," *Canadian Medical Association Journal*, 90:1373-1374, 1964.
20. "Generic Products as Equivalents," *Canadian Medical Association Journal*, 88:94, 1963.
21. P.P. Morgan, "Pharmaceutical Advertising in Medical Journals," *Canadian Medical Association Journal*, 130:1412, 1984; M. McCaffery, "The Muzzle Muddle," *Canadian Family Physician*, 21:7, November 1975.
22. D. Woods, "The Pharmaceutical Industry Needs Remedy for MacEachenism," *Canadian Medical Association Journal*, 126:337, 1982; D. Woods, "Antibusiness Attitudes Strangling Drug Research," *Canadian Medical Association Journal*, 127:559, 1982; D. Woods, "The Pharmaceutical Industry: A Prescription," *Canadian Medical Association Journal*, 129:675, 1983.
23. *Canadian Medical Association Journal*, 127:276, 1982.

24. D. Woods, "The Pharmaceutical Industry. Roche: Blending Independent and Commercial Research," *Canadian Medical Association Journal*, 129: 743-752, 1983.
25. M. Silverman, P.R. Lee and M. Lydecker, *Prescriptions for Death: The Drugging of the Third World*, University of California Press, Berkeley, 1982, p. 124.
26. A. Klass, "An Unholy Alliance," *Canadian Medical Association Journal*, 83:660, 1960; A. Klass, "The Unholy Alliance," *Canadian Medical Association Journal*, 107:848, 1972.
27. Montreal *Gazette*, October 26, 1982, p. A-8.
28. "Report of the Committe on Pharmacy," *Canadian Medical Association Journal*, 93:459, 1965.
29. Canada, House of Commons, Special Committee on Drug Costs and Prices, *Minutes of Proceedings and Evidence, No. 18*, Tuesday, November 15, 1966, Queen's Printer, Ottawa, 1966, Appendix A, p. 1265. Cited in: R.W. Lang, *The Politics of Drugs*, Saxon House, Westmead, England, 1974, p. 108.
30. R.W. Lang, *op. cit.*, p. 109.
31. "Report of the Committee on Pharmacy," *Canadian Medical Association Journal*, 97:700-701, 1967.
32. *Ibid.*, p. 701.
33. "Bill C-190," *Canadian Medical Association Journal*, 98:262, 1968.
34. R.W. Lang, *op cit.*, p. 108.
35. Canada, House of Commons, *op. cit.*, p. 1266. Cited in R.W. Lang, *op. cit.*, p. 109.
36. Canada, House of Commons, *op. cit.*, p. 1265. Cited in: R.W. Lang, *op. cit.*, p. 112.
37. "Improved Financial Picture for 1970 Forecast by Finance Committee," *Canadian Medical Association Journal*, 103:205, 1970.
38. "Come Out From Under That Bed," *Canadian Medical Association Journal*, 102:1306-1307, 1970.
39. M.G. Sanders, "The Sparce Index: Medical Excellence or Drug Dependence," *Canadian Medical Association Journal*, 102:531-532, 1970.
40. Toronto *Star*, November 6, 1980, p. F1.

CHAPTER 8. ADVERTISING

1. Vancouver *Sun*, March 24, 1960. Cited in: Director of Investigation and Research, Combines Investigation Act, *Material Collected for Submission to the Restrictive Trade Practices Commission in the Course of an Inquiry Under Section 42 of the Combines Investigation Act Relating to the Manufacture, Distribution and Sale of Drugs*, Queen's Printer, Ottawa, 1961, p. 117.
2. *Globe and Mail*, May 5, 1980, p. B11.
3. Cited in: R.L. Smith, *The Health Hucksters*, Beacon Press, Boston, 1967, p. 99. In 1965, the amount per doctor for all 58 PMAC companies was $2,100.
4. P.R. Garai, "Advertising and Promotion of Drugs," in: P. Talalay (editor), *Drugs in Our Society*, Johns Hopkins Press, Baltimore, 1964, p. 191.
5. Canada, House of Commons, *Second (Final) Report of the Special Committee of the House of Commons on Drug Costs and Prices*, Queen's Printer, Ottawa, 1967, p. 23.

6. B. Pazderka, *Promotion and Competition in the Canadian Prescription Drug Industry*, Unpublished Ph.D. Thesis, Queen's University, Kingston, Ontario, 1976, p. 239.
7. Restrictive Trade Practices Commission, *Report Concerning the Manufacture, Distribution and Sale of Drugs*, Queen's Printer, Ottawa, 1963, p. 226.
8. Pharmaceutical Manufacturers Association of Canada, *The Pharmaceutical Industry and Ontario*, Ottawa, 1978, p. 35.
9. Restrictive Trade Practices Commission, *op. cit.*, p. 258.
10. *Canadian Family Physician*, 30:97-100, 1984.
11. "MER/29 and Warnings on New Drugs," *The Medical Letter*, 4:6, 1962.
12. Restrictive Trade Practices Commission, *op. cit.*, p. 260.
13. *Ibid.*, p. 261.
14. "The Positive Role of Pharmaceutical Advertising," *Canadian Medical Association Journal*, 84:668, 1961.
15. P.R. Garai, *op. cit.*, p. 190.
16. C. Cocking, "The Abuse of Prescription Drugs," *Weekend Magazine*, June 18, 1977, p. 16.
17. Dr. Murray Katz develops this argument in an article he wrote for the Montreal *Star*, July 23, 1973, p. D1.
18. M.C. Smith, *Principles of Pharmaceutical Marketing*, Lea and Febiger, Philadelphia, 1968, p. 67.
19. J. Pekkanen, "The Impact of Promotion on Physicians' Prescribing Patterns," *Journal of Drug Issues*, 6:13-20, 1976.
20. R. Bowes, "The Industry as Pusher," *Journal of Drug Issues*, 4:238-242, 1974
21. A. Klass, *There's Gold in Them Thar Pills*, Penguin, Middlesex, England, 1975, p. 40.
22. Montreal *Star*, *op. cit.*
23. R.W. Bell, "Doctors: The Front Line of Drug Industry Promotion," *Perception*, 3:32-33, January/February 1980.
24. Montreal *Gazette*, October 26, 1982, pp. A-1, A-8.
25. G.M. Torrance, "The Influence of the Drug Industry in Canada's Health System," Prepared for Community Health Centre Project, February 1972, pp. 28-29, (mimeographed).
26. L. Reis and W.F. Morando, "Pinpointing the H.P.P.," *Pharmaceutical Marketing and Media*, 2:27-30, March 1967. Cited in: Task Force on Prescription Drugs, *The Drug Prescribers*, U.S. Government Printing Office, Washington, D.C., 1968, p. 10.
27. Pharmaceutical Manufacturers Association of Canada, *The Pharmaceutical Manufacturing Industry*, Ottawa, 1973, p. 8.
28. Canada, House of Commons, Special Committee on Drug Costs and Prices, *Minutes of Proceedings and Evidence*, No. 18, Tuesday, November 15, 1966, Queen's Printer, Ottawa, 1966, p. 1225. Cited in: R.W. Lang, *The Politics of Drugs*, Saxon House, Westmead, England, 1974, p. 113.
29. Canada, House of Commons, Special Committee, *op. cit.*, p. 1225. Cited in: R.W. Lang, *op. cit.*, p. 113.
30. Pharmaceutical Manufacturers Association of Canada, *Principles and Code of Marketing Practice*, Ottawa, 1972, p. 7.
31. "Findings and Conclusions of the NCCC Project on Drug Advertising," *Journal of Drug Issues*, 4:311-312, 1974.
32. M. Mintz, "Drug Ad Exports Pose a Problem," Washington *Post*, May

21, 1968. Cited in: M. Silverman and P.R. Lee, *Pills, Profits and Politics*, University of California Press, Berkeley, 1974, p. 65. In Canada, the drug is called Duretic.

33. C. Cocking, *op. cit.*, p. 19.
34. H.F. Dowling, *Medicines for Man*, Alfred A. Knopf, New York, 1970, pp. 131-132.
35. U.S. Senate, Committee on the Judiciary, Subcommittee on Antitrust and Monopoly, *Hearings on Administered Prices in the Drug Industry*, U.S. Government Printing Office, Washington, D.C., Part 18, 1960, p. 10288. Cited in: H.D. Walker, *Market Power and Price Levels in the Ethical Drug Market*, Indiana University Press, Bloomington, 1971, p. 87.
36. Montreal *Gazette, op. cit.*, p. A-8.
37. *Globe and Mail*, October 22, 1982, p. 5. Transderm-V is not a prescription item, so technically CIBA could promote it anyway the company pleased. However, in most respects CIBA has been treating it the same as it does its prescription drugs: it is advertised in medical journals; it is listed in the *CPS*; and CIBA has had it accepted for listing in Ontario's *Drug Benefit Formulary*, meaning that those people covered by the Drug Benefit Plan will receive it free if it is prescribed.
38. *The Medical Post*, August 24, 1982, p. 12.
39. Hearings on Administered Prices, *op. cit.*, p. 10372. Cited in: H.D. Walker, *op. cit.*, pp. 86-87.
40. U.S. Senate, Committee on Small Business, Subcommittee on Monopoly, *Competitive Problems in the Drug Industry*, U.S. Government Printing Office, Washington, D.C. Part 11, 1967, p. 4480. Cited in: R. Burack, *The New Handbook of Prescription Drugs*, Pantheon Books, New York, 1970, pp. 32-33.
41. Advertisement cited in: *Globe and Mail*, October 22, 1982, p. 5.
42. Montreal *Gazette, op. cit.*
43. Toronto *Star*, November 6, 1980, p. F1.
44. *Globe and Mail*, September 10, 1982, p. R2.
45. Montreal *Gazette, op. cit.*
46. *Globe and Mail*, May 5, 1980, p. B11.
47. Ben Gaffin and Associates, "Fond du Lac Study, A Basic Marketing Study made for the American Medical Association," Chicago, 1956. Cited in: H.D. Walker, *op. cit.*, p. 74. The sample sizes are small, so no definitive conclusions should be drawn.
48. Montreal *Gazette, op. cit.*
49. V. Ross, "Between Bliss and Beldam," *Maclean's*, December 8, 1980, p. 40.
50. *Modern Medicine of Canada*, 33:1623, 1978.
51. Montreal *Gazette, op. cit.*
52. W. Bell, "Accredited Pharmaceutical Manufacturers Representatives," *Canadian Medical Association Journal*, 120:1327, 1979.
53. *Summary Publication, Drug Symposium: Drug Information for the Health Care Team*, McGill University, May 30-31, 1975, p. 7, (mimeographed).
54. Montreal *Gazette, op. cit.*
55. Pharmaceutical Manufacturers Association of Canada, Principles and

Code of Marketing Practice, *op. cit.*, p. 14.
56. M. Silverman and P.R. Lee, *op. cit.*, p. 62.
57. All the information and quotes on MER/29 come from: R.A. Fine, *The Great Drug Deception*, Stein and Day, New York, 1972.
58. *Globe and Mail*, May 5, 1980, p. B11.
59. B. Pazderka, *op. cit.*, pp. 239-240.
60. The amount spent on direct mail was not given in the latest PMAC figures, but is generally about 4.2 percent of all marketing costs.
61. R.G. McAuley and F. Little, "Junk Mail," *Canadian Medical Association Journal*, 129:1174-1176, 1983.
62. B. Pazderka, *op. cit.*, pp. 42-43.
63. Restrictive Trade Practices Commission, *op. cit.*, p. 284.
64. *Canadian Medical Association Journal*, 83:553, 1960.
65. *Ibid.*
66. *Ibid.*
67. *Canadian Medical Association Journal*, 118:24, 1978.
68. Restrictive Trade Practices Commission, *op. cit.*, p. 231.
69. *Ibid.*, p. 226.
70. *Globe and Mail*, May 5, 1980, p. B11.
71. Restrictive Trade Practices Commission, *op. cit.*, p. 226.
72. *Ibid.*, p. 272.
73. *Ibid.*, p. 270.
74. *Ibid.*, p. 272.
75. Montreal *Star*, July 23, 1973, p. D1. The regulations on this matter have since been changed and now require doctors to sign a receipt for any samples they receive.
76. R.W. Fassold, E.L. Heath and C.W. Gowdey, "An Appraisal of Drug Sampling," *University of Western Ontario Medical Journal*, 38:42-46, 1967.
77. *Globe and Mail*, May 5, 1980, p. B11.
78. W. Bell, personal communication.
79. E.M. Berry, "The Evolution of Scientific and Medical Journals," *New England Journal of Medicine*, 305:400-402, 1981.
80. M. Mintz, "FDA and Panalba: A Conflict of Commercial, Therapeutic Goals?," *Science*, 165:875-881, 1969.
81. *Ibid.*, p. 878. It appears that the Council on Drugs' independence and forthrightness eventually led to its demise. The trouble began in January 1971, when proofs of the Council's first edition of a drug handbook came back from the printer. The head of the AMA's Board of Trustees asked that the proofs be sent to the Pharmaceutical Manufacturers Association (PMA) saying: "We [the AMA] have to keep in good with PMA because we derive a high proportion of our income from them, and because they are our friends." Distribution of the handbook was delayed for about three months while the PMA studied the proofs. The PMA was "highly critical of the book," according to Dr. John Adriani, one of the editors, and offered to pay for making "a whole lot of changes" it desired. The Council refused to let these changes be made, but when the book was finally distributed, unauthorized changes had been made and a preface from the AMA executive vice-president was

inserted which was, in effect, a disclaimer for some of the Council's advice. In 1972, the Council set about preparing for a second edition, but when the AMA demanded certain changes, the Council refused. At that point, the AMA disbanded the Council. *Globe and Mail*, February 8, 1973, p. W6.
82. Summary Publication, *op. cit.*, p. 16.
83. V. Coleman, *The Medicine Men*, Temple Smith, London, 1975, p. 96.
84. *Ibid.*
85. A. Klass, *op. cit.*, p. 159.
86. J. Pekkanen, *op. cit.*
87. Pharmaceutical Manufacturers Association of Canada, Principles and Code of Marketing Practice, *op. cit.*, p. 8.
88. Brief of the Canadian Pharmaceutical Manufacturers Association to the Restrictive Trade Practices Commission. Cited in: Restrictive Trade Practices Commission, *op. cit.*, p. 261.
89. Since its inception, the PAAB's code has superceded the PMAC's guidelines as far as journal advertising is concerned. In practice it makes little difference which code is used since they are almost identical.
90. D. I. Rice, "Misleading Advertising of Drug Products," *Canadian Family Physician*, 24:101-102, 1978.
91. W. Bell, personal communication.
92. S. Garb, "The Reaction of Medical Students to Drug Advertising," *New England Journal of Medicine*, 259:121-123, 1958.
93. S.E. Harris, *The Economics of American Medicine*, Macmillan, New York, 1964, p. 89.
94. P.R. Garai, *op. cit.*
95. "Buffered Tetracyclines and Antibiotic Blood Levels," *The Medical Letter*, 1:3, 1959.
96. "References Used in Drug Advertisements," *The Medical Letter*, 5:56, 1963.
97. R. Hargraves, "Introduction," *Journal of Drug Issues*, 6:1-5, 1976. Sometime between 1974 and 1976, the National Council of Churches dropped the "of Christ" from its name.
98. "Findings and Conclusions of the NCCC Project on Drug Advertising," *Journal of Drug Issues*, 4:310-313, 1974.
99. G.V. Stimson, "The Use of References in Drug Advertisements," *Journal of the Royal College of General Practitioners*, 26 (Supplement 1):76-80, 1976. Although this was a British study, using British journals, I feel that the results are equally applicable in Canada for two reasons. First, many of the companies and drugs are the same in the two countries, and second, the Code of Practice for the British pharmaceutical industry is generally similar to the Canadian one.
100. *Modern Medicine of Canada*, 37:1832-1834, 1982.
101. Advertisement cited by Dr. M. Katz in: Montreal *Star*, July 23, 1973, p. D1.
102. *Modern Medicine of Canada*, 37:1514-1518, 1982.
103. F.F. Sandor, P.T. Pickens and J. Crallan, "Variations of Plasma Potassium Concentrations During Long-Term Treatment of Hypertension with Diuretics Without Potassium Supplements," *British Medical Journal*, 284:711-715, 1982.
104. *Medicine North America*, 28/36 (1st series):2737-2738, 1982.
105. *Canadian Family Physician*, 28:1966, 1998, 1982.

106. *Physician's Management Manuals*, 53:217, May 1982.
107. E.M. Sellers, "Clinical Pharmacology and Therapeutics of Benzodiazepines," *Canadian Medical Association Journal*, 118:1533-1538, 1978.
108. A. Kales, M.B. Scharf, J.D. Kales *et al.*, "Rebound Insomnia: A Potential Hazard Following Withdrawal of Certain Benzodiazepines," *Journal of the American Medical Association*, 241:1692-1695, 1979.
109. F. Solomon, C.C. White, D.L. Parron *et al.*, "Sleeping Pills, Insomnia and Medical Practice," *New England Journal of Medicine*, 300:803-808, 1979.
110. *Ibid.*
111. *Canadian Family Physician*, 24:95-96, June 1978.
112. *Canadian Family Physician*, 28:2190-2191, 1982.
113. *Canadian Medical Association Journal*, 125:194, 1981.
114. *Modern Medicine of Canada*, 37:1562-1564, 1982.
115. *Canadian Medical Association Journal*, 124:1634, 1981.
116. *Modern Medicine of Canada*, 37:1682-1684, 1982.
117. *Canadian Family Physician*, 28:1791-1792, 1982.
118. *Canadian Family Physician*, 19:82-83, August 1973.
119. *Canadian Family Physician*, 19:4-5, April 1973.
120. *Canadian Journal of Psychiatry*, 27:A19, A21, 1982.
121. *Canadian Family Physician*, 20:26, 28, February 1974.
122. See for example: H.J. Osofsky and R. Seidenberg, "Is Female Menopausal Depression Inevitable?," *Obstetrics and Gynecology*, 36:611-615, 1970.
123. *Canadian Medical Association Journal*, 122:6, 1980.
124. *Canadian Medical Association Journal*, 124:848, 1981.
125. *Canadian Family Physician*, 28:1988-1989, 1982.
126. *Canadian Medical Association Journal*, 122:749, 1980.
127. *Medicine North America*, 28/36 (1st series):2666, 1982.
128. *Canadian Family Physician*, 28:1908-1909, 1982.
129. *Canadian Medical Association Journal*, 127:1150, 1982.
130. R. Seidenberg, "Drug Advertising and Perception of Mental Illness," *Mental Hygiene*, 55:21-31, 1971.
131. P.S. Stephenson and G.A. Walker, "Psychotropic Drugs and Women," *Bioethics Quarterly*, 2:20-38, 1980.
132. C. McRee, B.F. Corder and T. Haizlip, "Psychiatrists' Responses to Sexual Bias in Pharmaceutical Advertising," *American Journal of Psychiatry*, 131:1273-1275, 1974.
133. J. Prather and L.S. Fidell, "Sex Differences in the Content and Style of Medical Advertisements," *Social Science and Medicine*, 9:23-26, 1975.
134. I.K. Zola, "Culture and Symptoms—An Analysis of Patients' Presenting Complaints," *American Sociological Review*, 31:615-630, 1966.
135. J. Prather and L.S. Fidell, *op. cit.*, p. 26.
136. *Globe and Mail*, February 27, 1980, p. 13.
137. P.R. Garai, *op. cit.*, p. 194.
138. Calvin Kunin. Competitive Problems, *op. cit.*, Part 2, p. 731. Cited in: The Drug Prescribers, *op. cit.*, p. 10.
139. P.R. Garai, *op. cit.*, p. 195.
140. G. Teeling-Smith, "Psychotropic Drugs and Society," *Journal of the Royal College of General Practitioners*, 23 (Supplement 2):58-63, 1973.
141. Pharmaceutical Manufacturers Association of Canada, The Pharmaceutical Industry and Ontario, *op. cit.*, p. 35.

CHAPTER 9. WHAT DO DOCTORS KNOW ABOUT DRUGS?

1. H.L. Lennard, *Mystification and Drug Misuse*, Jossey-Bass, San Francisco, 1971, p. 29.
2. Pharmaceutical Manufacturers Association of Canada, *Principles and Code of Marketing Practice*, Ottawa, 1972, p. 4.
3. H.D. Cook, "Brand Names or Proper Names? (The Question in Perspective)," *Canadian Medical Association Journal*, 91:172, 1964.
4. For a summary of the Royal Commission on Health Services' recommendations on prescription drugs see: Canada, House of Commons, *Second (Final) Report of the Special Committee of the House of Commons on Drug Costs and Prices*, Queen's Printer, Ottawa, 1967, pp. 60-62. For the Special Commons Committee's recommendations see its report, p. 17.
5. O.L. Peterson *et al.*, "An Analytical Study of North Carolina General Practice: 1953-1954," *Journal of Medical Education*, 31:1-165, December 1956.
6. K.F. Clute, *The General Practitioner: A Study of Medical Education and Practice in Ontario and Nova Scotia*, University of Toronto Press, Toronto, 1963, pp. 300-301.
7. H.C. Neu and S.P. Howrey, "Testing the Physician's Knowledge of Antibiotic Use," *New England Journal of Medicine*, 293:1291-1295, 1975.
8. Montreal *Gazette*, October 26, 1982, p. A-8.
9. R.W. Fassold and C.W. Gowdey, "A Survey of Physicians' Reactions to Drug Promotion," *Canadian Medical Association Journal*, 98:701-705, 1968.
10. C. Cocking, "The Abuse of Prescription Drugs," *Weekend Magazine*, June 18, 1977, p. 18.
11. "You and The Ads," *Canadian Medical Association Journal*, 103:329, 1970.
12. "Around North America With Mefenamic Acid," *The Medical Letter*, 20:104, 1978.
13. *Physicians' Desk Reference*, 32nd Edition, 1978, p. 1277.
14. *Compendium of Pharmaceuticals and Specialties*, Canadian Pharmaceutical Association, Toronto, 1978, p. 522. There is even less information given in the Mexican *Diccionario de Especialidades Farmaceuticas*.
15. W.A. Parker, "The Compendium of Pharmaceuticals and Specialties as a Drug Information Resource for Treatment of Acute Drug Overdoses," *Canadian Family Physician*, 25:211-212, 214-215, 1979.
16. R.W. Bell and J. Osterman, "The Compendium of Pharmaceuticals and Specialties: A Critical Analysis," *International Journal of Health Services*, 13:107-118, 1983.
17. L.S. Linn and M.S. Davis, "Physicians' Orientation Toward the Legitimacy of Drug Use and Their Preferred Source of New Drug Information," *Social Science and Medicine*, 6:199-203, 1972.
18. Ben Gaffin and Associates, *Attitudes of U.S. Physicians Toward the American Pharmaceutical Industry*, Chicago, 1957. Cited in: R.A. Bauer and L.H. Wortzel, "Doctor's Choice: The Physician and His Source of Information About Drugs," *Journal of Marketing Research*, 3:40-47, February 1966.
19. Ben Gaffin and Associates, *op. cit.* Cited in: H.F. Dowling, *Medicines for Man*, Alfred A. Knopf, New York, 1970.
20. Pharmaceutical Manufacturers Association, *Survey of Physicians*, Washington, D.C., 1960. Cited in: J.J. Harris, "Survey of Medical

Communication Sources Available for Continuing Physician Education,"
Journal of Medical Education, 41:737-755, 1966; R. Ferber and H.G.
Wales, *The Effectiveness of Pharmaceutical Promotion*, University of
Illinois Bureau of Economics and Business Research Bulletin 83, Urbana,
Illinois, 1958.

21. J. Avorn, M. Chen and R. Hartley, "Scientific versus Commercial
Sources of Influence on the Prescribing Behavior of Physicians,"
American Journal of Medicine, 73:4-8, 1982.
22. Ben Gaffin and Associates, "Fond du Lac Study, A Basic Marketing Study
Made for the American Medical Association," Chicago, 1956. Cited in:
H.D. Walker, *Market Power and Price Levels in the Ethical Drug Market*,
Indiana University Press, Bloomington, 1971, p. 74.
23. H. Menzel and E. Katz, "Social Relations and Innovation in the Medical
Profession: The Epidemiology of a New Drug," *Public Opinion Quarterly*,
20:337-352, Winter 1955-56. Cited in: R.A. Bauer and L.H. Wortzel, *op.
cit.*, p. 43.
24. R.A. Bauer, "Risk Handling in Drug Adoption: The Role of Company
Preference," *Public Interest Quarterly*, 25:546-559, 1961.
25. R.W. Fassold and C.W. Gowdey, *op. cit.*, pp. 702-704. Twenty-five
percent gave commercial sources as the ones they preferred.
26. C.W. Gowdey and R.W. Fassold, "Survey of Doctors' Reactions to the
Promotion of New Drugs," *Canadian Pharmaceutical Journal*, 101:30-
36, September 1968. A 1979-1980 survey of Ontario doctors seems to
show that the better qualified the doctor the less s/he relies on pharmaceutical handouts. Over 15 percent of all primary care physicians
considered drug company literature an important source of continuing
medical education, but only 2.6 percent of doctors who were certified by
the College of Family Physicians held this view. E. Dunn, J.I. Williams,
A.M. Bryans *et al.*, "Continuing Medical Education in Ontario: A Primary Care Perspective," *Canadian Family Physician*, 28:1327-1328, 1330,
1332-1333, 1982.
27. M.H. Becker, P.D. Stolley, L. Lasagna *et al.*, "Differential Education
Concerning Therapeutics and Resultant Physician Prescribing Patterns,"
Journal of Medical Education, 47:118-127, 1972.
28. Ben Gaffin and Associates, Attitudes of U.S. Physicians, *op. cit.*, p. 17.
Cited in: R.A. Bauer and L.H. Wortzel, *op. cit.*, p. 45.

CHAPTER 10. PRESCRIBING AND PROBLEMS

1. G. Stimson, "Doctor-Patient Interaction in Some Problems for Prescribing," *Journal of the Royal College of General Practitioners*, 26 (Supplement 1):88-96, 1976.
2. *Globe and Mail*, October 21, 1977, p. 9; *Globe and Mail*, October 11,
1974, p. 13.
3. C. Archer and M. Benner, "Women's Use of Psychotropic Medication: A
Community Survey," *Canadian Family Physician*, 26:867-871, 1980.
4. IMS of Canada, *A Drug Profile: Psychotherapeutic Agents*, Dollard-des-
Ormeaux, Quebec, 1978, Figure 1.
5. R. Cooperstock, "Special Problems of Psychotropic Drug Use Among
Women," *Canada's Mental Health*, 28:3-5, June 1980. According to a
1982 survey by the Ontario Addiction Research Foundation the use of
tranquillizers may be dropping. In 1977, 13.2 percent of the people interviewed reported using tranquillizers in the past year, but by 1982 that
figure had dropped to 8.6 percent. The trend was even more pronounced

in women, falling from 17.3 to 10.6 percent. R.G. Smart and E.M. Adlaf, *Trends in Alcohol and Drug Use Among Ontario Adults, 1982*, Addiction Research Foundation, Toronto, 1982.

6. *Globe and Mail*, November 8, 1979, p. T3.
7. J.-D. Tu, "A Survey of Psychotropic Medication in Mental Retardation Facilities," *Journal of Clinical Psychiatry*, 40:125-128, 1979.
8. L.S. Linn, "Physician Characteristics and Attitudes Toward Legitimate Use of Psychotherapeutic Drugs," *Journal of Health and Social Behavior*, 12:132-140, 1971. Diazepam prescribing was compared in two groups of Montreal physicians: doctors in a group practice working on a fee-for-service basis and salaried doctors in health centres. There was little difference in the proportion of physicians willing to prescribe diazepam. However, the salaried doctors imposed stricter time limits on their prescriptions, gave clearer warnings about the risks of diazepam and were more likely to suggest non-chemical forms of therapy. M. Renaud, J. Beauchemin, C. Lalonde *et al.*, "Practice Settings and Prescribing Profiles: The Simulation of Tension Headaches to General Practitioners Working in Different Practice Settings in the Montreal Area," *American Journal of Public Health*, 70:1068-1073, 1980.
9. L.S. Linn and M.S. Davis, "Physicians' Orientation Toward the Legitimacy of Drug Use and Their Preferred Source of New Drug Information," *Social Science and Medicine*, 6:199-203, 1972.
10. IMS of Canada, *op. cit.*
11. *Toronto Star*, August 25, 1973, p. B7.
12. R. Cooperstock, *op. cit.*
13. S. Zisook and R.A. DeVaul, "Adverse Behavioral Effects of Benzodiazepines," *Journal of Family Practice*, 5:963-966, 1977.
14. P.D. Stolley and L. Lasagna, "Prescribing Habits of Physicians," *Journal of Chronic Diseases*, 22:395-405, 1969.
15. L. Kopala, "The Use of Cimetidine in Hospitalized Patients," *Canadian Family Physician*, 30:69-72, 1984.
16. *Globe and Mail*, December 5, 1979, p. 13. The response from Baxter Rowsell, manager of pharmacy and consumer affairs for Lilly, was that the company believes "re-education and not proscription" will solve the problems related to the drug.
17. "Poll on Medical Practice: Rheumatoid Arthritis (1966)," *Modern Medicine*, 34:75, 1966.
18. H.E. Simmons and P.D. Stolley, "This is Medical Progress? Trends and Consequences of Antibiotic Use in the United States," *Journal of the American Medical Association*, 227:1023-1028, 1974.
19. P. Heaton, "The Diagnostic Problem of Prescribing Antibiotics in URI," *Canadian Family Physician*, 19:55-58, May 1973.
20. T.L. Perry and G.H. Guyatt, "Antimicrobial Drug Use in Three Canadian General Hospitals," *Canadian Medical Association Journal*, 116:253-256, 1977.
21. M.R. Achong, B.A. Hauser and J.L. Krusky, "Rational and Irrational Use of Antibiotics in a Canadian Teaching Hospital," *Canadian Medical Association Journal*, 116:256-259, 1977.
22. E. Schollenberg and W.L. Albritton, "Antibiotic Misuse in a Pediatric Teaching Hospital," *Canadian Medical Association Journal*, 122:49-52, 1980.
23. C. Muller, "Medical Review of Prescribing," *Journal of Chronic Diseases*, 18:689-696, 1965; R.S. Myers, "The Misuse of Antibacterials in Inguinal

Herniorrhaphy," *Surgery, Gynecology and Obstetrics*, 108:721-725, 1959; A.W. Roberts and J.A. Visconti, "The Rational and Irrational Use of Systemic Antimicrobial Drugs," *American Journal of Hospital Pharmacy*, 29:828-834, 1972.

24. A.W. Roberts and J.A. Visconti, *op. cit.*, pp. 833-834.
25. *Globe and Mail*, February 10, 1973, p. 11.
26. This line of reasoning is summarized from: M. Silverman and P.R. Lee, *Pills, Profits and Politics*, University of California Press, Berkeley, 1974, pp. 260-261.
27. H.L. Lennard and A. Bernstein, "Perspectives on the New Psychoactive Drug Technology," in: R. Cooperstock (editor), *Social Aspects of the Medical Use of Psychotropic Drugs*, Addiction Research Foundation, Toronto, 1974, pp. 149-165.
28. *Ibid.*, p. 161.
29. Montreal *Gazette*, October 27, 1982, pp. A-1, A-6.
30. *Globe and Mail*, October 21, 1981, p. 4.
31. P. Lou, J.S. Campbell, I.W.D. Henderson *et al.*, "Drug Adverse Reactions in Autopsy Cases," *Rx Bulletin*, 5:2-3, January/February 1974.
32. R.I. Ogilvie and J. Ruedy, "Adverse Drug Reactions During Hospitalization," *Canadian Medical Association Journal*, 97:1445-1450, 1967.
33. I.T. Borda, E. Napke and C. Stapleton, "Drug Surveillance Data in a Canadian Hospital," *Canadian Medical Association Journal*, 114:517-522, 1976.
34. B.C. Hoddinott, C.W. Gowdey, W.K. Coulter *et al.*, "Drug Reactions and Errors in Administration on a Medical Ward," *Canadian Medical Association Journal*, 97:1001-1006, 1967.
35. *Globe and Mail*, June 4, 1973, p. 11.
36. *Globe and Mail*, September 26, 1973, p. 1.
37. *The Medical Post*, April 5, 1983, p. 11.
38. *Globe and Mail*, April 10, 1974, p. 8.
39. R.B. Talley and M.F. Laventurier, "The Incidence of Drug-Drug Interactions in a Medi-Cal Population," paper presented before a meeting of the American College of Physicians, Atlantic City, New Jersey, April 20, 1972. Cited in: M. Silverman and P.R. Lee, *op. cit.*, pp. 280-281.
40. "The Worst Interactions May Happen Most Often," *Drug Topics*, May 8, 1972. Cited in: M. Silverman and P.R. Lee, *op. cit.*, p. 281.
41. K.L. Melmon, "Preventable Drug Reactions—Causes and Cures," *New England Journal of Medicine*, 283:1361-1368, 1971.
42. E. Hemminki, "Adverse Reactions to Antibiotic Drugs: The Present Scope of the Problem in Outpatient Care and Possibilities for Improvement," *International Journal of Health Services*, 11:283-301, 1981.
43. There are an estimated 3.7 million hospital admissions in Canada each year. Each admission results in an exposure to an average of seven drugs, for a total of 25.9 million exposures. Based on the figures from the London study, 8.4 percent, or 2.18 million, of these will cause adverse reactions. If 6.2 percent of these adverse reactions are life-threatening, that amounts to 135,000 a year. Also, in the London study, at least 4 percent of reactions resulted in transient or permanent damage. On a national scale that would be 87,000 a year in Canada. Therefore, the total number of serious reactions could be as high as 222,000 a year. This number is an estimate of serious reactions in hospitals alone. No data exists on which to base an estimate of the number of serious reactions that occur yearly outside of hospital.

44. *Globe and Mail*, May 23, 1974, p. W6; W.M. O'Brien, "Drug Testing: Is Time Running Out?," *Bulletin of the Atomic Scientists*, 25:8-14, January 1969; R.B. Talley and M.F. Laventurier, "Drug Induced Illness," *Journal of the American Medical Association*, 229:1043, 1974.

CHAPTER 11. PATENTS

1. Pharmaceutical Manufacturers Association of Canada, *Principles and Code of Marketing Practice*, Ottawa, 1972, p. 5. At times though, the PMAC appears to have a split personality with respect to patents. In another document it has issued, it is self-congratulatory about what it claims is the level of competition in the industry and appears to give the credit for this situation to the lack of patent protection. Pharmaceutical Manufacturers Association of Canada, *The Performance of the Canadian Pharmaceutical Industry: A Supplement to the Pharmaceutical Manufacturers Association of Canada Suggestions for a Canadian Drug Formulary*, Ottawa, April 1975, Appendix I, p. 24.
2. Canadian Drug Manufacturers Association, *Pharmaceutical Patents: Compulsory Licensing. A Case for the Retention of Section 41(4) of the Patent Act*, Toronto, 1983, pp. 16-18. The figure $85 to $165 million is not the value of the sales of generic drugs in Canada. Rather it represents the CDMA's estimate of how much more the multinationals would have been able to charge if they did not face competition from generic equivalents.
3. See: "Schering's Structural Roulette," *Fortune*, August 1958, pp. 104-107, 158, 160, 162, for an example of how one company manipulated its basic drug.
4. P.K. Gorecki, *Regulating the Price of Prescription Drugs in Canada: Compulsory Licensing, Product Selection, and Government Reimbursement Programmes*, Technical Report No. 8, Economic Council of Canada, Ottawa, 1981, pp. 261-262. For 48 out of 62 drugs for which compulsory licences have been granted, the original patentee received an average of six patents. The effect of these additional patents was to extend the normal seventeen-year patent life by at least five more years. Consumer and Corporate Affairs Canada, *Compulsory Licensing of Pharmaceuticals: A Review of Section 41 of the Patent Act*, Ottawa, 1983, p. 44.
5. H.D. Walker, *Market Power and Price Levels in the Ethical Drug Market*, Indiana University Press, Bloomington, 1971, p. 50.
6. U.S. Senate, Committee on Small Business, Subcommittee on Monopoly, *Competitive Problems in the Drug Industry*, U.S. Government Printing Office, Washington, D.C., Part 12, 1967, p. 5067.
7. See for instance: D. Woods, "The Pharmaceutical Industry Needs Remedy for MacEachenism," *Canadian Medical Association Journal*, 126:337, 1982; C. Gray, "The Pharmaceutical Industry—Will Canada Become a Major Research Centre?,"*Canadian Medical Association Journal*, 124:910-918, 1981.
8. J. Randal, "Up for Adoption: Rare Drugs For Rare Diseases," *Science 82*, 3:31-37, September 1982.
9. J.J. Friedman & Associates, *Pharmaceutical Prices in Canada: Guiding Principles for Government Policy*, PMAC, Ottawa, 1981, p. 90.
10. *The Medical Post*, April 22, 1980, p. 12.
11. L.L. Dan, "The Drug Industry in Canada: A Position Analysis," *Business Quarterly*, 47:62-71, Autumn 1982.

12. PMAC, *The Pharmaceutical Manufacturing Industry*, Ottawa, 1973, p. 13.
13. A. Klass, *There's Gold in Them Thar Pills*, Penguin, Middlesex, England, 1975, p. 89. The argument on patents is summarized from Klass.
14. Restrictive Trade Practices Commission, *Report Concerning the Manufacture, Distribution and Sale of Drugs*, Queen's Printer, Ottawa, 1963, p. 509. From 1966 to 1969 there were a further fourteen applications.
15. Director of Investigation and Research, Combines Investigation Act, *Material Collected for Submission to the Restrictive Trade Practices Commission in the Course of an Inquiry Under Section 42 of the Combines Investigation Act Relating to the Manufacture, Distribution and Sale of Drugs*, Queen's Printer, Ottawa, 1961, pp. 225-226.
16. Restrictive Trade Practices Commission, *op. cit.*, p. 111.
17. P.K. Gorecki, *op. cit.*, p. 33.
18. Restrictive Trade Practices Commission, *op. cit.*, p. 509.
19. "High-Priced Drugs Are Still, Well, High-Priced," *Executive*, 13:26-29, February 1971.
20. Director of Investigation and Research, *op. cit.*, pp. 257-258.
21. Restrictive Trade Practices Commission, *op. cit.*, p. 523.
22. *Canada, Royal Commission on Health Services: Report*, Volume 1, Queen's Printer, Ottawa, 1964, p. 709.
23. R.W. Lang, *The Politics of Drugs*, Saxon House, Westmead, England, 1974, p. 59. The Information that follows on the history of Bills C-190 and C-102 comes mostly from Lang's book.
24. *Ibid.*, pp. 249-252. Lang is supported on this point by Dr. David Bond of Consumer and Corporate Affairs. C. Gray, *op. cit.*, p. 915.
25. W.W. Wigle, "A Pharmaceutical Industry in Canada?,"*Canadian Medical Association Journal*, 97:1361, 1967.
26. Canada, House of Commons, *Debates*, Monday, February 12, 1966, p. 6650. Cited in: R.W. Lang, *op. cit.*, p. 240.
27. "Letter Riles Knowles," Winnipeg *Free Press*, December 20, 1967; "Blackmail NDP Says of Letter Sent MPs by Toronto Drug Firm," Toronto *Star*, December 20, 1967. Cited in: R.W. Lang, *op. cit.*, p. 239.
28. PMAC, "Top Man Only," *Bulletin* No. 199/67, December 7, 1967. Cited in: R.W. Lang, *op. cit.*, pp. 239-240.
29. R.W. Lang, *op. cit.*, p. 242.
30. *Ibid.*
31. *Ibid.*, p. 136.
32. *Globe and Mail*, January 29, 1969, pp. 1,3.
33. *Report of the Advisory Committee on Central Drug Purchasing and Distribution*, Province of Manitoba, 1972, p. 30.
34. See: *Lilly v. S&U Chemicals Ltd.*, 9 C.P.R. (2d) 17 at 18. See also: *Gruppo Lepetit S.P.A. and Ciba-Geigy A.G. v. ICN Canada Ltd.*, 15 N.R. 51 at 59-60. Both cited in: P.K. Gorecki, *op. cit.*, p. 42.
35. P.K. Gorecki, *op. cit.*, p. 107.
36. *Ibid.*, pp. 108-109.
37. *Ibid.*, p. 110.
38. *Globe and Mail*, May 5, 1982, p. 4.
39. *Globe and Mail*, January 29, 1969, pp. 1, 3.
40. Canadian Drug Manufacturers Association, *op. cit.*, p. 5.
41. P.K. Gorecki, *op. cit.*, p. 76.
42. *Ibid.*, pp. 71-72.
43. P.K. Gorecki, *op. cit.*, p. 51.

44. M. Gordon and D. Fowler, *The Drug Industry: A Case Study in Foreign Control*, James Lorimer & Company, Toronto, 1981, p. 65.
45. P.K. Gorecki, *op. cit.*, p. 87. See Chapter 3 of the present book for an analysis of why it is so difficult for small companies to sell their drugs.
46. Bureau of Policy Coordination, *A Policy Analysis of the Compulsory Licensing of Pharmaceutical Patents in Canada*, Department of Consumer and Corporate Affairs, Ottawa, September 1982, p. 11, (mimeographed).
47. T.K. Fulda and P.F. Dickens, "Controlling the Cost of Drugs: The Canadian Experience," *Health Care Financing Review*, 1:55-64, Fall 1979; M. Gordon and D. Fowler, *op. cit.*, pp. 68-70; P.K. Gorecki, *op. cit.*, pp. 126-127; S. Jackson and G. Plet both referred to in: P.K. Gorecki, *op. cit.*, pp. 123-124; R.C. Kennett, *Profile of the Pharmaceutical Industry in Canada*, Supply and Services Canada, Ottawa, April 1982, pp. 22-23. Three government reports have tried to estimate the overall Canada-wide savings in drug bills resulting from compulsory licensing. The Industry, Trade and Commerce study states that there has been a price reduction of 5 percent at the manufacturer's level. The Biotechnology report says that the saving has been less than one dollar per capita per year at the manufacturer's level. Neither of these two presents any documentation for their conclusions nor do they say anything about prices at the retail level. Kennett makes the claim that pricing practices by the drug companies "neutralize the competitive pricing benefits arising from compulsory licences." However, he uses the Consumer Price Index for prescription drugs to back up his conclusions and as we saw in Chapter 3 the CPI is at best a crude measure of the changes in the cost of prescription drugs. Department of Industry, Trade and Commerce, *The Health Care Products Industry in Canada*, Ottawa, 1980, p. 12; Task Force on Biotechnology, *BIOTECHNOLOGY: A Development Plan for Canada*, A Report to the Minister of State for Science and Technology, Supply and Services Canada, Ottawa, 1981, p. 27; R.C. Kennett, *op. cit.*
48. Montreal *Gazette*, October 27, 1982, p. A-6.
49. *Ibid.*
50. *Ibid.*
51. *Ibid.* Drugs which originated from a single source and were relatively unlikely to have compulsory licences issued against them because of low sales volume, production technicalities and/or market penetration by innovators experienced a price rise of 42.52 percent between January 1, 1979, and January 1, 1982. Drugs which were resistant to competitive forces because of physician and consumer demand had their prices shoot up by 64.42 percent in the same three-year period. R.C. Kennett, *op. cit.*, p. 23.
52. *Globe and Mail*, December 18, 1979, p. 4.
53. C. Gray, *op. cit.*, p. 915.
54. J. Genest, "Address of Welcome," *Canadian Medical Association Journal*, 103:819, 1970.
55. For examples of recent criticisms of the 4 percent royalty rate see: A. Moriarty, "How Patents Nurture High Technology Industrial Development: Changes Needed for Canadian System," *Canadian Research*, 15:52-54, October 1982; J. Garner, "Ayerst Shutdown Demonstrates Some Patent Problems with Compulsory Licensing," *Canadian Pharmaceutical Journal*, 115:450-452, 1982; J. Partridge, "Painkiller Politics: Why the Drug Industry is in an Uproar," *Canadian Business*, 55:19-20, December

1982; W.E. Goodman, "Drug Substitution: Remedy or Rip-off?," *Canadian Medical Association Journal*, 128:198-202, 1983.
56. Bureau of Policy Coordination, *op. cit.*, p. 17.
57. *Globe and Mail*, August 22, 1978, p. B1.
58. Bureau of Policy Coordination, *op. cit.*, p. 20.
59. Pharmaceutical Manufacturers Association, *Survey of Potential Effects on U.S. Pharmaceutical Industry of Burke-Hartke Bill S.2592, 92nd Congress*, Washington, D.C., August 1972. Cited in: K.S. Palda and B. Pazderka, *Background to a Target: An International Comparison of the Canadian Pharmaceutical Industry's R&D Intensity*, Department of Industry, Trade and Commerce, Technological Innovation Studies Program, Report No. 71, Ottawa, 1980, p. 54.
60. Canadian Drug Manufacturers Association, *op. cit.*, pp. 37-40.
61. *Globe and Mail*, July 16, 1983, p. B1.
62. J. Partridge, *op. cit.*
63. Department of Industry, Trade and Commerce, *op. cit.*
64. P.K. Gorecki and I. Henderson, "Compulsory Patent Licensing of Drugs in Canada: A Comment on the Debate," *Canadian Public Policy*, 7:559-568, 1981.
65. *The Medical Post*, February 8, 1983, p. 80.
66. The Hon. Andre Ouellet, Letter to Mrs. Barbara Shand, February 23, 1983. Consumers' Association of Canada, *Brief to the Minister of Consumer and Corporate Affairs Concerning the Proposal to Change Compulsory Licensing Provisions Under Section 41(4) of the Patent Act*, August 31, 1983, p. 3, (mimeographed).
67. *Globe and Mail*, April 7, 1983, p. 8.
68. *Ibid.*
69. Canada, House of Commons, Health, Welfare and Social Affairs Committee, *Minutes*, 67:11, May 27, 1983.
70. The Hon. Andre Ouellet, Letter to Mr. Andrew Cohen, June 21, 1983. Consumers' Association of Canada, *op. cit.*, p. 3.
71. *Globe and Mail*, July 16, 1983, p. B1.
72. *Globe and Mail*, November 12, 1983, p. 16.
73. Canada, House of Commons *Debates*, Volume 126, No. 547, 1st Session, 32nd Parliament, p. 27244, September 19, 1983.
74. G. Beauchemin, "PMAC—Who, What, Where, Why?," *Canadian Pharmaceutical Journal*, 111:3-5, January 1978.

CHAPTER 12. THE GOVERNMENT: ACTIONS AND REACTIONS

1. L.I. Pugsley, "The Administration and Development of Federal Statutes on Foods and Drugs in Canada," *Medical Services Journal, Canada*, 23:387-449, 1967.
2. *Ibid.*
3. "The Evolution of Federal Statutes on Foods and Drugs in Canada," *Rx Bulletin*, 1:2-4, November 1970.
4. Montreal *Gazette*, October 23, 1982, p. A-4.
5. *Ibid.*
6. *Ibid.*
7. *Globe and Mail*, October 28, 1982, p. 5.
8. Montreal *Gazette*, *op. cit.*
9. Occasionally the PMAC claims that Canadian regulations unduly delay the appearance of new life-saving drugs on the Canadian market. The most recent example of such a claim came from Gordon Postlewaite, the

PMAC's director of communications: "There are many instances of a drug not clearing the regulatory hurdles here although it has been on the market in Britain for 6 or 7 years and saved countless lives." C. Gray, "The Pharmaceutical Industry: Promoting Research in the '80s," *Canadian Medical Association Journal*, 124:787-792, 1981. This kind of assertion is not even taken seriously by other people in the drug industry. A study of the introduction of new drugs into Canada, co-authored by the vice-president for scientific affairs at Bristol-Myers and the medical director at Astra, concluded: "If a drug is not available in Canada it is usually because the data have not been properly documented to show safety and efficacy." J.E. Knapp and R.S. Fynes, "Is the Introduction of Drugs into Canada Unduly Delayed?," *Canadian Medical Association Journal*, 124: 8-9, 1981.

10. Edmonton *Journal*, April 3, 1982, pp. 1, 3.
11. *Globe and Mail, op. cit.*
12. *Globe and Mail*, October 20, 1982, p. 4.
13. Montreal *Gazette*, October 25, 1982, p. A-6.
14. Toronto *Star*, November 19, 1983, p. H4.
15. M. Silverman and P.R. Lee, *Pills, Profits and Politics*, University of California Press, Berkeley, 1974, p. 31.
16. P. Tyrer, "The Benzodiazepine Bonanza," *The Lancet*, 2:709-710, 1974; "Choice of a Benzodiazepine for Treatment of Anxiety or Insomnia," *The Medical Letter*, 19:49-50, 1977; E.M. Sellers, "Clinical Pharmacology and Therapeutics of Benzodiazepines," *Canadian Medical Association Journal*, 118:1533-1538, 1978; M.G. Tierney and W.M. McLean, "Pharmacokinetics of Benzodiazepines—Lack of Clinical Relevance: A Commentary," *Modern Medicine of Canada*, 35:208-212, 1980; "Choice of Benzodiazepines," *The Medical Letter*, 23:41-43, 1981.
17. Montreal *Gazette*, October 23, 1982, p. A-4.
18. *Globe and Mail*, October 28, 1982, p. 5.
19. *Globe and Mail*, October 18, 1982, p. 5.
20. Montreal *Gazette*, October 25, 1982, p. A-6. This comradely relationship between the government and the industry extends beyond the HPB. Percy Skuy, President of Ortho Pharmaceuticals and a past head of the board of the PMAC, said that aside from the Department of Consumer and Corporate Affairs, most other branches of the federal government, such as the Ministry of Industry, Trade and Commerce and the Ministry of Science and Technology, "are willing to bend over backwards to help us." *The Medical Post*, August 10, 1982, p. 58. With the May 1983 announcement from the Minister of Consumer and Corporate Affairs that the Patent Act was going to be amended, that department too seems to have swung into the industry's camp.
21. Montreal *Gazette*, October 25, 1982, p. A-6.
22. *Ibid.*
23. Montreal *Gazette*, October 23, 1982, p. A-4.
24. Edmonton *Journal*, April 4, 1982, p. 1.
25. All the information and quotes about Oraflex come from: Montreal *Gazette*, October 25, 1982, pp. A-1, A-6.
26. *Ibid.*
27. M. Omatsu, "New Drugs and Human Experimentation," paper for Professor LeDain, Osgoode Hall Law School, York University, Toronto, 1974, p. 16, (mimeographed).
28. Montreal *Gazette*, October 23, 1982, p. A-4.

29. C. Cocking, "The Abuse of Prescription Drugs," *Weekend Magazine*, June 18, 1977, pp. 16-19.
30. H. Sjostrom and R. Nilsson, *Thalidomide and the Power of the Drug Companies*, Penguin, Middlesex, England, 1972, p. 136. The rest of the information on thalidomide is summarized from this book.
31. *Ibid.*, p. 143.
32. *Ibid.*, p. 146.
33. The study by Dr. Nulsen claimed that thalidomide had been tested by him and was "a safe and effective sleep-inducing agent which seems to fulfil the requirements outlined in this paper for a satisfactory drug to be used late in pregnancy." Later it was discovered that Dr. Nulsen had no formal training in obstetrics; that he did not even know whether the drug had been approved or rejected by the U.S. Food and Drug Administration; that his article was actually written by an employee of Merrell, although it appeared under his name; and that he had used as references studies he had never actually read. Montreal *Star*, July 24, 1972, p. C1.
34. M. Mintz, "FDA and Panalba: A Conflict of Commercial, Therapeutic Goals?," *Science*, 165:875-881, 1969.
35. *Globe and Mail*, September 9, 1979, p. T2.
36. In mid-1980, the federal government, after a two-year study, came to the conclusion that tranquillizers were being over-prescribed. An announcement was made that the Department of Health and Welfare was going to ask doctors to stop prescribing tranquillizers for everyday stress. To 1983, the actions of the government seem to have been limited to the production of a booklet: R. Cooperstock and J. Hill, *The Effects of Tranquillization: Benzodiazepine Use in Canada*, Health and Welfare, Ottawa, 1982; and a therapeutic monograph: T.A. Ban, W.T. Brown, T. DaSilva *et al.*, "Therapeutic Monograph on Anxiolytic-Sedative Drugs," *Canadian Pharmaceutical Journal*, 114:301-308, 1981.
37. "Guidelines for Review of Use of Stimulants and Sedatives in Medicine Discussed by CMA Committee," *Canadian Medical Association Journal*, 103:428-429, 1970; "Association Submits Second Brief on Non-Medical Use of Drugs to Le Dain Commission," *Canadian Medical Association Journal*, 104:738-742, 1971.
38. According to one article, 5 percent of high school students in London, Ontario, admitted to taking speed: C. Con and R. Smart, "The Nature and Extent of Speed Use in North America," *Canadian Medical Association Journal*, 102:724-729, 1970. In the United States, it was felt that about 50 percent of the production of amphetamines was finding its way into illegal channels of distribution: J.F. Sadusk, "Size and Extent of Problem," *Journal of the American Medical Association*, 196:707-709, 1965.
39. Toronto *Star*, December 29, 1972, p. 3.
40. These six were: narcolepsy, a rare condition in which a person tends to fall asleep uncontrollably; hyperkinetic disorders in children; mental retardation; epilepsy; Parkinson's disease, a disorder of the nervous system which involves, among other things, tremors in the limbs; and hypotension (low blood pressure) states associated with anaesthesia.
41. *Globe and Mail*, December 22, 1972, p. 11.
42. S. Duncan, "Reduce Prices of Drugs or Else...," *Drug Merchandising*, 51:29-32, July 1970.
43. Toronto *Star*, May 10, 1970, p. 5.
44. W.E. Granger, "QUAD Is Working Fine and There Are More Regulations To Come," *Drug Merchandising*, 54:68-69, April 1973; "PMAC Ends

QUAD Boycott," *Drug Merchandising*, 54:8, June 1973.

45. *Globe and Mail*, October 25, 1972, p. B7.

46. J.M. Parker, "Some Implications of Legalized Substitution of Prescribed Pharmaceuticals," *Canadian Medical Association Journal*, 87:1318-1321, 1962. Dr. Parker was head of the medical section of the PMAC.

47. Substitution is prohibited by Ontario doctors in only about one in 200 prescriptions. Toronto *Star*, January 7, 1982, pp. A1, A14. In Manitoba, where substitution is also allowed, one prescription in 120 bears the instruction, "do not substitute." J. Davis, "Prescription Cost Margins in Manitoba Pharmacies," *Canadian Pharmaceutical Journal*, 116:419-420, 1983.

48. G.W. Robb, "Product and Service Less Than Best," *Drug Merchandising*, 51:27-28, October 1970.

49. "Asks Ontario Abandon Formulary," *Drug Merchandising*, 59:36, September, 1978.

50. T.Kyriakos, "The Last Word on PARCOST: Fee Disputes Spell Demise of Ailing Drug Plan," *Drug Merchandising*, 64:12-13, March 1983.

51. *Report of the Advisory Committee on Central Drug Purchasing and Distribution*, Province of Manitoba, 1972.

52. "An Open Letter From Don Harper—No Threat Made by Dr. Wigle," *Drug Merchandising*, 53:56, 74, September 1972.

53. For a more detailed outline of the Saskatchewan plan see: *Saskatchewan Prescription Drug Plan, Annual Report 1981-1982*, Regina, 1982.

54. Maclean-Hunter Research Bureau, *A Survey of Prescriptions 1979*, Conducted for Drug Merchandising and Le Pharmacien, Toronto, July 1979, pp. 6, 7. For a more detailed description of provincial drug reimbursement programs see: P.K. Gorecki, *Regulating the Price of Prescription Drugs in Canada: Compulsory Licensing, Product Selection, and Government Reimbursement Programmes*, Technical Report No. 8, Economic Council of Canada, Ottawa, 1981, pp. 8-23.

55. W.M. Garton, "The Pharmaceutical Industry in Canada—Its Environment and Performance," *Canadian Pharmaceutical Journal*, 111:6-7, January 1978. Major-General Garton (Retired) was president of the PMAC.

56. Montreal *Gazette*, October 27, 1982, p. A-6.

57. Ontario Council of Health, *Review of the Ontario PARCOST Program*, Toronto, 1973.

58. R.R. Kerton and T.K. Chowdhury, "The Impact of the PARCOST Program on Prescription Drug Prices in Ontario," *Canadian Public Policy*, 7:306-317, 1981. Although the figures on the drop in Ontario drug prices produced by Kerton and Chowdhury are not disputed, their interpretation of them is. Other authors have attributed the decline in prices more to factors such as the patent law changes than the PARCOST program. See: P.K. Gorecki, "The Impact of the PARCOST Program on Prescription Drug Prices in Ontario: Some Queries," *Canadian Public Policy*, 8: 358-361, 1982; N. Ellis, "The Impact of the PARCOST Program on Prescription Drug Prices in Ontario: Some Queries," *Canadian Public Policy* 8:361-364, 1982.

59. The information and quotes on discount pricing are summarized from a Southam News story that appeared in: Sault *Star*, October 21, 1983, pp. 1, 2.

60. Vancouver *Sun*, November 3, 1983, p. A-9.

CHAPTER 13. MEDICALIZATION: THE IDEOLOGY OF DRUG USE

1. H.L. Lennard, L.J. Epstein, A. Bernstein *et al.*, "Hazard Implicit in Prescribing Psychoactive Drugs," *Science*, 169:438-441, 1970.
2. In fact, deaths from heart disease have started to decline, but it is far from clear that modern medical therapy has made a major contribution to this decline.
3. M. Renaud, "On the Structural Constraints to State Intervention in Health," *International Journal of Health Services*, 5:559-571, 1975.
4. J. Powles, "On the Limitations of Modern Medicine," *Science, Medicine and Man*, 1:1-30, 1973.
5. M. Renaud, *op. cit.*
6. *Ibid.*, p. 564
7. J. Eyer, "Hypertension as a Disease of Modern Society," *International Journal of Health Services*, 5:539-558, 1975.
8. *Ibid.*
9. G. Rose, "Epidemiology of Ischaemic Heart Disease," *British Journal of Hospital Medicine*, 7:285-288, 1972. Cited in: J. Powles, *op. cit.*, p. 8.
10. Most of the argument on how modern capitalist society generates hypertension is summarized from: J. Eyer, *op. cit.*
11. G. Andrews, S.W. MacMahon, A. Austin *et al.*, "Hypertension: Comparison of Drug and Non-Drug Treatments," *British Medical Journal*, 284:1523-1526, 1982.
12. Ontario Council of Health, *Hypertension*, Toronto, 1977.
13. J. Eyer and P. Sterling, "Stress-Related Mortality and Social Organization," *The Review of Radical Political Economics*, 9:1-44, Spring 1977.
14. This argument is based on information contained in a speech by Vincente Navarro in Toronto, October 24, 1980.
15. H.L. Lennard, L.J. Epstein, A. Bernstein *et al.*, *op. cit.*, p. 439.
16. H.L. Lennard and A. Bernstein, "Perspectives on the New Psychoactive Drug Technology," in: R. Cooperstock (editor), *Social Aspects of the Medical Use of Psychotropic Drugs*, Addiction Research Foundation, Toronto, 1974, p. 159.
17. H.L. Lennard, L.J. Epstein, A. Bernstein *et al.*, *op. cit.*
18. S. London, "Science as Ideology," *Health/PAC Bulletin*, No. 67, pp. 10-18, November/December 1975.
19. M. H. Brenner, "Health Costs and Benefits of Economic Policy," *International Journal of Health Services*, 7:581-623, 1977.
20. J. Harding, "The Pharmaceutical Industry as a Public-Health Hazard and as an Institution of Social Control," in: D. Coburn, C. D'Arcy, P. New, and G. Torrance (editors), *Health and Canadian Society*, Fitzhenry and Whiteside, 1981, p. 289.
21. R. Cooperstock and H.L. Lennard, "Some Social Meanings of Tranquilizer Use," *Sociology of Health and Illness*, 1:331-347, 1979.
22. *Ibid.*, p. 340.
23. *Ibid.*, pp. 336-337.
24. *Ibid.*, p. 336.
25. "Pharmaceutical Control: Part 3," *Ideas*, CBC FM, March 17, 1983.
26. R. Cooperstock and H.L. Lennard, *op. cit.*, p. 344.
27. "Pharmaceutical Control," *op. cit.*
28. *Globe and Mail*, February 28, 1980, p. T1.
29. H.L. Lennard and A. Berstein, *op. cit.*
30. *The Journal*, October 1, 1983, p. 1.
31. H.L. Lennard and A. Bernstein, *op. cit.*, make essentially the same points.

Annotated Bibliography

The sources consulted in writing this book were many and diverse. This annotated bibliography contains selected references which I found to be the most useful for understanding the Canadian pharmaceutical industry.

Books

R. Cooperstock (editor), *Social Aspects of the Medical Use of Psychotropic Drugs*, Addiction Research Foundation, Toronto, 1974. Ruth Cooperstock is widely known both in Canada and internationally for her work on mood modifying drugs. This collection of essays illustrates how social problems are being turned into medical ones and demonstrates the consequences of that transformation.

R. Cooperstock and J. Hill, *The Effects of Tranquillization: Benzodiazepine Use in Canada*, Health and Welfare Canada, Ottawa, 1982. This little book touches on the major issues connected to the use of tranquillizers. For a publication sponsored by the federal government it has a surprisingly political tone.

R.A. Fine, *The Great Drug Deception*, Stein and Day, New York, 1972. This book formed the basis for the second half of Chapter 5 dealing with MER/29, and details one of the lowest points in the history of the drug industry.

M. Gordon and D. Fowler, *The Drug Industry: A Case Study in Foreign Control*, James Lorimer & Company, Toronto, 1981. Written by two economists and using technical language, this book sometimes requires that you reread passages a few times to discover what is being said. As the title suggests, the book is an exploration of the effects of foreign control on the Canadian industry. The authors conclude that it would be in Canadian interests to increase the level of domestic control of the industry.

A. Klass, *There's Gold in Them Thar Pills*, Penguin, Middlesex, England, 1975. Alan Klass chaired the Manitoba inquiry into the drug industry in the early 1970s. His book is an iconoclastic, moderately left wing look at the industry. Although he uses a few Canadian examples, most of the information is either British or American. His conclusion, that it is ultimately up to doctors to defeat the tyranny of the drug companies is quite naive.

R.W. Lang, *The Politics of Drugs*, Saxon House, Westmead, England, 1974. This book is based on a Ph.D. thesis and at times reads like it. However, it is still a very useful and critical look at the way the PMAC functions as a pressure group.

P. Schrag and D. Divoky, *The Myth of the Hyperactive Child*, Dell, New York, 1975. This book is largely American in content, but when it talks about the drugging of children, what it has to say applies to Canada as well.

M. Silverman and P.R. Lee, *Pills, Profits and Politics*, University of California Press, Berkeley, 1974. This is the best book ever written about the American pharmaceutical industry, and much of what is in it is relevant to Canada. The book's only failing is that the authors lack an overall political perspective and instead tend to view the industry from a reformist point of view.

Government Studies and Reports

Director of Investigation and Research, Combines Investigation Act, *Material Collected for Submission to the Restrictive Trade Practices Commission in the Course of an Inquiry under Section 42 of the Combines Investigation Act Relating to the Manufacture, Distribution and Sale of Drugs*, Queen's Printer, Ottawa, 1961. This was the inquiry that set the ball rolling for future government action in the area of prescription drugs. Most of the material is dated, but it is still worth reading. The description of the industry shows why the government felt obliged to take further action, especially with respect to the price of drugs.

Restrictive Trade Practices Commission, *Report Concerning the Manufacture, Distribution and Sale of Drugs*, Queen's Printer, Ottawa, 1963. This was the follow-up to the report from the Director of Investigation and Research, and was based on evidence gathered during comprehensive hearings into the pharmaceutical industry. The Commission's most controversial recommendation was that patents on drugs should be abolished.

Royal Commission on Health Services, *Provision, Distribution and Cost of Drugs in Canada*, Queen's Printer, Ottawa, 1964. The first half of this report is largely a summary of what was contained in the study of the Restrictive Trade Practices Commission. The last half is a province-by-province description of programs for providing drugs to welfare recipients and a look at various kinds of drug insurance plans.

Canada, House of Commons, *Second (Final) Report of the Special Committee of the House of Commons on Drug Costs and Prices*, Queen's Printer, Ottawa, 1967. This was the report that recommended the changes to the Patent Act to allow for issuing compulsory licences to import drugs already being manufactured in Canada.

Report of the Advisory Committee on Central Drug Purchasing and Distribution, Province of Manitoba, Winnipeg, 1972. Of all the government reports, this is probably the most critical of the pharmaceutical industry. A product of the heady first few years of NDP government, it recommended central drug purchasing for all provincial pharmacies by the government.

Department of Industry, Trade and Commerce, *The Health Care Products Industry in Canada*, Ottawa, 1980. This discussion paper followed the release of five background papers a year earlier. The stated goal of this analysis was to provide government and industry with up-to-date information in order to develop policy options for the industry. What is most notable in the section dealing with pharmaceuticals is how the Industry, Trade and Commerce analysis of the drug industry is almost identical to the PMAC's analysis.

P.K. Gorecki, *Regulating the Price of Prescription Drugs in Canada: Compulsory Licensing, Product Selection, and Government Reimbursement Programmes*, Technical Report No. 8, Economic Council of Canada, Ottawa,

1981. A highly technical study that takes hours to wade through, but also a very important one. The author shows that, contrary to PMAC claims, compulsory licensing has not had a major impact either on Canada's balance of trade in pharmaceuticals or on expenditures for research and development.

Bureau of Policy Coordination, *A Policy Analysis of the Compulsory Licensing of Pharmaceutical Patents in Canada,* Department of Consumer and Corporate Affairs, Ottawa, September 1982, (mimeographed). This working paper reviews the major industry arguments against Section 41(4) of the Patent Act and shows how little basis in fact each of them really has.

Consumer and Corporate Affairs, Canada, *Compulsory Licensing of Pharmaceuticals: A Review of Section 41 of the Patent Act,* Ottawa, 1983. Consumer and Corporate Affairs issued this review in order to provide the justification for amending the Patent Act. What is interesting, though, is that little concrete evidence is presented which justifies the proposed changes.

Miscellaneous Studies and Reports

Summary Publication, Drug Symposium: Drug Information for the Health Care Team, McGill University, May 30-31, 1975, (mimeographed). This summary is particularly biting in its critique of the *CPS* and detail men. Unfortunately, unless you know someone with a copy of this report, it may be difficult to find.

B. Pazderka, *Promotion and Competition in the Canadian Drug Industry,* Unpublished Ph.D. Thesis, Queen's University, Kingston, Ontario, 1976. The conclusion that the author reaches is that the harder a drug is promoted, the better it sells. Pazderka's research into the marketing of drugs provides the evidence to back up this obvious finding.

J. Harding, "Pharmaceutical Control," *Ideas,* CBC Transcripts, 1983. This three-part radio series focused on: pharmaceutical use in the third world; the history of drug laws in Canada and the criminalizing of non-pharmaceutical drugs; and the prescribing of drugs to women.

Consumers' Association of Canada, *Brief to the Minister of Consumer and Corporate Affairs Concerning the Proposal to Change Compulsory Licensing Provisions Under Section 41(4) of the Patent Act,* Ottawa, August 31, 1983, (mimeographed). This ten page brief is a good summary of the case against changing the Patent Act.

Articles

Anonymous, The Peculiar Success of Chloromycetin," *Consumer Reports,* 35:616-619, October 1970. This is the story of how Parke, Davis kept the sales of Chloromycetin high even years after it should have been limited to use in a few life-threatening illnesses.

J. Avorn, M. Chen and R. Hartley, "Scientific Versus Commercial Sources of Influence on the Prescribing Behavior of Physicians," *American Journal of Medicine,* 73:4-8, 1982. The authors show that even in the 1980s, commercial sources of information about drugs continue to have a major impact on the prescribing habits of doctors.

R.W. Bell and J.W. Osterman, "The Compendium of Pharmaceuticals and Specialties: A Critical Analysis," *International Journal of Health Services,* 13:107-118, 1983. The information given in the *CPS* for 207 drugs was compared to the information in several standard pharmacological references. The authors conclude that the *CPS* had so many major flaws that it "is in fact the paragon of successful drug advertising."

E.M. Boyd, "The Equivalence of Drug Brands," *Rx Bulletin,* 2:101-102,

120A, 1971. The conclusion of this article is that the lack of physiological and clinical equivalency between brands of the same drug is probably of very minor significance.

C. Cocking. "The Abuse of Prescription Drugs," *Weekend Magazine*, June 18, 1977, pp. 16-19. If you want a short critical introduction to the major issues in the drug industry, this article, although slightly dated, is a good place to start.

R. Cooperstock and H.L. Lennard, "Some Social Meanings of Tranquillizer Use," *Sociology of Health and Illness*, 1:331-347, 1979. The authors interviewed groups of volunteers, most of them women, to find out how they viewed their use of tranquillizers. The majority of women were found to be using these drugs because of conflicts around their traditional roles as wife, mother and homemaker.

L.L. Dan, "The Drug Industry in Canada: A Position Analysis," *Business Quarterly*, 47:62-71, Autumn 1982. Leslie L. Dan is president of one of the largest Canadian-owned drug companies. He is also one of the major forces behind the Canadian Drug Manufacturers Association, and writes this general look at the industry from that bias.

M. Dowie, D. Foster, C. Marshall *et al.*, "The Illusion of Safety," *Mother Jones*, June 1982, pp. 35-49. This team of investigative journalists from *Mother Jones* has brought together page after page of examples of fraud in research on new drugs.

T.K. Fulda and P.F. Dickens, "Controlling the Cost of Drugs: The Canadian Experience," *Health Care Financing Review*, 1:55-64, Fall 1979. The authors conclude that between 1970 and 1974, federal and provincial programs aimed at reducing drug prices brought about a decline of 39 percent in the average price of the sixteen drugs studied.

P.R. Garai, "Advertising and Promotion of Drugs," in: P. Talalay (editor), *Drugs in Our Society*, Johns Hopkins Press, Baltimore, 1964, pp. 189-202. Pierre Garai was an executive with a leading advertising agency. Although still a staunch believer in free enterprise, Garai was honest enough to expose some of the more flagrant abuses of drug promotion. Even though this was written more than twenty years ago, it is still relevant today.

P.K. Gorecki and I. Henderson, "Compulsory Patent Licensing of Drugs in Canada: A Comment on the Debate," *Canadian Public Policy*, 7:559-568, 1981. This short article takes a critical look at the PMAC's position on the 1969 changes to the Patent Act.

J. Harding, "The Pharmaceutical Industry as a Public-Health Hazard and as an Institution of Social Control," in: D. Coburn, C. D'Arcy, P. New, and G. Torrance (editors), *Health and Canadian Society*, Fitzhenry and Whiteside, 1981, pp. 274-291. Jim Harding uses data from the Saskatchewan Prescription Drug Plan to analyse the use of drugs which act primarily on the central nervous system. Having described who receives the prescriptions, Harding develops his larger theme of drugs as agents of social control.

R.R. Kerton and T.K. Chowdhury, "The Impact of the PARCOST Program on Prescription Drug Prices in Ontario," *Canadian Public Policy*, 7:306-317, 1981. The authors conclude that "the PARCOST program helped to bring about a decrease in average drug prices in Ontario."

T. Kyriakos, "The Last Word on PARCOST," *Drug Merchandising*, 64:12-13, March 1983. PARCOST is almost a dead program in Ontario because of restrictions placed on the fees that pharmacists can charge.

J. Mitford, "Experiments Behind Bars," *Atlantic*, 231:64-73, January 1973. Prisoners in American jails used to be the favorite target of drug companies interested in testing new products. Mitford describes what happened to some of the men who took part in these tests and also looks at the attitudes of doctors in charge.

L.I. Pugsley, "The Administration and Development of Federal Statutes on Foods and Drugs in Canada," *Medical Services Journal, Canada,* 23:387-449, 1967. This article is purely descriptive, but it is the only place that details the evolution of Canadian drug laws and regulations.

V. Ross, "Between Bliss and Bedlam," *Maclean's,* December 8, 1980, pp. 38-44. A somewhat superficial look at the use of mood modifying drugs across Canada. One of the more interesting parts is the interview with the adaptable detail man who sees his job as "perceiving needs, or creating them."

M.G. Sanders, "The Sparce Index: Medical Excellence or Drug Dependence," *Canadian Medical Association Journal,* 102:531-532, 1970. The author reviews advertising in 40 medical journals. The *CMAJ* was unique in being the only publication to have advertising and scientific content on the same page.

F. Solomon, C.C. White, D.L. Parron and W.B. Mendelson, "Sleeping Pills, Insomnia and Medical Practice," *New England Journal of Medicine,* 300:803-808, 1979. The Institute of Medicine, American National Academy of Sciences, sponsored this review of the use of sleeping pills out of concern for the public health problems associated with their use. The basic conclusion is that sleeping pills are widely prescribed, often without adequate investigation of the problem and with little understanding on the part of many physicians about how these drugs work.

P.S. Stephenson and G.A. Walker, "Psychotropic Drugs and Women," *Bioethics Quarterly,* 2:20-38, 1980. The authors suggest that the difference in prescription rates of mood modifying drugs to men and women is rooted in the assumption that women who are unhappy with their traditional roles must be ill.

M.H. Van Woert, "Profitable and Nonprofitable Drugs," *New England Journal of Medicine,* 298:903-906, 1978. This article documents the fact that drugs that are expected to generate big profits get developed and those that are not, do not.

I. Waldron, "Increased Prescribing of Valium, Librium and Other Drugs—An Example of the Influence of Economic and Social Factors on the Practice of Medicine," *International Journal of Health Services,* 7:37-62, 1977. Ingrid Waldron shows, in this important study, how the rise in the use of Valium and Librium coincided with a period of rising social stress. Her conclusion is that fundamental solutions to the problems of drug prescribing will emerge only with far-reaching restructuring of our social and economic relations.

G. Weiss, E. Kruger, U. Danielson and M. Elman, "Effect of Long-Term Treatment of Hyperactive Children with Methylphenidate," *Canadian Medical Association Journal,* 112:159-165, 1975. Hyperactive children treated with methylphenidate (Ritalin) were compared to a similar group of children who received no treatment. After five years, no difference was found between the two groups in emotional adjustment, delinquency, IQ, visual-motor skills and academic performance.

Industry Sources

Pharmaceutical Manufacturers Association of Canada, *Principles and Code of Marketing Practice,* Ottawa, 1972. If only what were written here were really true.

Pharmaceutical Manufacturers Association of Canada, *Background Information on the Canadian Pharmaceutical Manufacturing Industry*, Ottawa, 1979. This collection of facts and figures about the Canadian drug industry can be put to uses not anticipated by the PMAC.

Canadian Drug Manufacturers Association, *Pharmaceutical Patents: Compulsory Licensing. A Case for the Retention of Section 41(4) of the Patent Act*, Toronto, 1983. Prepared by the "good guys" in the drug industry, this is a useful alternative to the attacks on the Patent Act that the PMAC grinds out.

Newspapers

Montreal *Star*, July 21, p. A-7; July 23, p. D-1; July 24, p. C-1; July 25, p. C-1; July 26, p. D-1, 1973. This series by Dr. Murray Katz ran under the title: "Thalidomide—Can It Happen Again?" The articles showed that the system of drug promotion and distribution which allowed the thalidomide disaster in 1962 remained basically unchanged in 1973.

Edmonton *Journal*, April 3, pp. A-1, A-3; April 4, p. A-1; April 5, pp. B-1, B-2, 1982. This series was concerned mainly with the question of how unsafe drugs reach and remain on the Canadian market.

Globe and Mail, October 16, pp. 1, 4; October 18, p. 5; October 19, pp. 1, 2; October 20, p. 4; October 21, p. 4; October 22, p. 5; October 25, p. 5; October 26, p. 5, 1982. This series, which ran at the same time as the one in the Montreal *Gazette*, is the inferior of the two. Although it occasionally presents some useful information, its analysis is generally quite superficial.

Montreal *Gazette*, October 23, pp. A-1, A-4; October 25, pp. A-1, A-6; October 26, pp. A-1, A-8; October 27, pp. A-1, A-8, 1982. This series touches on almost all the major areas of concern in the drug industry, and although the corporations' point of view is presented, the tone is generally critical of the industry. A comparison of the problems described in these articles with those described nine years earlier by Dr. Katz makes it obvious that not much had changed.

Sault *Star*, October 21, 1983, pp. 1, 2. This story ran in Southam papers across the country. It describes how the pharmacists and the drug companies have driven up the costs of most provincial drug plans and how the provincial governments, until recently, have mainly stood by and watched the situation develop.

Index

266